LADY ICARUS

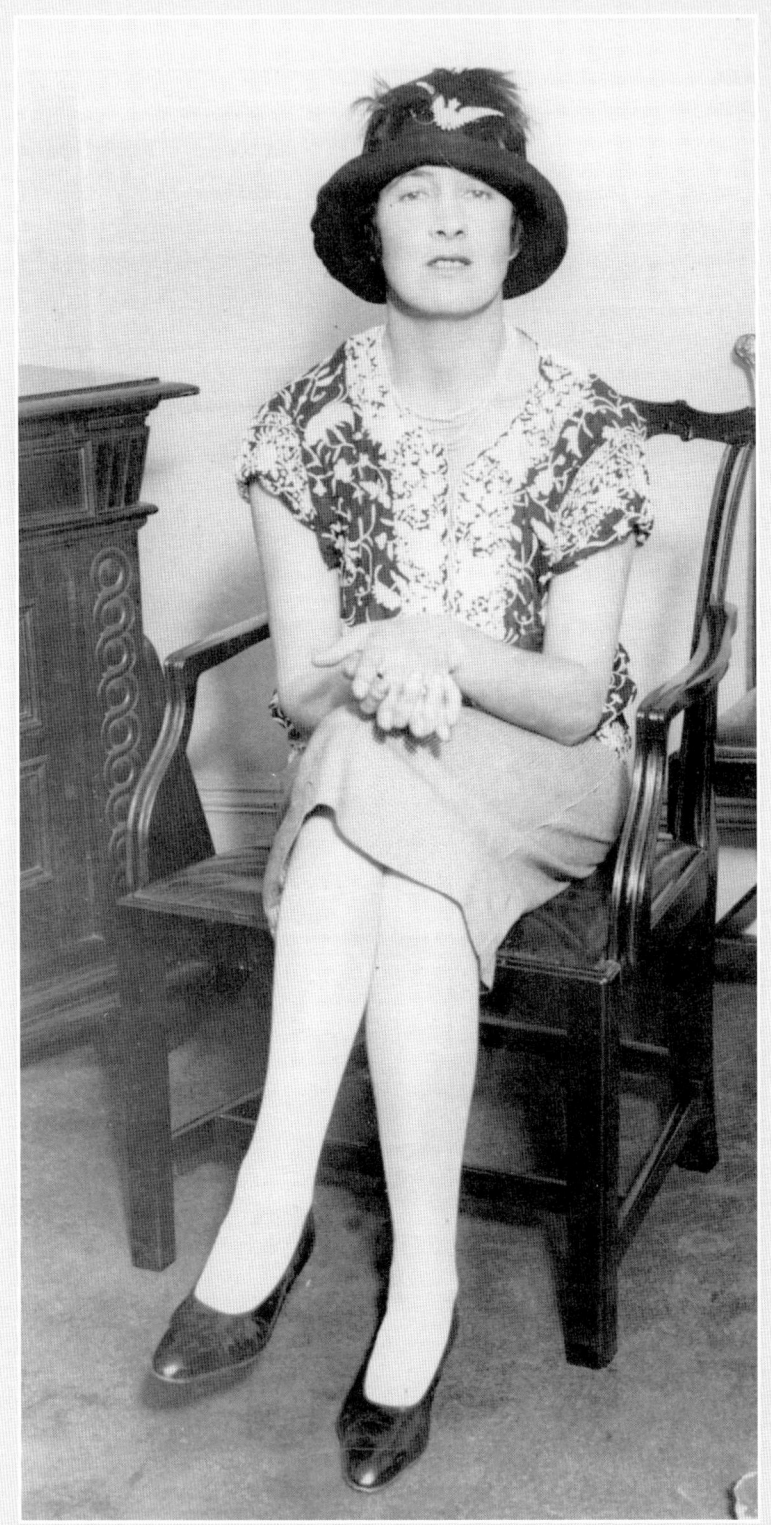

Lady Icarus

The Life of Irish Aviator Lady Mary Heath

LINDIE NAUGHTON

First published in 2004 by

ASHFIELD PRESS • DUBLIN • IRELAND

© Lindie Naughton, 2004

ISBN: 1 901658 38 4

A catalogue record for this book is available from the British Library.

All rights reserved. No part of this publication may be reproduced, stored in a retrieval system or transmitted in any form or by any means, electronic, mechanical, photocopying, recording or otherwise, without the prior, written permission of the publisher.

This book is sold subject to the condition that it shall not, by way of trade or otherwise, be lent, resold, hired out, or otherwise circulated without the publisher's prior consent in any form of binding or cover other than that in which it is published and without a similar condition, including this condition, being imposed on the subsequent purchaser.

Typeset by Ashfield Press in 12 on 15 point Adobe Garamond
Designed by
SUSAN WAINE

Printed in Ireland by
ßETAPRINT, DUBLIN

Contents

	Preface	7
	Prologue	11
1	A Family Tragedy	13
2	Growing up in Newcastle West	28
3	College days in Dublin	35
4	The War Years	44
5	Mrs Eliott-Lynn Athlete	54
6	Farming in Africa	62
7	Olympic Arguments	74
8	Sophie Takes Flight	83
9	Wings over Europe	95
10	At Last a Lady	112
11	The Flight from the Cape	125
12	A World Famous Flyer	143
13	After Earhart	159
14	The New World	176
15	The Women's Air Derby	190
16	Crash Landing	200
17	Back in Ireland	214
18	Her Final Days	228
	Postscript	232

Appendices
Sophie's Athletic Career 238
Lady Mary's Flying Career 241
From Cape Town to London 1928 243
Sources and Bibliography 244
Endnotes 253
Index 257

'How can I describe the splendid tonic effect of flying? To be up there alone, in the air, free and in space, is like being alone in a vast cathedral. There is something awe-inspiring and solemn about it. To fly is an adventure and at the same moment a time of spirit renewal and refreshment.'

LADY MARY HEATH

Preface

WRITING THE STORY of Sophie Peirce's life has been an exhilarating, though occasionally frustrating, task. Search the newspaper files and you will find plenty of information about her life; for a couple of years in the late 1920s, when known as Lady Mary Heath, the aviation pioneer born plain Sophie Peirce in Knockaderry, County Limerick, was one of the most famous women in the English-speaking world.

Look for primary sources and you have a bigger problem. Most of her contemporaries are dead; those who remain were eager to share their memories of a remarkable woman, but sadly, they were few.

Much of the information used in previous work on her life has come from an archive held by John Cussen in Newcastle West. This consists of books, cuttings, photographs and newspaper clippings proudly collected by her Aunt Cis, to whom Sophie remained devoted all her life.

As an ex-athlete, I had first come across Sophie in a history of Irish female athletes called *From Sophie to Sonia,* written by an old friend, Noel Henry. What intrigued me was not just her sporting prowess, but her sensational private life, as ineluctably grim as any Greek tragedy. Noel's book sent me first to my own collection of books on athletics, which provided snippets of information, but little more. Unfortunately, the early days of women's athletics in the UK are not well documented; meetings tended to take place in private houses, and valuable minute books and other material were all too often lost. However, the meticulous research undertaken by British athletics historians Eric Cowes, John Brand and Greg Moon and by Gertrud Pfister in Germany filled in many of the gaps, as did trawling the small print in Irish newspapers for the occasional mention of women's sporting achievements; not much change there then.

A visit to the Royal Aeronautical Society in London uncovered another treasure trove of material from the UK, USA and France, including a collection of typically spirited letters Sophie had written to the Society, of which she was a member. There was also the Public Record Office at Kew, where letters she had written to the Air Ministry and other government bodies are held. These files include much correspondence relating to her pilot's licences. Also held at Kew was a large and revealing file on the military career of her first husband, Captain Eliott-Lynn.

Other information came by sheer serendipity. While in the National Library, filling time while awaiting the arrival of yet another volume of the *Limerick Leader*, I decided to check through the indexes for any mention of the Royal College of Science. Imagine my joy when I discovered a couple of volumes of a students' magazine from the period around 1916, filled with articles either written by Sophie or mentioning her activities. A few more mysteries unravelled, such as the date of her first marriage.

Over the years spent researching, material occasionally fell into my lap. By chance, I found a yellowing biography of her friend and fellow aviator Bill Lancaster at my local library in Blackrock, County Dublin. A visit to Paris coincided with a Champs Elysées exhibition on the early days of aviation, which graphically underlined just how flimsy the early flying machines were, while in Geneva I came across a book on a pioneering Swiss flight from Europe to the Cape in 1926, with wonderful maps.

The internet proved helpful in establishing contact with overseas libraries and collections. When I got in touch with John Ahouse at the University of California Special Collections, he used my request for information as an opportunity to tidy up some files, faithfully photocopying anything he thought was of interest, and even sending on the sheet music for a contemporary song mythologising women aviators. Joan Hrubec at the International Women's Air and Space Museum in Cleveland was equally helpful and provided a stuffed envelope of newspaper clippings relating to Sophie's American career.

Perhaps the most special moment came through American film-maker Jayne Loader, who told me that the pioneering aviatrix Elinor Smith, who had written extensively about Sophie in her autobiography, was still alive. When contacted, Elinor, a sprightly woman in her nineties who had enjoyed a long and rewarding career as a pilot, was not only willing to share her memories of her old friend and mentor, but was wonderfully encouraging.

Thanks to Elinor Smith's letters and e-mails, I felt at last I was getting close to cracking the enigma of Sophie. Even better was to come when Pauline Godwin, then an archivist at RTE, got in touch. Pauline, a native of Newcastle West, had spent many years collecting film references to Sophie and, at her own expense, had sent off for a few newsreel films. She copied these for me on videotape; finally I could see Sophie in action on film and hear her talking, a poignant and moving experience. Later came a highly rewarding visit to Newcastle West and Knockaderry, where many still remember their most famous daughter with pride and fondness.

Despite the many years of research, I cannot pretend that this is the definitive book on Sophie Peirce. Because few of her personal papers survived her erratic life, many mysteries remain, particularly relating to her private life; oh, for a stash of papers perhaps even now hidden in somebody's attic! She had relatives in England for instance; so far, I have failed to find them. There was also the 'love of her life', a man called 'John'; another complete mystery. In athletics circles, rumours abounded about her sexuality, but even nowadays, women involved in sport have to cope with such innuendo, and in Sophie's case, nothing could be confirmed.

If anyone can cast some light on any of these mysteries, I would love to hear from them. In the meantime, what is on offer here is an admittedly biased account of a remarkable life, most of it from the subject's point of view. Sophie Peirce's story remains one of great achievement tempered by almost unbearable poignancy. She was a larger than life figure, highly intelligent, physically imposing and a lover of the limelight, conscious of the sensitive role she played as a woman in a man's world, if occasionally incapable of holding back her exasperation. In private, she was a loving and conscientious niece to her aunts and a caring friend to many. She polarised opinion – some liked and admired her, while others couldn't stand her; I suspect this will still be the case.

Whatever people think of her, like all truly fascinating personalities, Sophie Peirce will remain something of an enigma. Her reinstatement in the pantheon of great Irish women is long overdue.

LINDIE NAUGHTON.
Booterstown, County Dublin.
August 2004

Prologue

ON A CHILLY May afternoon in 1928, three tiny planes came into view above Croydon Aerodrome in south London. Two were DH Moths, which had taken off earlier, but the focus of everyone's attention was an Avro Avian biplane made of timber, wire and cloth, looking impossibly fragile as it hovered above the large crowd, its engine no louder than a motorbike.

By now the pilot was visible in the open cockpit and, in an exuberant greeting, she looped-the-loop before coming in for a perfect landing. No sooner had the plane taxied to a halt than it was surrounded by hundreds of men and women, including journalists, photographers and dignitaries, who had waited hours for this occasion.

At last a tall figure wrapped in a fur coat and wearing a cloche hat stepped carefully from the cockpit in her high-heeled shoes. Lady Mary Heath had just flown the final leg of a gruelling 9,000 mile journey from Cape Town, which had taken her three long months. Along the way, she had withstood sun, wind, rain and, on one occasion, a swarm of beetles blown into her face. She had fallen ill first with sunstroke and, later with glandular fever, and had battled officialdom again and again. Using pages stripped from an atlas, she had kept to her course by leaning out of her cockpit to see what lay below; happy the days when she found a railway line or a river, such as the Nile, to guide her. After every stage of the journey, she had donned a pair of overalls and given her engine a thorough going over. But she had also been careful to pack an evening dress and had found plenty of use for it.

In newspaper reports carried all over the English-speaking world the next day, Lady Mary was careful to underplay her considerable achievement. 'My Avian is as comfortable as a motor-car,' she had told waiting reporters. 'You really do not need special flying kit in these light planes. Why, I have flown practically from Cape Town in this outfit.' Flying along the Nile proved 'a delightful experience' when she had the opportunity to read a novel and eat chocolates as she flew along. 'So well was my Avian running that I decided after leaving Wadi Haifa to make a non-stop flight to Cairo, a distance of 700 miles,' she added casually. Even now, flying 700 miles non-stop in a small, open-topped aeroplane is no mean achievement, but Lady Mary managed to make it sound easy: 'As Cairo is an important place, I thought I must appear respectable, so I poked out a pair of silk stockings from the back locker and managed to put them on in mid-air.'

Her achievement, allied with considerable charm, turned Lady Mary into one of the best-known women of her time. What few suspected was that this forceful figure, wrapped in furs and basking in the adulation of her public, had been born not into the British aristocracy, as she allowed them to believe, but as plain Sophia Peirce Evans in Knockaderry, a small village outside the County Limerick town of Newcastle West.

She had indeed come a long way.

CHAPTER I

A Family Tragedy

O N 10 NOVEMBER 1896, Sophia Theresa Catherine Mary Peirce Evans was born in Knockaderry House, a substantial farmhouse on the outskirts of Knockaderry village, near Newcastle West in County Limerick. How much she knew of her origins, at least in her early years, is open to question. When older, calling herself 'an orphan', she would say that her father had died two months before she was born and her mother in childbirth. At other times, she liked to tell a tale of her father carrying her on his bicycle when she was little.

Whatever her stories – and the stories she had been told – her background was considerably more tragic. On 8 December 1897, her father, Jackie Peirce, had brutally battered her mother, Catherine Teresa Dooling, to death at their home. After a sensational trial in Limerick, he was declared mad; he was to spend the rest of his life at the Central Lunatic Asylum in Dublin, dying when Sophie was aged nineteen.

Growing up in her grandfather's house at Newcastle West, Sophie was educated at home and later sent away to boarding school, isolating her from the finger-pointers and the whisperers in a small, provincial town. Few in Newcastle West could have been unaware of her shocking and scandalous origins. Fuelling the interest was her fusty, bourgeois background; hers was a family sprinkled with clergymen, doctors and other pillars of respectable society.

On her father's side, the family encompassed a number of better-known local families. The D'Arcy Evans family of her grandmother were 'gentleman farmers' who had come to Munster as 'planters' following the Desmond rebellion in the seventeenth century. Knockaderry, where they settled, is a small village situated on a cross-roads four miles north-east of Newcastle West on the road to Ballingarry; Knockaderry House, the 'ancient seat' of the D'Arcy family, was 'pleasantly situated beneath the shelter of a hill and surrounded by thriving plantations,' says the historian Samuel Lewis in his contemporary history of Limerick city and county.

Sophie's paternal great-grandfather, John Peirce, was a doctor, originally from King's County, now County Offaly, where the family, originally from England, had

Dr George Peirce. *(Cussen Collection)*

settled in Cromwellian times. Early in the 1820s, a Dr McCarthy had been the only medical man in Newcastle West, but abandoned his practice after buying a brewery in the town. An advertisement was put in the Dublin newspapers looking for a replacement, and so it was that Peirce came to the County Limerick town.

He took over a house in The Square adjoining the estate of the Earl of Devon, a typical absentee landlord, who spent most of his time at the family's main property in Exeter. Across The Square lived Thomas Locke, a distant cousin of the Earl and agent of his vast interests in County Limerick. His daughter Frances caught the young doctor's eye and they married soon after. Three of their sons were to follow in the family tradition by becoming doctors; George, Sophie's grandfather, destined to take over the practice in Newcastle West, studied at the University of Glasgow.[1]

George Peirce married twice. His first wife, Sophie's grandmother, was Catherine D'Arcy Evans of Knockaderry.[2] The couple had eight children, with Sophie's father, John, usually known as Jackie, the eldest and only boy. From the start, he was wild and difficult, especially after the death of his mother in 1889 and his father's

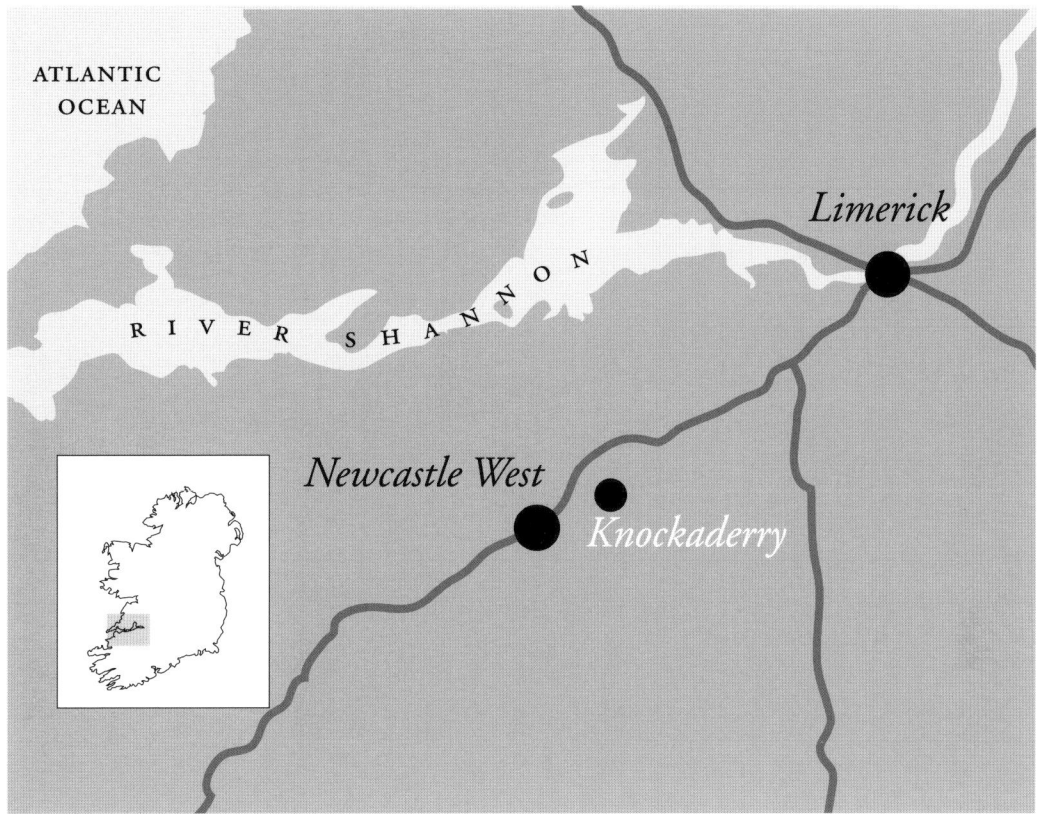

subsequent marriage to Henrietta Georgina Hewson from Ballybunion, County Kerry, a woman already in her forties, older than her new husband and completely incapable of coping with his large family.

While a good doctor and respected medical officer to the Newcastle West Union Board,[3] George was a hopeless father. At home, Jackie's exuberance was uncontrollable and in his maternal uncle, Thomas D'Arcy Evans, or Old Tom Evans, as he was called, he found a kindred spirit, only too delighted to find a replacement for two dead sons. Since the elderly man was an irredeemable drunk, George Peirce, none too pleased by this association, attempted to separate the pair by finding Jackie a job with the Provincial Bank in Kilrush, County Clare.

The dull routine of life as a banker, if anything, made Jackie worse. He was an inveterate prankster and after one escapade, the police were called in. Unrepentant, he devised a stunt to make them look foolish. For a few days, he went down to the Kilrush pier after bank hours, acting strangely enough to attract attention and then dodging away every time he saw a policeman. When he was sure the police were

Knockaderry House. *(Cussen Collection)*

following his every move, he arrived at the pier one evening with a coffin-shaped contraption on his back, put this in a boat and rowed off into the centre of the Shannon estuary.

By now, every policeman in the area had assembled on the pier. Certain that their binoculars were trained on him, Peirce stood up in the boat, theatrically threw the 'coffin' into the water and then calmly rowed back to the pier. There he was arrested while a couple of policemen rowed off to retrieve the wooden box. With some effort, they dragged it back to the shore, but when they opened it, found it full of stones and timber shavings.

Inevitably, Peirce lost his job with the bank and returned to Knockaderry, where, to the despair of his father, he continued to spend most of his time with Old Tom. At meetings of the County Limerick Hounds, at his coverts in Knockaderry and at local race meetings, he revelled in elaborate practical jokes. In one instance, he took the local shoemaker, a man who had never ridden before, dressed him in outlandish garb, sat him on a horse and entered him in a race.

On the death of his uncle, Jackie inherited Knockaderry, with the proviso that he add 'Evans' to his name. The slide into disaster began. Untrained for anything and utterly undisciplined, the new landlord's ideas on how to manage a property were curious to say the least. If a tenant owed rent, he would offer to fight him. If the tenant won, the rent in abeyance was forgotten on the spot. Soon, the Peirce house was a refuge for 'the lowest blackguards' from Newcastle West, frequenters of the workhouse and the jail; 'all respectable persons' avoided its owner, according to the judge during one of Peirce's many appearances in court.

Since none of his scandalised sisters was willing to help him manage the large house, Peirce was forced to advertise for a housekeeper. The first woman to take on this role was Catherine Keane, a labourer's wife. She was terrified of her new boss, with whom she was soon having a sexual relationship, and frequently attempted to run away; Peirce would then scour the countryside until he found her. His long list of appearances before the magistrates began after he was found guilty of assaulting first Mrs Keane's husband and later Mrs Keane herself, an offence for which he was sentenced to a month in jail.

The relationship horrified his father, who consulted the local Catholic bishop, Dr O'Dwyer, about his son's adulterous relationship with Mrs Keane. Denounced from the pulpit by Fr John O'Shaughnessy, the local Catholic priest, who seemed to find nothing strange in a man regularly beating up a woman, Mrs Keane fled the parish.

Not so lucky was the next housekeeper to arrive at Knockaderry House. Teresa O'Connor, as she then called herself, came from Castlemaine, County Kerry, which was in a different county and distant enough, so she may not have been aware of Jackie Peirce's notoriety, well documented though it was in the local newspapers. Even if she knew what he was like, the idea of living in a 'big house' with a 'gentleman' may have driven all fears for her personal safety out of her head, especially since her own origins, were, to say the least, unfortunate. The 'illegitimate daughter of an illegitimate mother', her real name was Catherine Dooling or Doolan; her father was a local farmer who had emigrated to the United States of America, while her mother was the illegitimate daughter of a Dr Mahoney from Ardfert, County Kerry.

Around 1888, Kate Teresa Dooling left her mother's home to work for a farmer near Ballybunion. After two years, she found a job in Mrs McCarthy's Hotel in Limerick. After that came the fateful move to Knockaderry. By then close to forty and about ten years older than Peirce, she was a 'fairly tall, good-looking woman of the peasant class, unequal to Evans' social position' according to later newspaper

John (Jackie) Peirce, Sophie's father
(Cussen Collection)

reports. She also had a drink problem 'from time to time'. She may have belonged to the Church of Ireland, because this time, Fr O'Shaughnessy kept his opinions about the irregular relationship at Knockaderry House to himself.

From the start, the liaison was stormy, and true to form, Peirce regularly assaulted his new housekeeper and expected her to share his bed. Inevitably, in those pre-contraception days, she found herself pregnant more than once, and was to spend at least one period in hospital after Peirce had given her a dose of sheep hash in an attempt to bring on an abortion. This followed an incident in May 1893 when he ended up in court for yet another assault against one John Liston. On this occasion, O'Connor, now styling herself 'Mrs Smyth', also prosecuted him for assault, but the charge was dismissed. In the evidence, she claimed she had married a soldier, Frederick Smyth, in June 1890 at a registry office in London, where a Mr Tottenham was the registrar. Her husband was now in Gibraltar, she said. Since she had been working in Limerick at the time of the alleged London wedding, the story was clearly a fabrication.

Just over a year later, in June 1894, a Limerick policeman, Constable O'Connor, had come across an angry crowd near the docks area of the town. In the middle of the crowd he found Peirce and a badly beaten woman, lying unconscious against a wall. In his hand Peirce held a revolver. Earlier in the day, the woman, calling herself Mrs Smyth, had visited a local doctor to seek an abortion.

After the abortion attempt had failed, Smyth had given birth to a baby boy, she called John, at the Protestant Hospital in Limerick in July 1894; she had brought the child back to Knockaderry. She had told the hospital staff that her boss was the father and that he was well able to support the child. When she had returned to Knockaderry with the baby boy, she was again calling herself 'Mrs Smyth', the wife of Thomas William Smyth, at present in Malta, whom she claimed to have married in September 1887. About the only fact coinciding with the previous story of her marriage was the name Smyth. The child then disappeared. It had died in Cork, according to its mother, because Peirce had refused to let her nurse it. The police had their suspicions, but Cork was a day's journey away and they could find nothing to suggest that the child had not died naturally.

Peirce continued to deny that he was the father. 'My relations were perfectly moral with this woman. She had a child in July last. I asked her who the father was and she said Smyth – I never saw Smyth nor did I desire to,' he said in his evidence to a sensational trial that was to come a few months later and followed allegations of rape against a neighbour, William Power, by Peirce and Mrs Smyth. By then, Mrs Smyth had suffered at least one other miscarriage, known to Dr George Peirce, who had treated her at the time. She was again pregnant, which may have triggered the events that followed.

All began late one night in February 1895, when Jackie Peirce banged on the door of his neighbour, William Power, and accused him of raping Mrs Smyth. Power, who had suffered the half-crazed Peirce's antics for years, immediately contacted his solicitor and sued Peirce for slander. In April, the case was heard in Dublin's High Court, with the outraged Power seeking the considerable sum of £1,000 in damages. By then, Peirce had withdrawn the accusation of rape but still insisted that Power had 'had immoral intercourse' with Mrs Smyth.

Power, a wealthy Catholic bachelor farmer in his fifties, lived with his sister at Chesterfield House, a large farm next door to Knockaderry House. The model of respectability, he was a regular Mass-goer and a well-known horse trainer. Peirce, on his uppers and desperate for cash, probably invented the rape story as a means of extracting money from him.

In the confusion of evidence given to the court, the true story gradually became clear. Earlier that day, Peirce had given Mrs Smyth a severe beating, perhaps because she had told him she was again pregnant. Dr John Bouchier-Hayes, a medical doctor from Rathkeale, confirmed this in his evidence. Although he made no mention of rape, she had 'marks of vile usage about the generative organs and finger marks and nail scrapes on the buttocks', the result of 'considerable violence committed on her by some person'.

After Peirce had stormed off, the badly beaten woman had run away, taking short cuts through the fields of the neighbouring farms. Her plan was to get to Rathkeale, because she was terrified that Peirce was going to shoot her and felt that she would be safer in a town with lots of people around her. At the house of a neighbour, Mrs Harrold, she asked to come in and was offered a glass of water and a cup of tea. She told Mrs Harrold what had happened and revealed the wounds on her back where Peirce had beaten her that morning with a whip. After saying that she was expecting another baby in six months time, she asked if she could wait in the house until it was dark. She was 'in dread' of being seen, although later that afternoon, Fr O'Shaughnessy visited the house and gazed in curiosity at the 'scarlet woman' of the neighbourhood. He later described her with telling lack of insight or compassion as a cold, brazen creature.

Later, when she thought it was safe, Mrs Smyth had left the Harrold house, pleading with two other women not to tell Peirce they had seen her. By this stage, Peirce was cycling around the neighbourhood, frantically trying to find her; she was always telling lies and as soon as they got back, he would lock her in a room and blacken her sides with a whip, he told one neighbour. He had spent £20 in goods for her and, three weeks earlier, had been about to pack her off to America but had changed his mind, he added.

His initial thought was that she might have taken the train to Kerry, which she had done in the past, but when he heard she was heading for Rathkeale, he abandoned his bike, ran across a field and burst out on to the road, where he found her talking to a policeman and presumably telling her story. At the sight of her tormentor, she fainted away with fright, but for some reason, probably lack of choice, opted to go back to Knockaderry House after she was revived.

In presenting the case, one counsel described Peirce and Smyth as 'half mad' and they were duly thrown out of court when the jury failed to agree. Later, the state authorities discussed prosecuting the pair for concocting a 'conspiracy for the purpose of extracting money from William Power' but sensibly abandoned the idea.

A month later, on 29 May 1895, Peirce married Mrs Smyth in the Dublin Registry Office. They were still in Dublin attempting to sort out the aftermath of the case, since Peirce not only had to pay Power but also had to underwrite all the costs of an expensive week in court. It was to ruin him and his family. Even before they left Dublin, the newly-weds were fighting, and their rows were often public, with the bride on occasion giving as good as she got.[4] Back home, Peirce continued to abuse his wife and was convicted several times for assaulting her; after one court appearance, both were sent to jail. In August 1896, a Kate Smyth was charged with drunkenness and 'grossly obscene' conduct in Limerick. She did not appear to be right in the head, the court heard, before she was sentenced to two months in jail.

After her birth on 10 November 1896, Sophie was baptised by the Reverend Joseph Vance, Church of Ireland rector of Newcastle West and canon of Limerick. Her arrival had no effect on her parents' troubled life, although her father was clearly fond of her and had the habit of carrying her around with him on his bicycle, as Sophie would later relate. His behaviour was as erratic as ever and, in one of his periodic fits of temper, he set off from Knockaderry for Queenstown, now Cobh, and the boat to America, carrying Sophie in a travelling bag under his arm. With him ranting and relaying his story to every passing stranger, he and the child were soon spotted, first in Charleville and later in Cork. There, he had wandered the streets looking for lodgings until the police were alerted by a concerned woman, who kept him in her house on Glanmire Road on the pretext of finding him a bed. Peirce was arrested and taken to Police Court, where he pleaded domestic unhappiness caused by his wife's behaviour. After his wife arrived in Cork the following day, the magistrate let the pair off, hoping for a reconciliation. The unhappy family returned to Knockaderry. In later years, Sophie would tell the tale of being found in a travelling bag when her father had attempted to board a ship for New York, but since by then she had a well-deserved reputation for telling tall tales, her listeners may not have realised that this particular story was close to the truth.

By now, Peirce was destitute. The fine building at Knockaderry was stripped of all but the most basic furniture and the family lived in the kitchen. After Peirce was declared bankrupt following the disastrous rape case, the bank sold his possessions in an effort to pay off his debts, while his property was placed into receivership. Since they had only a small allowance, and no money to pay for help, Peirce, his wife and child were the sole occupants of the large house and were ostracised by their families. Indeed, Peirce's despairing father registered a new Will in January 1897 mentioning neither his eldest child nor his newborn grandchild.

Peirce continued to feud with William Power and, in late January 1897, stood before the Newcastle West Petty Assizes yet again on charges of assault and using abusive language. This followed a similar case, just months earlier, when Peirce had escaped a long period in Tralee jail only when friends intervened. The magistrate bound both to keep the peace and dismissed the case.

The following month, Peirce was pleading to the Newcastle West Union board of governors 'that his wife was in no way destitute', that she had his house, garden and allowance which was quite enough for her support. She had taken his child from his care, he informed the guardians, and he was concerned 'lest she should dishonour herself and me by making application at any Poor Law board or elsewhere for relief'. His poor, addled wife had indeed sought refuge in the house for a couple of days before being taken to Cork as a witness against her husband. This presumably related to the incident when Peirce had abducted Sophie. Following her husband's plea, the cost of her stay at the Poor House was considered a loan to be repaid.

That March, Peirce was again in court at Limerick, where Martin Rohan claimed he had kept Peirce supplied with food and wine while in jail for a month and had also supported his wife. He was now looking for the defendant's clothes, worth £5, as part repayment of his debt.

In Newcastle West, his father, his stepmother and his sisters looked on in despair. So far, no harm had come to the infant Sophie, despite one story that he had created a sling with a baby basket attached so that he could haul her into a tree and keep her out of his way when he was busy. Although it sounds outlandish, such a tactic was not entirely unknown in farming families, where children could come to serious harm if left to run around.

Despite his good moments, it was abundantly clear that Sophie's father was mad and her mother a simple, ill-educated woman, who lived in terror of her husband's mood swings. That Sophie emerged as such a strong character from this calamitous mixture of genes was something of a miracle. Unfortunately, it was to take one final, violent act from her father before she could be delivered into anything approaching a normal childhood.

On 8 December 1897, a small paragraph appeared in the Dublin newspaper, the *Evening Herald,* about a horrific crime that had taken place the previous night in County Limerick. 'A shocking wife murder is reported from Knockadery [*sic*], Co. Limerick. John Peirce Evans, a farmer, had repeatedly quarrelled with his wife, and yesterday morning her dead body was discovered in her house,' it said under the headline 'Alleged Wife Murder in Co. Limerick.'

This was the first the outside world was to hear of the grim happenings of 6 December, when Peirce had bludgeoned his wife to death. The case became celebrated as 'The Knockaderry Murder', and it packed the courtrooms, where the perpetrator was gaped on with awe and horror, his every gesture analysed and discussed. In the *Limerick Chronicle,* the death of Sophie's mother was described as a story 'so startling and revolting that the townspeople were slow to believe the news, although fully aware that the two parties concerned in the tragedy have led an unhappy life'. Initially, the newspapers reported that Mrs Peirce had been shot. Later

> **ALLEGED WIFE MURDER IN CO. LIMERICK.**
>
> A shocking wife murder is reported from Knockadery, Co Limerick. John Pierce Evans, a farmer, had repeatedly quarrelled with his wife, and yesterday morning her dead body was discovered in her house, presenting unmistakable marks of violence, death appearing to have been caused by blows of some heavy instrument on the head. County Inspector Hayes was apprised of the murder by telegram, and left Limerick at once to investigate the facts of the tragic occurrence. Subsequently Evans was arrested on the charge of having murdered his wife.

Evening Herald, 8 December 1897.

it became clear that her death was the result of a 'fiendish attack' of kicks and blows from her husband which had lasted for an entire day. So badly battered was the woman that the shinbone on one of her legs was visible through the blood and skin.

Since Peirce was well known to be at the very least eccentric, few had any difficulty believing that the murder was the result of a bout of temporary insanity. The initial hearing took five hours before the resident magistrate, J.M. Dickson, and before proceedings began, there was an affecting scene between Peirce and his father, Dr George Peirce, with the son sobbing loudly.

According to observers who managed to squeeze into the packed room, Peirce appeared calm but 'of no fixed idea' when he was formally charged, 'that on the night of the 6th of December or morning of the 7th, he did with malice aforethought kill and murder one Kate Teresa Peirce-Evans.' During the hearing, he looked 'drowsy and fatigued', saying little apart from the occasional remark to his solicitor, Patrick T. Liston, and burying his head in his hands when a piece of clothing belonging to his late wife was produced.

Thomas Hannon Junior, a neighbour, recalled for the court the last day of the unfortunate Mrs Peirce's life. His father, Thomas senior, grazed his cows at Knockaderry and early on the fateful morning, the young lad arrived to milk them, chatting briefly with Mrs Peirce who seemed in 'her usual health' after the job was done. Later that afternoon, Thomas returned to Knockaderry House, this time with his young sisters, Kate and Annie, and while they tended to their cows, all three could hear a loud commotion from the shed built over the kitchen door of the house. 'Get up, get up!' Peirce was shouting, banging loudly on the door.

Terrified, the two girls abandoned the milking and fled, leaving Thomas to put the cows back in the field. Peirce then appeared in the yard, demanding to know where the girls had gone. At first, he told Thomas to stand at the door and not let 'the Mrs' out while he went after the young girls, but he then changed his mind and invited the young lad into the house. 'The Mrs' was very bad and he wanted someone to speak to her, he said. When Thomas went into the kitchen, he saw Mrs Peirce lying on the floor with a quilt wrapped around her, clearly unwell.

After Thomas had spoken to her for about five minutes, she appeared to recover and he helped her to her feet and then followed her as she walked into the next room. By now, it was dark and it was only when Mrs Peirce had lit a lamp that he could see a fresh cut over her eye. With Peirce's help, he then lifted her on to the bed in the kitchen, where she rested for about an hour before sitting up and making a pot of tea. After sipping a mug of tea, she vomited. When she had recovered sufficiently, she invited young Thomas to stay and have supper with 'the boss'. The young lad, increasingly uneasy, insisted that he must leave. Finding the door locked, he threatened to break it down if Peirce would not let him out. As Peirce grudgingly relented and approached the door, he took the opportunity to hit his wife across the face, following this up with a vicious kick to the shins, all the while calling her what the court described as 'opprobrious' names. The terrified witness could only remember that she failed to hit back and appeared 'very weak'.

The local police sergeant, Sergeant Thomas Mongey, told how they had arrived at Knockaderry House early the next morning to find the cold, stiff body of Mrs Peirce lying on the floor, covered with old clothes. 'Near her was the little girl, who was wrapped in peaceful sleep,' said the sergeant. The woman was dead: 'I put my hand on her face and found it cold and rigid'. There were marks over each eye and on the nose and jaw, with no blood evident, although the wounds were clearly fresh. The room 'was all in confusion'. Near the body was a bent tongs, fragments of a broken hazel stick and a basin containing dirty, reddish water. Mongey had previous experience of Peirce; as early as 1892, he had considered him 'a dangerous lunatic' but could find no grounds to lock him up.

When arrested, the still raving Peirce made a long, rambling statement, admitting that he had killed his wife and that it was the result of bad temper on both sides: 'I killed my wife and that's the long and short of it with my scolding and my temper and without knowing what I was doing and my heart is broken. My wife and I were over-worked and were irritated and afraid of each other.'

Peirce said that he had asked Tom Hannon's son and daughter to stay with them the previous day: 'We asked Tom Hannon to allow his son and his daughters to associate with us, for we were irritable and fight terrible when over-worked. They refused to stay yesterday morning through a disagreement. My wife took it to heart so that it put her into a fit and that sent me frantic for it upset my business and we were all day scolding and fighting and starved and the child starved and nobody with us to make peace.'

He hadn't hurt his wife until the evening: 'We both went out at cow-time and as we couldn't get the Hannon girls to come in, I almost forced Tom Hannon to come in and we both forced him to stay to keep the peace between us for four hours until he threatened to break the door if we didn't let him out. He left us no milk, though we had not a drop in the house.' After Hannon left, Peirce's temper had become uncontrollable and he took his anger out on his wife: 'I struck her repeatedly on the arms and body with my blackthorn stick and she got convulsions in the stomach and told me she was afraid she was going to die and that there was blood in her throat. I stopped my brutality then…and I got my coat and put it around her and got her on my lap and tried to warm her up'.

The dogs outside had started to bark: 'She was breathing slower and slower so I wrapped her up as well as I could to keep her from the cold and covered her legs and I kissed her lips and they were getting colder and colder.' As his wife stiffened in his arms, Peirce realised the enormity of what he had done and, after checking that the child was safe, ran off to the Hannon's house, barefoot and wild with panic. According to his statement, his wife had been 'delicate' and he had told Kate Hannon that she had not long to live; he had done his best for her, and the previous week had gone into Limerick and bought her 'every delicacy'. 'She and I were both afraid that our mad, devilish rows would bring on the convulsions and choke her,' he said. 'Now I have only the little one left for her mother. God help me,' he concluded with heartfelt emotion.

After all the evidence had been heard, the jury's verdict was that 'Kate Teresa Peirce aged about 40, died at her residence, at Knockaderry on Tuesday morning the 7th inst., from injuries inflicted on her by her husband John Peirce-Evans.' It refused to add a rider that Peirce was insane, although he had pleaded not guilty to the murder of his wife and the case was referred for trial to the Limerick Spring Assizes the following March. In the meantime, Peirce returned to Limerick Prison, travelling by the night mail train with a small escort.

The dead woman was buried at Churchtown Cemetery outside Newcastle West on 11 December. In prison, her husband was watched day and night before being transferred to the local asylum. He was to spend the next three months there, along with about 600 other patients. Details of the case had been sent to the authorities at Dublin Castle and newspapers reported that the Lord Lieutenant would probably order the prisoner's removal to the Criminal Lunatic Asylum in Dublin after his trial.

When the case was finally heard the following March, the defendant's ability to plead was the subject of a long discussion and much medical opinion. In the end it was decided that although he suffered from what they described as 'impulsive mania', probably manic depression in modern terminology, he was currently going through a lucid phase and was fit to stand trial.

After he was formally arraigned for having 'wilfully and feloniously and with malice aforethought' murdered Kate Theresa Peirce Evans on 7 December, Peirce was asked for his plea.

'I did not wilfully murder my wife,' Peirce replied, slowly and with considerable emotion, according to newspaper reports. The judge took that to mean not guilty on the grounds of insanity.

With the Crown case closed, his lawyer Mr D.B. Sullivan, QC pleaded eloquently for Peirce. His client had lost his comfortable property through mismanagement and had but a pittance from the court to support himself, his wife and child, he said. When these recurring fits came upon him, he seemed to be aware of what was happening and he tried to get someone, like the Hannons in this case, to protect himself and others from his own violence. From the evidence, the only conclusion to be drawn was that the man 'was not a responsible being' and could not be answerable for his acts.

After a short absence, the jury returned a verdict: Peirce was guilty of the murder but was insane at the time. The judge then ordered the prisoner to be detained as a criminal lunatic in Limerick Prison 'until the pleasure of the Lord Lieutenant was made known'.

Peirce was eventually transferred to what is now the Central Mental Hospital in the Dublin suburb of Dundrum. This institution, functioning since 1850 as an asylum for 'criminal lunatics', remains the only psychiatric facility for the criminally insane in Ireland. The overwhelming majority of its patients are referred from within the prison system and suffer from illnesses such as schizophrenia, psychosis and manic depression. Based on a 35-acre site, the prison accommodation consisted of small cells with barred windows. Once locked up within its walls, prisoners could expect to see little of the outside world again.

In May 1904, Thomas Hannon senior took out a seven-year lease on Knockaderry House and the 56 acres of land surrounding it. His son, Thomas Junior, became the tenant, paying an annual rent of £36 3s 9d. Three years later, in April 1907, the Hannons bought the house for £502 under the Land Purchase Acts. Their descendents still own the property.

By then, Jackie Peirce's only daughter was a young girl living in Newcastle West. Despite the efforts of her family to give her a normal upbringing, it must have been hard for them to forget her dreadful beginnings. From an early age, she was clearly her father's daughter, fearless and difficult to control. Whether or not she would also inherit his mental instability only time would tell.

CHAPTER 2

Growing up in Newcastle West

IMMEDIATELY AFTER the tragic death of her mother, Sophie was brought to the house of her grandfather, Dr George Peirce, in Newcastle West. While his wife did her best, she was neither young nor capable and the day-to-day job of looking after the infant girl soon fell to her aunts, in particular Ann Maria, usually called 'Cis', and Sophia Louisa, called 'Lou'.

Sophie was to spend her childhood in the prosperous and busy market town, twenty miles south-west of the city of Limerick.[1] Dominated by the Earl of Devon's estate, society in the Newcastle West of Sophie's youth was still strictly divided. While the Protestants and planters, the landlord's support class, were neighbours of the Peirces in The Square, the poor of the parish, mostly Catholic, were kept remote and out of sight, though not entirely neglected, with the Earl of Devon contributing generously to the local Catholic church and to a school for all the poor children of the neighbourhood.

Through marriage, the Peirces were related to the owners of many of the big houses in the locality. Heathfield belonged to Edward Locke Lloyd and Castleview to Thomas Locke, and later to Sophie's grand-uncle, Robert Peirce. Perhaps the best known of the big houses was Cahirmoyle, where the artist Dermod O'Brien, a son of the Irish rebel William Smith O'Brien, lived until 1920; he was an acquaintance of the Peirce family.

In 1910, the fabric and character of Newcastle West changed forever when the town was sold off by the Earl of Devon, who was experiencing financial difficulties. In the prospectus for the auction, it was stated that Thomas E. Lloyd, a cousin of George Peirce's and the executor of his Will, was paying the ground rent for the Peirce house on The Square.

Time was running out for the landlord class in Ireland. The disestablishment of

The house at No 1, The Square, Newcastle West (on left), where Sophie was brought up. *(Cussen Collection)*

the Church of Ireland in 1869, followed by the Irish Land Act a year later, allowing tenants to buy out their landlords, heralded the beginning of the end for the Protestant ascendancy. As Roman Catholicism and Irishness became synonymous, it cannot have been easy for ordinary Protestant families like the Peirces, who, simply because of their religion, were associated with all that had been bad about English rule; many simply left the country they had lived in for centuries. Ironically, the impetus for a Gaelic cultural and social revival had come from well-educated, middle-class citizens just like them, such as Douglas Hyde, John Millington Synge and William Butler Yeats.[2]

Others, especially those deeply rooted in their rural communities, refused to leave a country they saw as their own. But they lived in fear, especially in the volatile early 1920s, when gangs of excitable youths, stoked up on alcohol and Republican ideology, considered anyone living in a big house to be the enemy and roamed the countryside looking for trouble.

This was the background to Sophie's childhood and adolescence, though there is no evidence that she ever took any interest in Irish politics and the cataclysmic events that were to alter the country's political landscape forever during those years. All her life, she believed unthinkingly, like so many of her class, that the British Empire brought civilisation and improved prosperity to its dominions and subject nations. She never had any difficulty describing herself as both Irish and British.

In Newcastle West, she was brought up in the same stiflingly strict manner as her four aunts before her. None of the girls had attended local schools and since they were not allowed on the streets of the town alone, their only experience of the outdoors was in a special play area behind the house, accessible by a private gate.

The arrival of a baby in the house must have been cheering for the remaining aunts, but as the years went by, money was increasingly a problem, especially after the murder trial, with a broken-hearted Dr Peirce unable to maintain his medical practice. At the turn of the century, the family had two servants, few enough for a family of its status; a decade later, they had just one. By the time Knockaderry House was sold off to the Hannon family in 1907, Dr Peirce's health was failing and later that year, on 20 October, he died of senile dementia. Despite his failing faculties, he is said to have instructed Cis and Lou, the two daughters remaining in Newcastle West, to look after young Sophie, then almost ten years old. He left £4,712 in his will to be administered by his wife and his cousin Thomas E. Lloyd, all of it going to his wife and daughters.

Cis, then in her early thirties, was the eldest of the aunts. She was Sophie's favourite – 'my mother aunt' she called her in her letters home as an adult, signing herself 'Baby'. Remembered as a small, busy woman with a shock of dark hair that she attempted to control with a large floppy hat, Cis was well-liked locally and Sophie was lucky to have her, according to those around then. Cis occupied her time with painting, including portraits of local children, some of which still exist. She particularly loved dogs; at one time she owned one so small, it could fit in a tea-cup, her distant relative Helen Allott remembered.

Sophia Louisa ('Lou') was altogether a more fragile character and the only other sister still living in Ireland. By the early part of the century, Frances Thomasina and Margaret had both moved to England, while Aphra Jane married a man called Pepper and moved to Canada. After the sale of the house in 1915, Lou finally found the courage to leave Newcastle West for England, a move Sophie approved of. She appears to have settled in the Isle of Man, but later on would meet Sophie on regular trips to London. Both Lou and Aphra suffered from depression all their lives.

For a vivacious child like Sophie, the atmosphere in the house on The Square was suffocating, especially while her grandfather was still alive. Even before the dreadful murder case, the Peirce family had little contact with the world outside, despite their father's continuing involvement with the local workhouse. Their names do not appear in the lists of guests for the hunt balls and other glittering social occasions, despite their family connections to several of the local 'big house' families. As she grew into a lively child, the aunts did their best to keep Sophie protected from taunts or insults, but she did not always understand this and all her life aspired to be part of the 'county' set she was excluded from when young.

According to local anecdote, the young Sophie was occasionally seen in the town; once rescuing a kitten, or 'pusheen' in the local dialect, from the river. When asked what she would call it, she replied, 'Moses – because I found him on the banks of the river.' By her own account, she could not play games and was permitted only a half-hour's walk each day. As a result, before she was sent away to school in Dublin at the age of twelve, she weighed twelve stone, very heavy even for a tall child like herself. 'My childhood has made me love freedom of every kind today,' she was to say.

She claimed that her aunts disapproved of sport for girls and moved her from one school to another when hockey or athletics figured too prominently on the timetable: 'I was taken away from one school…on account of the fact that not only was hockey played there, but one match in the term was played against a boys' school! I was at once transferred to another school where the girls went out, two and two, every day for a nice long walk in galoshes!'

Judging from photographs taken at the time, Sophie's childhood included regular outings to Ballybunion, where she could visit either her Uncle Robert's cottage at Doon Bay or another called 'Raven Cliff', which belonged to her D'Arcy cousins. Ballybunion, with its cliffs, caves, long beaches and the crumbling ruin of the Fitzmaurice castle, was not only breathtakingly beautiful but designed to enthral any child and she always remembered Kerry with delight:

> This delicate fairy grass, with seeds all shrouded and shaking.
> I used to gather it, quaking, where the Kerry highroads pass.

she writes in a poem after spotting similar grass on a visit to Africa in the 1920s.

Photographed with her as a child were a couple of Creagh Langford cousins, and later, Richbel Curling, by then the Earl of Devon's agent in County Limerick, an unmarried man Sophie disliked intensely all her life, and on whom centred a certain amount of local rumour.

Despite the best efforts of her aunts – or maybe because of them – Sophie was a wild youngster and did not change much as she progressed into early adulthood. Even in her young days, she must have been a striking figure. From her mother she

A family group portrait, probably in Ballybunion. *(Cussen Collection)*

took her mass of dark hair and her height, reaching almost six feet tall, at a time when the average height for a woman was at least six inches less. With her height and her intelligent, mobile face, she was hard to ignore. Like her father, she was quick-witted, loved playing pranks and craved attention.

In one instance, while at boarding school, she discovered a secret passage and took it upon herself to hide mutton bones there together with a message in 'blood' (red ink) supposedly from a prisoner who had been tortured to death. On another occasion, she hoodwinked a headmistress by pretending to be the aunt of a pupil and taking the said girl out to tea. Another escapade found her climbing from her dormitory into the grounds of another school to steal some of the refreshments laid out for a garden party. Or so she claimed – another of her gifts was the ability to tell a good yarn and, all her life, she was prone to exaggeration, making it difficult to take anything she said at face value.

Life opened up for Sophie after the death of her grandfather and in her early teens, she was at last permitted to leave the stifling confines of the house in Newcastle West for boarding school. Judging from her own comments in an article written for a magazine published by the School for the Deaf in Nova Scotia called *School-Days*,[3] she attended at least one other school before finally arriving at St Margaret's Hall in Dublin. Then a small day and boarding school for Protestant girls on Mespil Road, St Margaret's was run by the formidable Edith F. Badham, daughter of a Church of Ireland rector, who had graduated with a first in history from Newham College, Cambridge, in 1888, and in 1909 was Trinity College Dublin's first woman LL.D. She was rarely to be seen without her splendid crimson graduation gown.[4]

In common with most of the buildings in the area, St Margaret's, facing the Grand Canal, was a large Victorian house with steps leading to the front door. Dr Badham had a drawing room, a study and presumably a bedroom somewhere. Another teacher, Miss Hensman, a woman rarely seen without a pork-pie hat firmly pinned to her head, also had a room of her own. At the back, there was an extension with space for two forms and, behind that again, the kindergarten for girls and boys. Upstairs were two dormitories for the twenty or so boarders. Across from the school and to one side, a large oblong plot of land held two tennis courts and a garden tended by the redoubtable Miss Hensman which kept the school supplied with fruit and vegetables. At an impressionable age, Sophie was presented with two striking models of independent and self-sufficient women.

At St Margaret's Hall, Sophie received the same classics-based education as any boy of her background. While Catholic schools followed the French tradition of educating young ladies for home and family duties, the Protestant schools were more progressive and had been the first to put forward girls as candidates for the Intermediate Education Examination. In 1879, the Royal University Act had allowed girls to compete for university places and in 1884, nine women graduated from the Royal University; this sparked off a huge row with the Roman Catholic bishops. The curriculum covered all the usual subjects approved of by the Department of Education – Latin and physics as well as English and French literature. Students who attended the school later remembered that the facilities included a well-equipped science laboratory, undoubtedly fuelling Sophie's interest in biology, botany, physiology, physics and chemistry.

For hockey, the girls travelled the short distance to the Pembroke Wanderers grounds in Ballsbridge on Mondays and Thursdays and Sophie soon became a keen player, also enjoying tennis. When it was too wet to play sports, pupils visited the National Gallery of Ireland, Christ Church or a museum until school finished officially at five o'clock. For Sophie, coming from an oppressive small-town existence in a house ruled by penny-pinching and the need to keep up appearances, it must have been heaven.

St Margaret's also provided the intellectual stimulation she craved as a gifted and intelligent young woman. From the start, she was a brilliant student and before she left, her name was engraved on the school's Board of Honour, prominently displayed in the entrance hall. Dr Badham felt she was destined for great things. 'When my sister, a pupil there later on, asked about her, Dr Badham had said that of all the pupils she had over the years, Sophie was one of just two that she felt was certain to go places. She had everything – she was well mannered, clever and good at sports. So her form was known even then,' said Robert Oliver Villiers Lloyd, whose father Robert was a second cousin of Jackie Peirce's.

While her school days were drawing to a close, money in the Peirce household continued to be tight and her wealthier uncles and cousins, some living in Dublin and others in England, were probably helping to pay for Sophie's education. Her father's escapades had ruined the immediate family financially and Dr Peirce had not left enough money to keep his family of non-earning daughters comfortably. For the rest of her life, Sophie would remain preoccupied by money and, despite the norms of the time, adamant that she had to earn her own living. She had no intention of turning into one of her aunts.

CHAPTER 3

College Days in Dublin

In 1914, with her school days over, the seventeen-year-old Sophie enrolled in the Royal College of Science for Ireland as an associate student to take a variety of scientific courses. The family's financial problems had cast a shadow over her ambitions and she had abandoned plans to follow the male members of her family into the medical profession, which even then would have proved costly.

With the help of relatives, she found lodgings with a Miss Merrick at 127 Leinster Road, Rathmines, then still a distinctly Protestant suburb of Dublin. Almost across the road from her, in number 22, was a distant cousin, John D'Arcy Evans, while nearby was the residence of Count Markievicz and, presumably, his fiery and slightly unbalanced wife, who was to become the first woman to be elected a member of the British House of Commons, although as an Irish Republican, she did not take up her seat.

Dublin at the time was the second city of the Empire, a bustling and lively city with a growing population.[1] Large shops were packed with the latest London fashions and there was a thriving arts scene. Thanks to the trams, clattering and banging their way from the inner suburbs to O'Connell Street, the city was easy to negotiate, making it a pleasant place for the more comfortably off, so long as they could ignore the grindingly poor tenements and the notorious red light district around Montgomery Street, known as 'the Monto'. With Bewley's opening its first establishment in 1894, café society had arrived, providing respectable venues where young ladies could meet and mingle. Others were to follow, such as the Café Cairo at the St Stephen's Green end of Grafton Street, a favourite student haunt in Sophie's day.

But for all its modern veneer and growing consumer culture, Ireland remained inward-looking, bourgeois and conventional. An elite class of wealthy farmers and a celibate Catholic clergy set the tone and, while they may have differed on other matters, they certainly agreed that a woman's place was in the home, looking after her husband and children. Even women's suffrage was seen as contrary to natural law; since a woman and man became 'one' when they married, why ever would they need two votes?

Grafton Street, Dublin, in the early 1900s.

Still, Sophie, never one to pay much attention to what others wanted or expected, was all set to enjoy her college years. Some regarded the Royal College of Science for Ireland, housed in an imposing building on Merrion Street,[2] as no more than a technological college for farmers, but in 1911 the newly crowned King George V had reopened it with full university status as a college providing vital skills for the go-ahead, modern Ireland.

The students' handbook from the period makes its function clear: 'The Royal College of Science for Ireland provides a complete and thorough course of instruction in those branches of science which are connected with agriculture, engineering and manufacture.' A four-year course led to an Associateship of the College – the equivalent of a bachelor's degree in other colleges; there were also more practical courses in poultry instruction, butter-making and bee-keeping. Throughout her life, Sophie would proudly append the letters 'ARCSc.I' to her name.

The college was open from 9am until 4pm on weekdays, except for Wednesdays when it closed an hour earlier. On arrival each morning, students had to sign the roll book in the entrance hall and, if they had been absent, provide the Dean with a reasonable excuse, a source of much irritation.

Terms ran from October to December, January to Easter and Easter to June, when examinations took place. The college's highest authority was the Dean, H.H. Jeffcott, while the college itself was answerable to the Department of Agriculture and Technical Instruction for Ireland, housed next door.[3] Among Sophie's lecturers was Michael Govern, the professor of botany, who later took an interest in her career as an aviator.

In her first year, Sophie achieved consistently high marks in all subjects and in her second year did even better, earning herself £2 when she took a first prize for geology, also finishing second in zoology. By now she was well-settled in the college and was among a small group of students who decided to publish a students' magazine. *The Torch* was a lively publication, mixing reports from the various debating societies and sporting clubs with poetry and opinion pieces. As part of the editorial board, Sophie 'exercised her censor's blue pencil with some skill', noted the editor later on, and contributed numerous articles, snippets and poems.

From the first issue, we discover that she was active in the Agricultural Debating Society. At a lecture on 'Fertilisers' by Mr Milne on 14 January 1916, she commented on the scarcity of fertilisers, telling the story of a gardener who, to supply potash to his forget-me-nots, was compelled to:

Dissolve in anguish by his scalding tears
His treasured love-letters of forty years.

The second issue of *The Torch* appeared in February 1916, with the editor complaining that some students had condemned the first issue as 'pretty rotten' before it had even appeared. Sophie was praised for her involvement with the hockey club, which had organised a whist drive at the Café Cairo. The club played mostly mixed matches, with Sophie a stalwart in defence as well as looking after the all-important post-match refreshments. Over the season, the club won 23 of its 40 mixed matches, drawing two and losing fifteen, while the men on their own lost all three of their matches. For a club without its own grounds, it was not a bad record

In that same issue of *The Torch*, a piece on the pivotal importance of the roll book in RCSc.I student mythology describes the signatures of the various students, among them 'the inimitable S-P (always a two part keystone)'.

She was clearly a popular student:

P's for Peach. We call her Miss P——ce
Tho' rather a 'deer', she's really not fierce.

goes a line in a verse from the fourth issue of *The Torch*. The June issue again pokes gentle fun at her. With term now over, the students will disperse for the summer:

> Court martial held in registrar's office. Sentenced to Rustication but commuted to three days hard labour
> President O'Conagh
> Countess Fierce.

Also in the issue is 'The First Law of T.D.', a lengthy satire on the college's rules, signed 'Sophia Peirce', though she later denied she had written it, possibly realising belatedly that she had gone too far and hoping to escape the wrath of the college authorities. It was not the last time her impulsiveness would cause her trouble. Cleverly written as a daydream in the style of the H.G. Wells novel *The Time Machine*, the article gives a good idea of the severe strictures facing students:

> Rule 19.1211. Prohibition 4.2: Smoking is prohibited in the Hall or Halls; Corridor or Corridors in about, above below; or off the step or steps; in front, behind, beside or beyond the College. On the roof, in the subways, on the ledge around the roof or down the ventilated airshafts or in the areas surrounding the basement. Any student or students, man or many, who shall or shall not be found breaking, violating or contravening this rule and regulation shall be hanged, drawn and quartered; shot at dawn (3 a.m. shooting hour!) or fined five bob and their flesh used to feed the guinea pigs and rabbits and their blood for watering on the roof.

As for Rule 19.292, this ordained:

> Students and others in and out of the precincts of the college shall not within the hours of 12 a.m. and 11.59 p.m. breathe or otherwise inhale or exhale without permission of the Registrar and Council.

The authorities can't have been too pleased, although there is no record of their reaction to this fairly innocuous piece of undergraduate humour.

Sophie's wild streak was never too far from the surface. Once, when 'dared' by fellow students, she stepped out of a college window several stories off the ground and walked around the entire building, leaping from one precarious foothold to the next and from windowsill to windowsill when necessary. She admitted to her independent nature later on, clearly thinking it was genetic:

Wherever a stream has flowed, or a winding road may lead,
That's the blood of my breed. The lust of the open road.

On 22 June 1916, her father died of 'general paralysis' in the Dundrum Lunatic Asylum. An inquest was held two days later, which was standard for people held in state custody. Nothing untoward was found. Local legend has it that his body was returned to Newcastle West by train for burial in the D'Arcy Evans family tomb at Churchtown cemetery, close to that of his wife. Almost no one was present at the funeral. It seems unlikely that Sophie, although protected from her family history during her childhood, could have remained entirely ignorant of this, or of how her father's illness had affected the family circumstances. She must surely have been aware that although he died intestate, he left a tidy sum of £1,138, probably from the sale of Knockaderry House, with administration granted to her Aunt Cis.

Money was probably on her mind when she met someone that summer who would alter the course of her life. Captain William Davies Eliott-Lynn was an officer with the Royal Engineers based temporarily in Beresford Barracks at the Curragh, County Kildare, not much more than an hour's drive from Dublin. Eliott-Lynn, originally from Liverpool, was not a regular army officer. Despite living in South Africa at the time, he had volunteered in August 1915, taking a few years off his true age, and is listed under 'temporary and acting captains' for the duration of World War I.

Hardly an ideal candidate for the horrors of trench warfare, Lynn had fortuitously lost part of a finger in a motorcycling accident at Poperinghe just a month after arriving at the Front and, when he recovered, was sent to Ireland in the aftermath of the 1916 Rising. Although this was the beginning of 'The Troubles', which would eventually result in Irish independence, nowhere does Sophie mention the circumstances that brought her future husband to Ireland, although she must have been aware of what was going on.

Aged forty-one and unmarried,[4] Lynn somehow or other met Sophie that summer, probably at one of the many social functions British Army officers attended, and was immediately taken with her originality and spirit. He seems to have met her family, and there is a photograph of the couple looking relaxed and happy at Ballybunion. Sophie, by now very aware of her family's impoverished status and the impending sale of their house in Newcastle West, probably saw marriage as her only salvation from a life of penny-pinching and poverty and was unlikely to dismiss a reliable earner with a healthy bank balance, even one who had escaped matrimony until this late stage in his life.

Sophie with her first husband, Captain William Davies Eliott-Lynn, in Ballybunion. *(Cussen Collection)*

In the autumn, Sophie was back in Dublin and embarking on the third year of her studies. *The Torch* continued to flourish. Its self-imposed task, the editorial committee proclaimed in Volume 2, No. 1, was to make life more interesting for the student. Again it is not difficult to pick out references to Sophie in the less serious articles:

> …his eye fell upon a girl who was taller than the rest and who seemed to command them all.

There is more criticism of the distressingly impersonal nature of the college, where the cloakrooms were the only communal meeting-place. The public, according to one writer, saw science as nothing more than a hobby for the idle rich. Despite its imposing facade, which included a seated figure representing Science and full-length figures of the Irish scientists Rowan Hamilton and Robert Boyle, few Dubliners even knew the college existed.

On 26 November 1916, Sophie stunned her fellow students by marrying Captain

Lynn, by now officer commanding No. 1 Works Company, Royal Irish Rifles:

> Considerable interest was manifested in college when it became known that Miss S.C. Peirce, one of our most popular lady students, had been married to Captain W.D.E. Lynn, R.E., on November 26 in Rathmines Parish Church. During the past few years, Mrs Lynn has occupied a prominent position in the social, athletic and literary life of the College. From its inception, she has taken a deep interest in *The Torch* both in her capacity as a member of the committee and as a constant contributor. On the hockey field, she is a leading figure, her fine defensive play contributing materially to the success of the club last year, while she also earned the thanks of that club by her able management of their teas. The students of the College will be pleased to hear that she purposes finishing her course here and we are sure all will unite in wishing Captain and Mrs Lynn every success and happiness.

Reverend E.H. Lewis-Crosby had performed the marriage in the Holy Trinity Church, near Sophie's Dublin residence. Witnesses were Violet C. Kelly and R.P.N. Swayne. The groom's father, William, is described as a 'minister'; the bride's as a 'gentleman'.

It was a year full of personal drama for Sophie. A month later, on 12 December, her step-grandmother Henrietta Peirce died, leaving less than £300 to be divided among four step-daughters and Sophie.[5] In January, her father's estate was finally settled, presumably bringing her a small income. Soon after, the house on The Square was sold to the Ulster Bank, and when Cis moved to Doon Cottage in Ballybunion, where she was to live for the rest of her life, the family's links with the town ended.

At a College Social held in late January, 'Mr D. Dowling called on Miss Browne to present Mrs Lynn with a very pretty teapot as a token of esteem from the students on the occasion of her recent marriage'.

Sophie's decision to marry was sudden even by her impulsive standards and for such an outgoing character, remarkably low-key. Because she had just turned twenty, it is difficult to believe that her aunts approved of her marrying so young, although possibly they hoped that she would now be financially secure, which was the most likely motive for her marrying a man twice her age. But thanks to her childhood, raised as an orphan by maiden aunts, Sophie had little idea of what marriage meant and there are indications that the entire experience came as something of a shock.

Initially at least, her life appears to have continued as normal after the wedding. Her new husband was based in the Curragh during the week, while she remained in 'digs', continuing to pursue her studies and her literary endeavours with *The Torch*. A

Sophie poses with her much loved Harley-Davidson J-11 motorbike.
(Newspaper cutting, Cussen Collection)

florid article signed 'Agricola', published in February 1917, could have been written by no one else and won a prize as the best article in the issue. A farmer, says Agricola, 'lives in the midst of beautiful nature. Can a man be melancholy who has a garden to dig or a byre to bed down with straw for a heifer or a kid?' Tea at Mitchell's or Café Cairo could not possibly compare, she argues:

> A child brought up amongst these surroundings will not miss the excitement of the picture house, skating rink, the degrading music hall song or cynical catchphrase cheapening earthly life. Yet how many of our young men do we see year after year leaving the beautiful country for the lowest bars in our great cities, where congregate the most degraded wretches of society?

Less than six months after her marriage, the new Mrs Lynn offered her services to the War Office as a motor dispatch rider, abandoning her studies at least temporarily. For the two previous years, newspapers had reported regularly on the work of the 'splendid women' who had been helping the war effort by taking over men's jobs, eventually making conscription possible. To cover for the men, women learned to drive, to operate complicated machinery in factories and to dig the earth. Skirts became shorter and clothes more practical. Female dispatch riders wore khaki overcoats, high lace-up leather boots and riding breeches, becoming the first generation of women to wear trousers. They also carried with them an appealing sense of daring.

When she volunteered, Sophie could have been following the example of her new husband, swept up in the prevailing spirit of patriotism. Alternatively, she may have been attempting to escape both him and the mundane reality of domestic life. There was also the perennial question of money. Her work as a dispatch rider meant that Sophie would be earning her own income for the first time. More crucially, she would be embarking on her first great adventure, unchaperoned and free to come and go as she wished, with no aunts or husband holding her back.

According to the *The Torch*, no sooner had Sophie been accepted by the War Office than she took the ferry to Wales and rode her new motor bike from Holyhead to London in a women's record time of eleven and a half hours. How they came up with this fact is unknown since there was no official race between the two places; more than likely, the newly minted Mrs Lynn invented the story of a record to embellish the report. Judging by photographs of the time, her mode of transport was a Harley-Davidson J-11 two-cylinder motorbike capable of reaching speeds of up to 60 mph. At the time, the War Office was using these American bikes extensively and, later, Sophie would bring her much-loved Harley with her to Africa:

> I, at Tangata, with its sand and ooze,
> Was forced to wait while twenty 'boys' or more,
> Half-naked, laughing – in two lashed canoes
> Ferried my Harley o'er.

CHAPTER 4

The War Years

Later in 1917, Sophie was back in Ireland recovering from an unexplained accident, and contributed an article on her war experiences to the December issue of *The Torch*. She had been based with the Women's Auxiliary Army Corps somewhere near Salisbury, probably at Boscombe, just north of the city, and was not entirely enjoying her work: 'There's a solo bike in the pouring rain outside, waiting patiently to endanger my life and limb by skidding all over the awful clayey roads that look so topping in decent weather.'

The working day, she reports, had been fairly simple, starting with parade at 8 am and 'knocking off' no later than 6 pm: 'Now they have practically halved the transport here. All the light lorries are driven by girls, which means all night work for some of us nearly every night'. Although she was driving or riding from sixty to a hundred miles each day, she considered herself fortunate: 'Personally, I've been jolly lucky, not being later than 10.30 any night yet since I came back.'

She expected changes when she returned: 'They are going to put us girls on guard after this month. That means sleeping in the main guardroom all night with your clothes on, and cursing the telephone operator every time he wakes you to take wires and dispatches and things.' With the rest of the 'girls', Sophie was billeted in a hut at the camp's 'Married Quarters', about a mile from the aerodrome: 'The quarters themselves are rather jolly, two in a room, and there's a priceless sort of rivalry between us as to who should have the most "*outré*" Kirschner pictures up and the largest amount of "frillies" negligently laid in conspicuous places the day the Colonel inspects the billets!' It was not a huge leap from the boarding school existence she had relished just a few years earlier.

The women were paid the same wages as the men, and, for the purposes of overtime, were classed as second air mechanics, earning what seems like a miserly five pence an hour (less than 3 cent in euro currency). There were lighter moments, with dances about once a fortnight and joyrides into Salisbury. At the local cinema, the previous month's Pathé newsreels and out-of-date Charlie Chaplin films were on view for three old pennies (about 2 cent in euro currency).

During World War I, Sophie drove one of these vans. (*Cussen Collection*)

Driving the Crossley tenders, to pick up the pieces and clean up after air crashes, provided the most interesting work at the station. Other accidents were more mundane, with many of the drivers breaking their arms when their machines backfired. There was the occasional encounter with civilians:

> One of our girls was sent to fetch an officer from a station about twelve miles away at 11.30 the other night. On the way back, she did a farmer's cart in. She says he was asleep and drunk and all over the road. He says he was driving with one arm, the other being 'occupied'.

So life wasn't all easy – but 'there isn't one of us that would go back to "civvy" life without regret', said Sophie, clearly speaking from the heart.

Soon after, she was sent to France. Since the first detachment of the Women's Army Auxiliary Corps had arrived in France towards the end of March 1917, the numbers of women in service had risen to 6,023 within a year and they fulfilled all sorts of non-military functions, freeing up men for the trenches. While close to the Front, Sophie possibly worked with an ambulance unit, since she claimed later in life to be an experienced nurse. She would certainly have witnessed the horrors of war at first hand, since women operated first-aid stations close to the action, although, officially, they were not allowed within three miles of the trenches. Sophie's knowledge of motorbikes and cars would certainly have come in useful, given the woeful lack of skilled drivers for the heavy Napier ambulances and an assortment of other vehicles. The experience undoubtedly formed the basis of her enduring skill with engines.

Life was tough for the nurses and their drivers, and while, according to later friends such as Elinor Smith, Sophie never spoke of her experiences, many others did, giving a graphic picture of those dreadful times – the ever-present mud, the shattered villages of northern France and Belgium, the constant threat of death. The women tended to the wounded as best they could in the cellars of bombed-out houses and spent long days under heavy fire in buildings that were likely to collapse in flames around them at any time. For diversion, the more adventurous or foolhardy would hop on the side of an ammunition bus 'to see the fun' as they became inured to the constant bombardment and to the eerie screams of the shells before they hit the ground and exploded.

The steady stream of hideously damaged human beings was more difficult to endure: '…it was more like hell than anything I can imagine. The never-ending processions of groaning men being brought in on those horrible blood-soaked stretchers, suffering unimaginable tortures, the filth, the cold, the stench, the hunger, the vermin and the squalor of it all…' said one contemporary witness.

When exhausted, they would retreat to Folkestone for three days' rest, or they could go to Paris, where two popular nightclubs were called 'Heaven' and 'Hell'. Although Sophie had learned early on how to block out anything unpleasant in her life, what she witnessed in France can hardly have left her unmoved.

Meanwhile, her husband had resisted all attempts to send him back to the horrors of the front line, clearly having seen enough on his brief first visit. After his year in Ireland, he was pronounced fit for action and ordered to embark for France, but he was having none of it and wrote a letter to the War Office pleading his case:

> Sir – I have been a contracting engineer in South Africa for the last 13 years and, during that period, have had contracts for both road and railway construction. I have considerable experience in excavating, banking, culvert and bridge erection and am well accustomed to working with native labour.

Sophie in uniform during her years as a driver. (*Cussen Collection*)
Detail from John Lavery's portrait of Sophie in uniform painted in 1918. (*Cussen Collection*)

Scribbled in red on the letter was a note commenting that Captain W.D.E. Lynn should do very well for a job in Africa. So he was spared a return to the dreaded trenches of Europe and, by April 1917, was on his way to British East Africa. In August, he was appointed works officer at the coastal town of Lindi in Tanganyika Territory and later given other jobs in the area, finally promoted to the rank of temporary major in October 1918. The war ended just weeks later on 11 November 1918. On the New Year's Honours List of 1919, Lynn was awarded an OBE. All was going well until early 1919, when he contracted a life-threatening case of malaria and, from Tanganyika, was sent to hospital in Alexandria in Egypt, where he lingered between life and death, losing three stone in weight and becoming very depressed. By April, he was claiming that he had recovered his strength and energy. Since he was quite cheered up and had suffered no recurrences of the malaria, he was pronounced fit for service, providing he avoided malaria zones, and ordered back to London.

There he suffered relapses in June and again in August, and since his condition was considered to be 'fair only', it was recommended that he be demobbed. A flurry of letters from his London address at Lancaster Gardens followed, in which he claimed the right to be 'repatriated' to South Africa. 'I came home from Johannesburg, South Africa, specially to join up and I wish to be repatriated before being demobilised,' said one of them. His request was turned down, and in January 1920, Lynn gave up the fight and formally left the army while still in London.

Although her husband was struggling with a serious and recurring illness, Sophie remained in France until at least July 1919, where, dressed in the uniform of a transport unit, she had her portrait painted by Sir John Lavery.[1] At the time, Lavery, like his fellow Irish painter William Orpen, was an official war artist; both men were later knighted for their work. Commissioned to produce a series of paintings for the 'Women's Work' collection at the newly established Imperial War Museum, Lavery had travelled to France, recording the work of women in hospitals, canteens, graveyards and improvised offices. Of the Voluntary Aid Detachment Motor Convoy at Étaples, the British base camp on the French coast near Le Touquet, he wrote: 'They do all the ambulance driving for a large district and contain some of the finest golfing and sporting women among the personnel'; hence possibly the golf club in a photograph of Sophie from the same period as the portrait. Lavery was expected to emphasise the women's comradeship with their male co-workers, but prudishly declined an invitation to paint a group of women playing football at Dieppe. It is tempting to speculate that among the footballing women was Sophie Eliott-Lynn, whose duties certainly included driving ambulances.

By autumn of that year, she was seriously considering her future and applied to the Department of Agriculture and Technical Instruction in Dublin for a training grant so that she could resume her studies in Dublin. Although such grants were available only to men, the Department took up her case and applied for a grant on her behalf to the Treasury office in London:

> Mrs Eliott-Lynn was a student of the Royal College of Science for Ireland before joining the Women's Army Auxiliary Corps…. Her grading in the Army was that of Driver-Mechanic, and the Department understands that she acted as Motor-Cyclist Despatch Rider in France for a considerable period.

Her first battle with the authorities for equal treatment of men and women ended in failure. While there was some sympathy for the case of ex-servicewomen undertaking training schemes for 'shorthand typists, tailoring, domestic service, etc' in order to earn a living after the war, Sophie's request was turned down because she was a married woman, presumably supported by a husband, and failed to make it clear why she could not afford to pay for her own further education, considered a luxury for a woman, especially one who was married.

Sophie emerged from the war a mature and self-sufficient woman and, like many others, found readjusting to 'civvy' life difficult. The war had changed women's lives beyond recognition. Social conventions had broken down in all classes of society, and women, earning their own money for the first time in their lives, had enjoyed living away from their families in hostels or lodgings. Single women could distract themselves from the horror of war by spending money on clothes, restaurants and the 'pictures', while married women went out with their friends. Although the pub remained an entirely male preserve, mixed groups socialised in nightclubs and at organised dances, which were recognised as valuable morale boosters. The cage door had been unlocked and there was no going back.

Her experiences abroad did nothing to calm Sophie's exuberance and, on one visit home, she would confirm that she was still very much her father's daughter. Her cousin Creagh Langford of Ardagh relayed the following tale to the Newcastle West solicitor Robert Cussen, many years later:

> One summer towards the end of World War 1, Sophie visited her Auntie Cis, by then living in Doon Cottage, Ballybunion. This particular evening, there was a lovely moon shining and close to midnight, when the tide was full in, nothing would do Sophie but to go down to Doon Bay and, guided by the moon's rays, to swim through the opening in the Virgin's Rock.
>
> Auntie Cis was against the engagement, but Sophie pooh-poohed her. So Auntie Cis sat on the edge of the cliffs watching Sophie get into the water and making for the opening. Well, Sophie swam in but never came out, while poor Aunt Cis died many deaths on the cliff waiting for her. At last, when Aunt Cis had given up all hope, Sophie appeared, all cut and torn. It appears that when she had swum into the opening, she experienced a terrible suction of water.
>
> This kept throwing her up against the top of the opening and she found she could neither go on nor turn back. There was also a turn from one opening to the other and the sucking and heaving not only imprisoned Sophie but also kept dashing her against the inner rock and roof.
>
> Luckily, Sophie was strong and fit, and having been heaved up and down and here and there, at last got the hang of things and, by great strength and constant trying, found her way out. So exhausted was she that she had to float on her back in the water for a time to get her strength back and then having made for the shore, collapsed on the strand.

The experience gave her a life-long respect for the power of the sea; she was always reluctant to fly over water, even stretches as short as the Irish Sea.

After she was demobbed, 22-year-old Sophie returned to Dublin where, in July 1919, she was reunited with her husband. After eight uneasy months together, Lynn set sail for Africa the following April and his young wife was free to revisit her old haunts. In August 1920, a small piece appeared under 'Cricket Notes' in the weekly *Sport* newspaper. It proposed starting a ladies' cricket club in Dublin, following the success of the girls' matches played at the Leinster Cricket Club's grounds in Rathmines over the summer. 'The keenness shown by the players and the interest taken in these games by the public would appear to justify the formation of such a club,' adds the report. Anyone interested was invited to contact Mrs Eliott-Lynn, care of the United Arts Club, 44 St Stephen's Green. If there was enough support, the new club would be launched the following year. So presumably Sophie planned to remain in Dublin.

Her husband had other ideas. Before he set off, Lynn had explained his financial position to Sophie:

> I told her I had managed by careful living to save £1,600 during the war with which I hoped to be able to get a farm, which she could work and develop, while I continued to practise my profession until the farm had been developed sufficiently to support us comfortably.

Sophie would return to college and complete her studies in agriculture while he would immediately set sail for Africa and find work as an engineer. When compared to the stifling dullness of life in rural Ireland, it seemed like a good plan, and in autumn 1920, Sophie returned to the Royal College of Science. Her address by this time was at Adelaide Road, near Dublin's city centre and a short walk from the college.

But the rifts already apparent in the marriage were steadily growing wider. Sophie's inability – or perhaps unwillingness – to manage money was a source of frequent disagreements between husband and wife. After she had confessed to her aunt that she was afraid to tell her husband of her financial problems, Aunt Cis had written him a long letter on her behalf in January 1921. Lynn defended himself robustly in a detailed reply, dated April of that year, which gave revealing insights both into his mental state and the state of his ill-advised marriage. The previous November, he wrote, Sophie had asked him to cable her £50 immediately, since otherwise, some of the local tradesmen would summons her: 'This letter was brought to me with my weekly food supply into one of the barren districts of British East Africa. It was utterly impossible to cable money from there, so I sent a cheque on the 7th January last, just a week before you even wrote your letter.'

Before they were married, Lynn had lent Sophie £60 for her trousseau, which she had promised to repay 'when the courts eventually paid her'. Following the deaths of her father and her step-grandmother, she was possibly due some money and although clearly anxious to make her own way in the world, the habits of the previous generation of women who did not work and survived on the outcome of anxiously awaited court cases and settlements for their financial survival were clearly ingrained.

As far as her husband was concerned, Sophie seemed incapable of managing her money; perhaps because she had never had any when younger, she spent wildly and then expected him to give her more when she got into trouble. After sailing for East Africa 'the first time', Lynn had given his wife a considerable sum as a nest egg in case of illness or accident to either of them. When she did have an accident,[2] she was treated in the hospital's free wards, because she had not a penny left. She even wrote to her husband's bank and got them to cable him for £30 – not caring, as he put it, what the bank manager thought of him for neglecting to provide for his wife.

In his letter, Lynn comes across as something of a loner. Sitting on the banks of the Nile, he revels in the beauty of the landscape: 'Battling with nature to overcome her vastness or to wrest her treasure from her, on the very edge of civilisation is the place for me.' The social whirl did not appeal to him: 'Dallying in a ballroom or handing round tea in a drawing room, I feel like a fish out of water.'

Sophie, on the other hand, was bright, attractive and flamboyant and always seeking attention; she 'bubbled at a time when women were not supposed to bubble' was how one relative described her. Despite her war experiences – or perhaps because of them – she was quite unready for the humdrum life of the typical wife. 'She is just at the age when she thinks herself very much wiser than half-a-dozen aunts or husbands,' said her exasperated husband. Neither did he approve of her friends, criticising 'her present habit of squandering every penny just as soon as she gets hold of it, and mostly on people that don't think any the better of her for doing it'.

Taking on such a young wife had proved to be an expensive indulgence for Lynn. Between the time Sophie had arrived back from France at the beginning of July 1919 until the following April, when he sailed for Africa, she had cost him £528. This included paying off debts, which she passed on to him, although she had been drawing her usual allowance from the bank. 'I am being rather forced to the conclusion that Sophie's idea of marriage is to extract just as much money as possible from one's husband and have as good a time as possible,' said Eliott-Lynn. On the evidence, it is hard to disagree.

Under the Soldier Settlement Scheme, Eliott-Lynn was awarded a large farm in East Africa on easy terms to be paid back over thirty years. Over the next few years, he seemed to divide his time between Pangani in Tanganyika Territory and Nakuru, hundreds of miles away in Kenya, so the couple possibly owned two farms. Lynn was delighted with this chance to make a new life, but Sophie felt from the start that developing a farm on her husband's savings would be impossible: '…yet she never made any effort to help by cutting down her expenditure in any way'. Claiming not to be extravagant, she would artlessly tell him in a letter that she had bought herself two hats: 'a black velour and another one!' Such a woman was unlikely to settle gladly in one of the fly-blown 'cow-towns' of East Africa, had Eliott-Lynn been blessed with the wisdom to see it.

At the moment, he feared, Sophie was frittering away the money he had left her to be used in time of sickness or for her eventual passage to East Africa. He could not understand how she was failing to manage on an income of over £300 a year: 'This surely is sufficient even nowadays in Dublin for a girl in Sophie's position.' He despairs at her lack of foresight. Pointing out that she was likely to live longer than him by a good many years, he wished she could see that every penny invested now in a farm, or in anything else for that matter, would double itself 'in seven years or less', meaning all the more for her after his death.

In his opinion, Sophie was hopeless at budgeting and had a bad habit of only part-paying debts, which got her into trouble with tradesmen: 'In her letter acknowledging my cheque, she says, "I am only paying them part; it would not be good for them to get the whole amount at once" and that is typical of her mental attitude to debt.'

Lynn tells Cis that Sophie would not even take the trouble to send him an occasional Irish newspaper as he had requested, although 'she must surely have a paper in the house sometime'. Lynn had been attempting to follow political developments in the country: 'I am very sorry that poor old Ireland is in such a bad way…the last I saw was that there was every chance of some sort of settlement being made between Lloyd-George and the Irish Catholics.'

Cis has clearly told Lynn something of Sophie's background: 'From what you have told me of her parents, I should think most of her faults in this particular line are hereditary, and she is more to be pitied than blamed.' He wonders if it might not be a 'real kindness' to force her to earn her own living: 'When she has finished her college training, she will be fitted to earn quite a good salary even in Ireland, and I know of no better way of teaching anyone the value of money than to let them earn it before they spend it.'

With a mark of 80 per cent, Sophie graduated first in her class on 7 July 1921, giving her an associateship in basic agriculture, although she appears never to have received her certificate. Her forwarding address at the time was given as c/o The Arts Club, then the intellectual and social hub of Dublin society, dominated by her County Limerick neighbour Dermod O'Brien, and to which she was to remain attached, off and on, all her life.

Lynn's big regret was that he had never refused Sophie money and, once she graduated, he gave her an ultimatum, insisting that she must find herself a job. So it was that in the autumn of 1921, his profligate young wife ended up at the University of Aberdeen in Scotland, apparently studying for a postgraduate degree and earning some money as a zoology demonstrator. For reasons that are unclear, she lasted only a few months, moving to London the following March, but during her period in Scotland, she made quite an impression on the hockey field, where she excelled in her usual defensive position. The Aberdeen University students' magazine of the time records her prowess: 'Mrs Lynn as right-back inspired terror in all opposing teams. Her swiftness in recovery allowed her to tackle far up the field, and the power of her stroke was often underestimated by our forwards.'

More crucially, Sophie had discovered the emerging sport of women's athletics. 'I once entered for the sports at a famous college when I was attending a post-graduate course,' she says in her book *Athletics for Women and Girls,* published in 1925. On the programme were four events for women. Sophie, an increasingly reluctant wife, had found herself a new passion, one that would bring her the attention she craved and distract her from the querulous admonishments of her faraway husband.

CHAPTER 5

Mrs Eliott-Lynn, Athlete

WHEN SOPHIE had enjoyed that sports day at the University of Aberdeen, women's athletics was still something of a novelty. The years from 1914 to 1918, which women spent driving jeeps, fixing engines, working in factories and cheerfully undertaking what had been seen as men's work, accelerated social changes already evident before the war. Now, for the first time, women had cast off their corsets, girdles and long dresses to become involved in organised sport, and the short dresses worn by the French tennis player Suzanne Lenglen at Wimbledon from 1919 to 1926 were considered a defining moment in social as well as sporting history.

Girls as well as boys love to test themselves in the simple disciplines of running, throwing and jumping, and although women's athletics was making steady progress in the United States of America, it was the European nations, such as Austria, and especially France, which were the pioneers. In 1918, the French woman Alice Milliatt, who had founded the Federation Feminine Sportive de France a year earlier, asked the Olympic Council to consider including women's track and field in its programme. The answer was an emphatic 'no'. At that time, the founder of the modern Olympic movement, Baron Pierre de Coubertin, was still in charge and,

although women had competed at the Olympics since the second games in 1900, it was against the wishes of the great man, who believed that women existed for nothing more than to present the male heroes with their victory garlands.

The first step towards organising international athletics for women came in May 1921, when Camille Blanc, Mayor of Beaulieu and president of the International Sporting Club in Monaco, attracted some 300 athletes from Italy, Norway, Switzerland, England and France to the '*Olympiades Feminines*' held in the glamorous surroundings of Monte Carlo.

[54]

The English team was organised by three men: Joe Palmer, a well-known athletics official and boxing referee, Ted Knowles, secretary of Kensington Athletics Club (and later Sophie's coach), and Major W.B. Marchant, formerly of the Army Physical Training staff and newly appointed director of physical education at the Regent Street Polytechnic in London. Women were welcome to try athletics at Regent Street, where Sam Mussabini, brought memorably to life in the film 'Chariots of Fire', was coach and, after trials conducted by Joe Palmer, a team, dominated by Regent Street women, was assembled. Arriving in Monte Carlo, the well-drilled English won five of the eleven events and shared a sixth, despite competing on an uneven and sloping track. With three wins, Mary Lines, a 27-year-old Lyon's Corner House waitress, became a household name, and, thanks to rapturous accounts in the British press, the Monte Carlo meet captured the imagination of a generation of adventurous young women.

Already an enthusiastic hockey, tennis, golf and lacrosse player, Sophie was immediately inspired to take up athletics, beginning her competitive career in the summer of 1921. With a few months to spare following her graduation before moving to Scotland, she competed frenetically at all the larger events held in and around Dublin city and also in a number of the sports days which were then an important feature of rural life in Britain and Ireland. Later she was to remember her first attempts at the high jump, an event eminently suited to her because of her height: 'The first time I ever jumped in 1921, I could not clear 3 feet 10 inches.'[1]

At the Moate Sports in County Westmeath in early July, she did a lot better than that for her first recorded high jump, jumping 4ft 1ins in a high jump 'exhibition'. Two days later, she was in Birr, County Offaly, jumping even higher, although these results are impossible to confirm. Compared to modern leaps of over two metres, the heights she jumped may appear low, but in those pioneering days, the high jump was an event requiring much courage. Athletes jumped straddle-style either over a rope attached to two upright poles, or (better for record-keeping purposes) a piece of stick balanced between the poles, landing in a pit of soft sand with nothing to break a knee-jarring fall. The modern athlete enjoys the benefits of special shoes, a synthetic take-off surface and a cushioned landing mat so large that flipping over the bar head first and landing on the back, 'Fosbury'-style, poses no risk of injury.

Sports days provided welcome summer entertainment in rural Ireland and were mostly frequented by locals, all hoping that a decent handicap would give them a chance of picking up a modest prize, such as candelabra or a dinner service. While some male athletes had become notorious 'pot hunters', planning their campaigns

Note the outfit in this early image of Sophie high-jumping over a (drooping) rope.

after careful reading of the fixture lists in the weekly *Sport* and other newspapers, Sophie's appearances must have caused a stir and, although she was often competing against girls five and more years younger, she would have enjoyed the attention. The low-key sports days served as a useful warm-up for Sophie's Dublin debut. Before a large crowd at the Dublin Tramway Sports in Lansdowne Road, she beat twelve others to win the high jump with a modest height of 4ft (1.219m). 'Not a bad effort for the sex in these days of general male mediocrity,' says the report in *Sport*. The women's high jump was regarded as 'a real novelty' by another newspaper, the *Irish Weekly Mail and Sports,* and a considerably better jump of 4ft 6ins (1.371m) at the Clonliffe Harriers Sports in Lansdowne Road was enough to rank her second in Britain and Ireland for the year 1921.

Even better was a leap of 4ft 9ins (1.447m) in Ballygar, County Galway; that equalled the best-known performance in the world at that time. Quite how seriously we can take this mark is open to question; although the Ballygar meet was a highlight of the Connacht calendar, there is no official record of any women's high jump taking place there that year.

After an enjoyable summer in Ireland with no husband to dampen her high spirits, Sophie travelled to Aberdeen in the autumn of 1921. Her first athletics coach was 'Mr J. Simpson,' presumably John Simpson, a recognised coach of the time, who helped her out 'before ever the WAAA was started'.[2] Like most women athletes of the time, Sophie was an all-rounder, prepared to have a go at anything, though she admitted later that her tendency to false start meant that she was never to win a sprint race: 'I never won a short distance sprint in my life, and can never hope to. I realise how bad it is, both for oneself and the starter's work, to get away before one should, but time and again I am brought back and reprimanded and penalised, only, with the best of intentions, to do it again.'

Her greatest achievements were to come in the high jump and the javelin, which she regarded as the ideal event for women. She also represented club and country in the high hurdles, shot putt and discus. The hurdles she always found a problem, with dozens of things to remember: '…if you drop your practice for the winter or for half the season, your body forgets them all and they have to be re-learnt'.

Meanwhile, women's athletics continued to progress at a heady rate. So encouraged was Alice Milliatt by the success of the Monte Carlo games that she called a meeting in Paris to establish an international body to govern women's sports. At the same time, she invited England to take on France in the first-ever international match, held on 30 October 1921. England won the match, with Mary Lines again the star.

A day later, representatives from England, Czechoslovakia, France, Italy, Spain and the USA formed the *Fédération Sportive Feminine International* (FSFI). Its function would be to establish technical rules for individual and collective sports, to ratify world records and to improve communications between existing women's sports federations all over the world. At last women's athletics had a set of standards, although the weights and distances still used today were not formally agreed until 1927.

A few months later, early in 1922, Major Worsech, director of physical training at the Regent Street Polytechnic, received a letter from Alice Milliatt asking if he could form a British women's athletic association that could then join the FSFI. The trio of Major Marchant, Ted Knowles and Joe Palmer set about the preparatory work, inviting Sophie along with Florence Birchenough of the Regent Street Polytechnic, a member of the original Monte Carlo team, to help them out. They then called an inaugural meeting to form a Women's Athletic Association.

Sophie, with clear pretensions to the grand life, was now calling herself Sophie Eliott-Lynn rather than plain Mrs Lynn, and although just a few months in the sport, had somehow emerged as an outstanding athletics talent and administrator. At the first annual meeting of the Women's Amateur Athletic Association (WAAA), held in the autumn of 1922, Major Marchant was elected president and chairman and Sophie secretary and treasurer. Unlike the men's organisation, which had paid office staff, committee members covered a number of roles and a lot of work was done in private houses.

As the women's organisation grew stronger, the men's Amateur Athletic Association withdrew its support. Although it had recommended that the women apply to the AAA for affiliation, their application, when it was received in October 1922, was thrown out on the dubious grounds that the WAAA had not been properly formed. Still, the AAA was happy to take credit for helping to establish women's athletics when it suited. The programme for the first women's international event at London's Stamford Bridge in 1925 brazenly states that the WAAA was founded at the suggestion of the AAA, blithely side-stepping the truth. Even years later, a hard core of stuffy male administrators continued to consider women's athletics as 'unladylike'.

Despite the men's unhelpful attitude, the universities and many big businesses, keen to improve the general physical fitness of the population in the wake of the war, were quick to pledge their support for the newly formed WAAA. Soon, companies and factories started to affiliate, while private clubs were set up in cities and towns all over the United Kingdom. Well-supported international meets took place annually, all of them abroad until the great meeting at Stamford Bridge, now the grounds of Chelsea Football Club, in 1924. By then, the women's organisation had several hundred affiliated clubs and some 23,000 members. Sophie herself claimed that, by 1925, as many as 25,000 women were members of 500 clubs; clearly athletics, a sport which is open to all – the tall, the short, the fat and the thin – and doesn't require a dozen or so others to make up a team, had touched a chord. Many of the women coming into athletics were office workers and when their firms organised annual sports days, they rediscovered activities they had enjoyed at school and rushed to join one of the many clubs. Adding to the appeal were organised dances, annual dinners and cream teas following competitions and training, which gave women a much-needed social outlet.

There is no evidence that Sophie competed in Ireland in 1922, her second year in athletics; quite simply, she didn't need to, since there were plenty of competitions taking place in the London area where she was now based after her brief time in Aberdeen. She competed for the first time that year in May at a sports day organised by the King's College, at Mitcham, London, where she may have been working, winning the high jump and 220 yards and finishing third in the long jump. Later that year, she organised the first of several trips to Torquay where she holidayed each year, while in early August, at a meet in Paddington, she made her first appearance in a two-handed javelin competition, where the best of three throws with the left arm and three with the right were added together for the total. She finished a commendable second.

Highlight of the season for Sophie was the first Women's Modern Olympic Games at the Pershing Stadium in Paris, organised by Alice Milliatt to coincide with the second conference of the FSFI on 20 August. At the British trials a few weeks earlier, Sophie did enough to get selected for the shot and, as one of the team organisers, sent a letter of instructions to her sister athletes:

> Will you please provide yourself with close-fitting black knickers reaching to not more than 4 inches from the ground when kneeling, a loose white tunic of stout material belted, with elbow sleeves, reaching 10-12 inches below the waist. The use of stockings is optional, but most of the team will compete without them. It is advisable to bring two pairs of running pumps and a warm coat.

The letter instructed the women to meet under the clock at Victoria Station, where their chaperone, Mrs Goold, could be recognised by a white handkerchief tied around her arm. The team duly assembled and on 18 August, a nervous and excited British squad set off for Paris by train and ferry. On the first day of the games, the women were up and about at 6 am, despite having their sleep disrupted by the noise of the city traffic. The competition was eagerly awaited and attracted 20,000 spectators, or a few more, if we are to believe Sophie:

> The first Women's Olympiad was held in Paris in 1922 before over 30,000 spectators at the Stade Pershing. All of the above nations [Belgium, Switzerland, Italy, Czechoslovakia and England] were present, with the addition of a small and enthusiastic band of pretty American girls in the charge of two qualified women trainers and two doctors.... It was my first experience of meeting American girls and I loved them all.

After the ritual of the opening ceremony, with the teams marching into the stadium behind their national flags, an emotional Alice Milliatt declared open the first

Sophie throws the javelin in the old two-handed style.

Women's Olympic Games. Despite having just thirteen competitors in action, Britain still finished top of the overall table, ahead of the American girls and the home nation, France. Mary Lines got most of the points, not only winning the 300m and long jump, but helping the 4 x 100m relay team to victory in a world-record equalling time. In the two-handed shot, Sophie finished ninth.

    The games proved a milestone. For the first time, a women's sports event had been treated with respect, with the extensive coverage by the local and international press guaranteeing large crowds. Exhilarated by the reaction, the FSFI meeting, held just before the competition began and attended by Sophie, voted to hold the games every four years, just like the regular Olympic Games, from which women's athletics was still excluded.

    Back in London, Kensington Ladies, with Sophie in the line-up, won a women's inter-club match held at the Croydon Sports Club ground at Plough Lane, in Wallington. This, the first competition of its kind to be held in Britain, included the first English Women's Championships for the 120 yard hurdles and the 220 yard sprint.[3]

Sophie had learned much from her experiences over the summer, and after she finally arrived in Africa that autumn, she trained every day, knowing she could do better the following year:

> When in East Africa, I used to practise throwing for twenty minutes every morning with these native spears (used by Masai warriors), and I had two semi-clad natives to throw back to me, who thought the 'memsahib' was utterly mad to do this sort of thing.

She learned from the Masai technique: 'I noticed that they always held their spears well behind the centre of gravity and so ensured that they came down point first.' Her style would still have been unrecognisable to the modern athletics fan. Apart from being 200 grams heavier than today's standard weight at 800 grams, the javelin was held low with both hands, one balancing the spear at the end, the other on the grip. After examining a film of her throwing, she describes her own technique in her book;[4] there is no mention of the side steps and cross steps of the modern thrower, but the rest sounds like a normal, if technically unrefined, throw. What is most remarkable about her account is her diligence: by going to the trouble of having her throws filmed, indeed by training so conscientiously at all, Sophie was way ahead of her time. She deserved her big throws of a few years later.

CHAPTER 6

Farming in Africa

In October 1922, Sophie had finally set sail for East Africa to join her husband at their farm at Pangani, in Tanganyika Territory. This small provincial settlement on the coast near the Kenyan border was about 300 miles from Nairobi. With the primitive dirt roads making travel difficult, it meant that the Lynns were at least a week's travel from the centre of British colonialism in East Africa. Pangani could not have been farther from the bright lights of London or even Dublin. From the start, her trip did not go well: she was to claim later that she travelled 'steerage' to save costs and that when she arrived, she had a terrible time of it, taking months to locate her husband. Allowing for her typical hyperbole, she probably did find it hard to find him, especially since it was her first visit to Africa, where communications were far from European standards.

During this visit, Sophie spent time not only in Pangani, but also in the Kenyan 'cow town' of Nakuru because she mentions a Caledonian dinner she attended around Christmas time in an estate there. Her relationship with her husband, when she finally made contact with him, continued to be fraught. According to a later newspaper article about 'Air-Minded Women', written by a male journalist, she insisted on joining Lynn on a safari in the African jungle, despite his protestations that it was no place for a woman. When her husband later refused to allow her to supervise part of the expedition, Sophie allegedly stormed off, making her way out of the jungle alone, entirely unconcerned at the risk she was taking.

Conventional wisdom at the time in Africa was that women could not enjoy slaughtering animals on safari; hunting was a man's pursuit and those women who insisted on joining in were mere attention-seekers. Yet hunting was a traditional part of British and, even more so, Irish rural life. Sophie's aviation rival Lady Bailey, who never attracted the same kind of criticism as her more extrovert friend, was an expert horsewoman, riding to hounds from an early age in her native County Monaghan.

Although Sophie had never hunted because of the family's lack of money, her father had been a keen horseman and from him she had inherited a love of stalking animals in wild places. She wrote about it in one of several poems from this period:

Dressed for a safari. (*Cussen Collection*)

> All alone with gun and moonlight, all alone beside the river...
> There were two men in the firelight drinking vermouth, mixed, and gin,
> And they never knew the thrill that comes from tracking hidden hippo,
> And stalking dusky clumps of shrubs, with waterholes within.

She may even have wished to share a common interest with her husband:

> But the clothes that you carry the best, dear, with the most accustomed swing,
> That interpret yourself the truest, that I loved you in first, old thing,
> Are, when I'm alone beside you...Before us the open track,
> That shirt and the shorts of Safari, with a train of boys at our back.

These verses come from the small book of poetry called *East African Nights*, published in London by Robert Scott in 1925, and originally printed under the pseudonym

'Mary' in the *East African Standard* ('The Settler's Paper'). 'All these scraps – I cannot call them poetry – have been written on episodes I have met or been told of in Kenya and Tanganyika,' she says in the preface to the book. Writing poetry seems to have come naturally to her.

The intriguing 'scraps' explore her mixed feelings about the colonial experience, marriage and much else besides. They come closer than anything else she wrote to revealing the character of this complex woman. In the clearly heart-felt preface, she says that East Africa is a wonderful place for women as well as men: 'Adventures are not tied to men in this glad new country. She who wishes it may share the camp-fire at night with the hunter, and at noonday, the blazing sun on the track.... There is scope for the eager woman with the man's soul to express herself in action, and organisation, and play.' Always aware of her less adventurous audience, she then softens the blow: 'There is a great field for the domestic woman to bring the traditions of the Mother Country with her, and to give them to Kenya.' Expanding on this argument, she borrows from Thomas Gray to praise the 'mute inglorious Miltons of Empire' living hard, lonely lives in out-of-the-way farms with their husbands and children.

The poems hint at more complex feelings. Never likely to be either mute or inglorious by choice, and much as she craved an entrée into high society, Sophie Eliott-Lynn clearly had trouble conforming to the social norms expected of colonial wives and found the restrictions and hypocrisy hard to stomach:

> Either do the women settle,
> Never coming off their shambas
> Or they butterfly and scatter,
> Violets and Crimson Ramblers.

She must have found her situation frustrating:

> People either love or hate you,
> Either praise you or talk slander.
> 'She's the sort we want in Kenya.
> What a gas-bag, I can't stand her.'

As for the weather, in the book's preface, she says: 'To leave the rains of England, with its cold and fog, its conventions and restrictions, and to go to a wild land of sunshine and great spaces. That is a great joy.' Yet her verse hints at depression caused by the weather: 'But I'm suffering from the weather/And I cannot leave my home', she says in one poem, while in another, she admits that the heat of Africa enervates her: 'Give me the sting of Autumn/The stirring chill of Spring'.

Judging from the poems, at Pangani, the Lynns attempted to farm sisal, a fibrous plant of Mexican origin used in the making of rope: '…ordered sisal, growing line on line' and possibly coffee at either Pangani or Kisumu: 'It pleases me to watch my coffee grow….'

Like any woman of her time and class, she had an ambivalent attitude to the 'natives'. She can paint a sympathetic portrait of her cook, forgiving him his filth for his glorious stews, cakes and puddings. But she can equally write of a beautiful young girl with 'a strain of white somewhere':

- Such Beauty – pity 'tis waste
When alien races wed.

At least, she mainly observed the local population sympathetically, unlike her more hide-bound husband: 'They have no arts or crafts and no traditions, and except for the power of speech, are no higher than the animals they live amongst', he believed.

By the following spring, Sophie was back in England, immersing herself in athletics. At the third Monte Carlo meet in early April, again dominated by the British women, the training she had put in while in East Africa paid off when she finished third in both the high jump and javelin. These were her first international medals, appropriately at the meet that had inspired her to take up athletics in the first place. Controversy surrounded her high jumping activities that summer. On 14 July in Wembley, she jumped 4ft 10ins (1.473m) to finish third behind old rivals Hilda Hatt and Ivy Lowman, with Hatt jumping an inch higher. Later, on 6 August at Brentwood, Sophie was to claim that she had jumped 4ft 10ins (1.485m) and for some reason, this mark was listed by the FSFI as the best jump of the year and a world record, although among the British women alone, Hatt had jumped higher and Ivy Lowman had equalled this mark. Apart from its appearance on an FSFI list, which even Alice Milliatt apparently queried, no evidence for this jump can be found. A meet certainly did take place at Brentwood, with Hilda Hatt jumping 4ft 10ins (1.473m) to win ahead of Sophie, whose jump was not recorded. There is no evidence of a second high jump competition or even an exhibition where Sophie could have jumped the height she alleged.

On 18 August 1923, the inaugural English Women's Athletics Championships took

Sophie Eliott Lynn jumping at two unknown locations. She is using the scissors style.

place at the Oxo Sports Ground, Bromley, and Sophie became the country's first women's javelin champion, also finishing second in a poorly supported 120 yard hurdles and third in the shot. There is no evidence that she competed in the high jump; she certainly did not appear among the medal winners.

There are two letters to Cis Peirce, her 'darlingest auntie' from this period. In the first, dated 29 July and with an address at 29 Courtfield Garden, she says that she will have to be very careful, presumably with her money, since she has decided to postpone returning to Africa: 'I was to have sailed on September 4 but now it's put off to somewhere near the 24th as there is an international on and I have been asked to delay my departure until it is over.' She clearly looks after her aunt when she can and had sent her a coat and skirt that she no longer wanted. She had also attempted to sort out a matter concerning 'Hughes the ironmonger'. She is glad to be busy: 'I would be fretting and chaffing terribly at London if I were not so busy. As it is, I have no time to long and hunger for the sea and the dear West of Ireland as I do when I have time on my hands.' She had seen her Aunt Lou three weeks previously: 'She was looking unusually well and neatly dressed, also much thinner, not a day older. Both you and she seem to have taken years off since leaving Newcastle.'

In this letter comes a hint that the unhappily married Sophie may have taken a lover: 'John, the one and only man in my life, is passing through London on Wednesday – tomorrow – and going to stay the night. It will be very sad and poignant seeing him again but God is very good to have let me have such a fine beautiful thing in my life as my love for him….' The only known John in her life was John Simpson, her first coach, presumably at Aberdeen, but there is no evidence that they were lovers. For a married woman living in an era when adultery and divorce were still very much frowned on, her easy discussion of this matter with her aunt seems startling and indicates that her marriage was over.

Her fondness for her aunt shines through in the letter; the private Sophie was a more likeable character than the more portentous individual who sometimes came across in her public pronouncements. 'Do try and write to me soon, my dear mother-auntie. I do so love your letters,' she writes before signing off, in her usual manner, as 'Baby'.

In an even more breathless effort, dated a month later and written while on a weekend break 'from the city and work' in the South Downs, she discusses 'doggy papers', wishes she could do more for her aunt, says that she meets Auntie Lou about once a fortnight ('I don't think she is nearly as happy as you') and mentions that she will be sailing from Amsterdam on 1 October, presumably for Africa. Almost in passing, she says: 'I broke the world's record on August 6 by jumping 4ft 11ins high and on August 18, I won the British javelin throwing championships so I am on the international team again.' She adds that she would be off to Barcelona with a team on the weekend of 8 September and then to Paris a fortnight later. Her comment adds further fuel to the mystery of her high jump record; her disputed height at Brentwood was half an inch shy of 4ft 11ins. But why mention it in a private letter to her aunt, someone she would not have been trying to impress?

Whatever happened in Spain, of which there is no record, Britain beat France at the annual match held on 23 September in Paris with Sophie being one of the outstanding performers. Her all-round ability and splendid 'teamwomanship' saw her finish second in the javelin and the hurdles and win the long jump.

By the end of the year, her controversial mark of 4ft 10ins (1.485 m) for the high jump had her sharing the women's world record on the FSFI lists with Elizabeth Stine of the USA. These lists were not entirely reliable; apart entirely from the doubts surrounding Sophie's mark, there was some evidence of a German jump of 5ft 1 inch (1.50m) set in 1921 over a proper, modern-style bar. Since Weimar Germany was none

Some of the victorious British team in Paris during the 1923 international against France; Sophie is fourth from left.

too popular after the war, and women's athletics there was regulated by two organisations, this outstanding mark did not come to light until some years later. Officially at least, Sophie was now the only remaining British-based female athlete credited with a world record, while standards all around the world were improving.

Despite her marital difficulties, Sophie departed for East Africa as soon as the athletic season was over. It was to be her last prolonged visit. Although there were many aspects of colonial African life that she loved, she was not happy there, as was clear from another of her poems:

> Which peace is best, the peace before a storm,
> When one must fear the menacing unknown,
> Or the peace afterwards, when safe through harm,
> Craft into quiet haven is gently blown?

What can such a strong woman have feared? In later years, when none too sober, she would claim that she had left her first husband because he had 'beaten her in the bush', implying that she had been physically abused. This, of course, could have been self-excusing fantasy, especially as her husband was so clearly exasperated, both with her spendthrift habits and her unwillingness to become a traditional settler's wife. They had been a mismatched pair from the start and whatever love existed between them was gone, although she puts a brave face on it:

> And there are other lovelier things,
> The spring, the hills, the sea.
> What matter it if love be gone,
> If these be left to me.

In 'Fortitude', a poem that contains a graphic description of a wild dog's death, the tone is starkly introspective:

> I think, dead thing, as I look down on you,
> I wish I could my little sufferings bear
> As you your great one bore, without a cry,
> Could meet my fate with such a stoic air.
> I squirm and I cry out like any child at the
> least pressure of the hand of fate.

All her short life, Sophie comes across as a woman torn between the need for adventure and a longing for acceptance in 'society'. There is little doubt that like many women of her time, she married for money. Unlike other women, accepting that their part of the deal was to stay at home and look after their husbands and children, Sophie married precisely so she wouldn't have to stay at home; little wonder that her husbands failed to understand her. She may also have become prone to bouts of depression, which when contrasted with her usual outgoing and positive attitude, leads to suspicions that she could have inherited a mild form of her father's manic depression. In the same poem, she writes despairingly:

> We higher beings oftentimes forget to learn our
>   code, until it is too late.
> Even this verse, it is a kind of cry,
> Afraid of living, and afraid to die.

She was never to have children and, as far as we know, never became pregnant: although in another poem, she claims that she had hoped to start a family with her husband:

> We dreamed of little children
> How children's voices thrill,

> Their wistful voices haunt me yet,
> Unborn and shapeless still.

Despite their constant clashes of personality, she must have loved her husband once – or at least, she pretended to:

> I have seen you and loved you in khaki, in boots with spurs at the heel,
> Your feet firm fast in the stirrups, the reins in your hands of steel,
> Your breast aflame with your ribbons, the buckskin white at your knees,
> …And I've seen you in tweeds, all tattered, I've seen you and loved you in these.

Sadly she admits that their love did not endure:

> We built a house with kisses,
> And we pull it down with tears,
> The mortar of our happy hopes,
> Could not withstand the years.

Compounding their marital problems was the failure of their farming efforts; their coffee crop failed and their animals died, which was not untypical of the time, when voracious tropical pests, along with an assortment of animal and plant diseases and the weather conditions, posed huge problems for Western-style farmers, who did not understand African conditions. She writes:

> Long lines of beans lie shrivelled, yielding nil,
> Idle the waterwheel is standing still.
> And sickness ravages the oxen teams.
> Nothing is left to us beside our dreams.

With the experiment in farming a failure, Sophie returned to England in early 1924. Although some aspects of life in East Africa, most notably the hunting, had greatly appealed to her, she was not the type of woman who could sit quietly in an isolated farmhouse, ordering the servants about and waiting for her husband to reappear. If anything was obvious by this stage in her life, it was that she enjoyed being centre stage, that she came to the fore in any organisation she joined and that her restless nature craved constant stimulation.

As for Lynn, his background in the practical world of engineering meant he was unlikely to understand the fickle nature of agriculture, so dependent on the weather and local conditions. His battle with malaria continued, leaving him listless and depressed for months and incapable of the physical effort vital for farming. His wife's return to London meant that their marriage was effectively over. After sorting out their business affairs, he was to follow her back to London, but whether or not they ever lived together again is unclear. Later Sophie would claim that Lynn had objected to her flying and that this was one of the reasons for them splitting up. Possibly for Lynn, his wife's new and expensive hobby was the final straw.

East African Nights is dedicated to 'J. – best friend one ever had', presumably the John mentioned in the letter to her aunt. Whatever his role in her life, she had obviously decided that the relationship could not continue. What effect this relationship had on her marriage we shall probably never know.

On her return to London, Sophie joined the newly formed Middlesex Ladies Athletic Club, which had taken much of its membership from the dissolved Kensington club, of which Sophie was a member; the new club had been officially launched while she was in East Africa. Winter training consisted mainly of cross-country runs at Horsenden Hill, Perivale, and from the start social events were given priority, with the first of many regular dances taking place at Kensington Town Hall just a month after the club's formation. This mix of physical endeavour and social activity proved immediately popular and the club rapidly became one of the largest in the country.

When she arrived back in England, Sophie threw herself into the club's activities and invited its members to her annual sports day and jamboree in Torquay. She was still regarded by some in athletics as a 'gold digger', only attracted to the sport because of the glamour attached to international games, such as the competition held in Monte Carlo, then, as now, the playground of the rich. But while Sophie certainly felt that associating with the rich was one way of generating an income, she was no snob – her coach, Teddy Knowles, a great supporter of women's athletics, was a house painter.

Her outgoing personality and athletic success meant that Sophie had become a well-known public figure and articles under her name frequently appeared in the newspapers. The pursuit of beauty is part of our fundamental aspiration towards perfection, she argues in a faintly ludicrous article published in the *Daily Mirror*:

> Beauty, as we understand it, in any form, is a harmonious blend of perfection of colour, form and line. Whether it be the still beauty of wonderful scenery – the quiet lakes with the sunset upon them or the blue spaces of misty uplands – or the living beauty of the young girl as she sways across a ballroom floor, laughing up at

her partner, it catches the heartstrings, holding our eyes and our minds with the emotions that Wordsworth must have felt when he said 'Earth hath not anything to show more fair'.

If the human being is the most wonderful thing in the world, she argues, then the well-built human body is the most beautiful thing. Men and women have different duties in the scheme of things. It is man's work to provide a home and food for his woman, while women's function is to be beautiful, not just for her husband, but as a visible sign of spiritual as well as physical health:

> Whether the woman be fortunate enough to have a home and love, or has to go down into the city or the field to work, her beauty (and all it signifies as the expression of her physical and mental well-being) is her strongest and most abiding asset.

So, according to the public Sophie at least, a woman is neglecting her duty if she fails to make the most of herself and, if not blessed by nature, then at least she can aspire to the attractive glow of perfect health by taking part in sport:

> Thirty years ago, the women who played games, who used the muscles and limbs she had been born with as they were meant to be used, was looked upon as hoydenish and rough, inclined to be coarsened by her pursuit of sport. Nowadays, we have changed all that and our girls are beginning to realise that clean, fresh air is the best external skin food there is, and that the heart which beats quickly, when its owner runs and chases the elusive ball, is the best of beauty doctors.

The suggestion that women have the right to take part in sport, just like men, was quite radical for the time. Cannily judging her audience as always, she emphasises the need for restraint: 'Too strenuous devotion to physical exercises…will mean that there is too much output of energy, too much waste of tissue. General tiredness will ensue, together with that nasty anaemic look that always comes from overdoing things.' Rose Thompson, holder of the world record for 100 yards, trains for half-an-hour twice a week and races at weekends, she points out, clearly feeling that this level of activity would be acceptable to her readers. She certainly doesn't pass on the information that she herself had been known to train for longer than that every day for weeks on end, without any damage to her health. The article concludes with the view that the battle for beauty is won on the playing fields of England, an interesting angle, probably designed to reassure mothers that a modicum of gentle sweating won't turn their daughters into unmarriageable crones.

With winter approaching, the *Daily Chronicle* persuaded her, as vice-president of the WAAA, to provide them with a course of exercises for their readers. The article she wrote mercifully refrains from quoting poetry and sticks to more practical matters: 'This is the period of the year when so many of us begin to feel the loss of open-air recreation. The short evenings make it impossible for us to get away from business or office in time for a round of golf or a set or two of tennis.'

Health, good looks, complexion and temper can all suffer, she said. We cannot hibernate 'like so many dormice' but must find something to take the place of our summer games and guard us from developing the 'desk stoop' or the 'city slouch'. The young woman of today wants 'to stay slim, and to preserve her poise and balance'. So, with Florence Birchenough, a member of the British Association of Physical Training, she had picked half-a-dozen exercises that can be practised in the morning 'halfway through dressing'. The exercises, based on the Swedish system, graduate from simple, elegant movements to a final rapid one to get the heart pumping. None of them takes longer than a minute to complete and the effort would pay off:

> American women with their well-known clarity of skin and vivacity and grace of movement, are firm believers in the daily practice of a few simple exercises, not alone for the sake of beauty but to keep themselves fit and ready for the time when open air summer games are possible again.

The British should follow their example: 'If one permits one's body to become utterly soft and one's muscles idle and useless in the winter, it will be far more difficult to take up the game again and to bring flaccid muscles up to concert pitch.' No one could argue with that.

With her new-found fame as a spokesperson for healthy women, Sophie was in her element. Her only problem was money. Much as she loved athletics, it could not provide a living. Although she took secretarial work where she could find it, with her husband now gone, she needed to find a means of allowing her to continue associating with the upper echelons of society, where clearly she felt she belonged.

CHAPTER 7

Olympic Arguments

SOPHIE'S FINEST MOMENT as an athlete came at the second annual English Women's Championships in the Woolwich Stadium, London, on 28 June 1924, where she was dominant in both high jump and javelin. Underlining just how sloppy record-keeping was in those days, she set what was described as a new English record of 4ft 9ins (1.447m) for the high jump, although it lasted only until Ivy Lowman jumped 4ft 10 ins (1.485m) on 4 August – and both these heights were lower than Hilda Hatt's jump of a year earlier and Sophie's own 'world record'.

But in the two-handed javelin, there was no disputing her magnificent aggregate total of 173ft 2ins (52.78m), the best athletics performance of her life. Although this outstanding effort obliterated the British and world records and no other woman was to come close to it for years, a slight wind meant her performance was never officially classed as a record. Sophie was far from happy. 'As there was a slight wind, the record could not be accepted, although the wind was blowing *against* her' was how she described the occasion in the third person when writing about it in her book *Athletics for Women and Girls*, not mentioning at all that she was the unhappy record-breaker in question.

Earlier in the season at a meet held in Stamford Bridge, Sophie had won the high jump and come second in the shot putt. But she was not very active that year, perhaps because the championships came so early or maybe lacking the incentive of a glamorous overseas trip. There may even have been personal problems, concerning her aunt, her marriage, her health or even her need for work.

Still, towards the end of July, Sophie was most probably in Paris for the Third Congress of the FSFI. There, representatives from nine countries decided that, in future, the congress would be held only every two years, since assembling its growing membership annually was proving impossible. It was also decided to extend the Women's Olympics to two days.

The highlight of the 1924 season was the United Kingdom's first international

Sophie proudly displays the many medals she won during her athletics career. (*Cussen Collection*)

women's athletic meet at Stamford Bridge on 4 August, a Bank Holiday Monday. Called the 'Women's International and British Games', it was promoted for several weeks in advance by W. Power-Berrey, the editor of the *News of the World,* and that newspaper's enthusiastic athletics correspondent, Joe Binks. Countries represented were Belgium, Czechoslovakia, France, Italy, Switzerland and Britain, all marching into the stadium in uniform behind their national flags. Thanks to the widespread publicity, the meet attracted 25,000 spectators and they watched, among others, the Swiss athlete Louise Groslimond set an unofficial world record for the two-handed javelin of 156ft (47.55m) – far below Sophie's throw of two months earlier. Overseas competitors took the first four places in the javelin and there appears to have been no British representative. It seems astonishing that Sophie was not there, especially since she was the reigning British high jump and javelin champion, but judging from her poor performances later in the season, she could have been injured or, for reasons already alluded to, out of training.

On the track, the British women won four of the five events, while Mary Lines, with three victories, was the individual star of the meet. Of the eleven events contested, world records were set in seven and, the following day, the *Daily Mirror* devoted its entire front page to the meeting, underlining just how popular women's athletics had become.

In early 1925, her small book of poetry, *East African Nights,* was published. In writing the preface, dated 25 February, she gave her address as the Ladies' Athenaeum Club at 17 Stratford Place, where she may have been working as a secretary. She soon became immersed in other administrative activities with the newly established National Playing Fields Association and on 15 April a letter under the heading 'More Playing Fields for Girls' appeared in *The Times*.

She wrote, she said, not alone as the vice-president of the WAAA, but as an individual personally affected by the lack of suitable open spaces for sport, and as one who had worked on social schemes in areas where boys and girls could play only in the roadway or gutter. Her letter was a characteristic mixture of overblown prose and good sense:

> I maintain that play is one of the four great essentials of life, whether it takes the form of the brilliant play of words and wit of a man like Disraeli, or the hopscotch of the little child of the slums.

Work, food and sleep were the other three essentials for good health, happiness and efficiency, she maintained, and were all the more vital as the population moved inexorably off the land and into cities. 'I suggest that every woman's society working in the interests of our girls should publicly associate itself with this movement,' she concluded.

Her life was to take another huge turn after she attended the 8th Olympic Congress in Prague from 29 May to 4 June as part of the FSFI delegation, travelling by aeroplane for the first time in her life. The Prague conference, attended by 62 delegates, was divided into two parts – a 'Pedagogical Congress' and a 'Technical Olympic Congress' – and Sophie presented two papers on 'Women's Participation in Sport'.

In the first, she began by pointing out that since men and women are more similar than different, women should enjoy much the same sports and physical exercises undertaken by men. Clearly conscious of her audience, Sophie then argued that sports likely to tax a muscular frame intended for child-bearing, are 'of course, wholly unsuitable for the feminine organism, which is more delicate and should conserve its energy for the great work before it'.

Thanks to her experience as an active athlete, she had come to the conclusion that women were capable of achieving three-quarters of what men could do without undue strain. She took the example of the high jump, citing her own disputed record, which was exactly three-quarters of the current men's best. She added that there was no proof that women had less endurance than men: 'Their very heritage of housework and child-bearing seems to indicate that they have these powers in a marked degree.'

In public at least, she was against any activity requiring heavy boots or implements 'as these cause unnatural development'. Neither could any sport where women suffered blows to the body be recommended. Running she considered an ideal sport: 'if starting practice be not too much indulged in'. Although faithfully reflecting current thinking, Sophie's knowledge of physiology appears out-of-date to the modern reader: 'Women's energy is slightly more available than a man's, in that her temperature is a fraction higher, and she recovers less rapidly from the expenditure of it. Excessive running also tends to ossify certain ligaments in the pelvic area which in normal parturition become soft and elastic.'

Sophie, despite her science degree, was merely reflecting the prejudices of her time and could hardly have forseen the flurry of long-distance swimming and running records set by women that would come half-a-century later. As a canny woman, she was also aware that she should not upset her audience too much by presenting her private view, which was that women were fit for anything. She is very much in favour of the field events: 'The swaying and bending movements entailed especially by the throwing events are invaluable from the point of view of improvement of the intestinal circulation.' The link between sport and general fitness, which she emphasises, has been almost completely lost since then, thanks to the modern obsession with winning at all cost.

For a woman, says Sophie, the years between fourteen and eighteen when she reaches puberty are critical, and during these years, violent physical exercise should be avoided as the body stabilises. But an interest in sport must be kept alive under the guidance of experts and she concludes with one of her customary florid touches: 'It is one of the most beautiful things I can imagine to see a group of young girls in summer happily competing with each other, full of camaraderie and *joie de vivre*.'

Sophie's second paper, entitled 'The Views of the English Women's Games Associations on the Question of Violent Games for Women', was more radical in its opinions. She argues that games are necessary for both girls and boys as an outlet for the primitive fighting instinct in all of us: 'Man shares with all animals who pass through a period of youth, the biological need to play.... If this is accepted, it is plain that games are as necessary to girls as boys.'

In her view, there was no conclusive evidence that any game was bad for girls. The causes of sterility and difficult labour were 'most numerous', while amenorrhoea, or the loss of periods, brought with it no symptoms of ill-health, with normal menstruation returning once a less strenuous life is led.[1] She quoted Miss Gray, headmistress of St Paul's School: 'If all the harm that games ever did to girls were multiplied a hundredfold and that again a hundredfold, I would regard it as insignificant and trifling compared with the good they do.'

In conclusion, the committee decided (with considerable wisdom) that taking it too seriously 'to the detriment of character' was the only possible damage sport might cause girls: 'On the whole, it would seem that there is no clear proof that strenuous physical exercise has any special influence either upon the prospect of motherhood or upon the difficulty of labour.'[2]

During the main congress, the International Olympic Committee ordered the FSFI not to use the term 'Women's Olympic Games' for their games; the FSFI, not without some argument, agreed to change the title of the games to the 'Second International Ladies Games' and, later, to the 'Women's World Games'.

On her return to London, Sophie, thrilled with her visit to Prague and at the reception her two papers had received, wrote an impassioned letter to *The Times* on the congress's findings and the importance of sport for young people. Britain, she argued, was lagging far behind other European counties and the USA in promoting physical activity for adolescents. Not only were there medical examinations for both boys and girls during their school years in those countries, but links are encouraged with sporting bodies 'so that they may – even to the poorest of them – have facilities for games and sports that will help to make them better and finer citizens'.

Other European nations 'envied Britain' the volunteers that introduced young people to sport in schools and clubs in their spare time: 'But…is it fair to put such a responsibility on the shoulders of the voluntary workers of the nation?'

Despite the 'self-sacrificing teachers' who organise sport after school hours, the majority of young people are left on the sidelines: 'It is only the results that the other nations see, the cream that comes to the top in international and record matches. I wonder if they know of the great masses of young people who never get a chance to play at all.' Sound words and still valid.

One man impressed by Sophie's arguments in Prague was Brigadier General R.J. Kentish, vice-chairman of the British Olympic Council and honorary organiser of the National Playing Fields Association, who was delighted to write an 'appreciation' for the book she had just written called *Athletics for Women and Girls*. Her views on whether or not all games are beneficial to women 'are so soundly conceived and so

Frontispiece of *Athletics for Women and Girls*. (*Cussen Collection*)

clearly stated that I have suggested to Mrs Eliott-Lynn that she should embody them in this book'.

The BBC broadcast the preface of the book on 9 April 1925, with Sophie reading it herself. When it was published later in the year, the book incorporated her addresses to the Prague conference, as suggested by Brigadier General Kentish. It is a small but remarkably sensible volume, written without too many flowery embellishments, which has worn well. In her preface, she quotes Dr Leonard Hill:

> Women and men are evolved together from the same parent stock …what is good for one is good for the other … but we must not forget the weakening effect of civilisation on women, of the years and decades of tight-lacing and restrictions, and we must accordingly begin by taking things very slowly.

Substitute 'sedentary living' for 'tight-lacing and restrictions' and that advice still holds good. She is opposed to the wearing of corsets, still a common practice then:

'If you feel your back wants some support, do some exercises that will strengthen the natural body-wall of muscles and do not utterly destroy it by adding an external and quite foreign body-wall of string and coutille and whalebone.' She stresses the importance of supervision, especially since young girls, just like young boys, tend to overdo it when they find a new pastime.

Though she believes, like her peers, that racing over a distance of more than 1,000m is not good for women, Sophie later devotes a full chapter to the joys of cross-country running: 'Of all branches of athletics, cross country seems to me the most classic and the most natural'. She also accepts that there are certain 'steady, indefatigable' women runners 'who although they have no powers of sprinting, seem to be incapable of wearying'. Running is vital for everyone and even field event specialists should run two or three miles regularly in winter 'to lay up a store of stamina and muscle power and wind' for the following summer. The previous autumn, she had run cross-country or gone beagling twice a week. Yet she views the women's 250 yards as the equivalent of a men's 440 yards; a 'middle distance' race over a long enough distance for tactics to matter. Today, the slightly longer 400m is regarded as a sprint.

The glory of athletics, she feels, is that all the competitors in a race are putting in a maximum effort at the same time. But while moderate running is the perfect exercise, she believes that the field events are more suitable than running for the majority of women because they are less tiring: 'One can quite happily throw a javelin for half an hour steadily without feeling too tired, whereas five minutes equal effort in running is exhaustive [sic].' While she fails to understand that five minutes of running is strenuous because the body is merely warming up, her appeal for a greater variety of events for women who are not natural runners could be echoed today.

About her only concession to the conventional wisdom of her time concerns child-bearing. Women, she believes, 'are primarily designed as mothers, and the opportunities must never be given for harm to happen either now or in far-reaching consequences in the future'. She quotes with approval a 'great authority' who believes that athletic women may regret their moments of sporting glory when it comes to having babies. Later, she unwittingly contradicts herself by remarking that fit women have an easier childbirth.

Most of the book is devoted to detailed technical advice on the full range of athletic disciplines, making it one of the first of its kind written by a woman for her sister athletes. But there are plenty of wise words, clearly based on experience; Sophie, for instance, points out that 'happiness...is a great factor in the make-up of the successful athlete', a point many modern coaches tend to forget. She emphasises that training must be moderate and gradual and observes that too much emphasis on 'record-breaking and championship fever' at an early age is disastrous for boys as well as girls:

> Many of the finest authorities, although they encourage team races and team competitions, are most strongly against anything in the nature of individual championships or record-makings, knowing that the star of today will not be the star of tomorrow, whereas the star of tomorrow, if its growth to brilliance be gradual and supervised, may be the star of the day after.

That, along with a lot of her advice, is strikingly apposite. Nor is she above a swipe at the male-dominated Olympic Games. Describing the prizes of 'a pair of strong oxen and a beautiful and good woman or wife' offered to male winners in the ancient Greek games, she caustically observes: 'History does not relate whether or not the Spartan girls were awarded "a beautiful and good man for husband" in their competitions.'

When it comes to mental preparation, so much a part of modern professional sport, she has her own simple routine:

> I always lie down quite flat on the ground with an old blazer, or something to keep my legs from the damp, wrapped round them, as well as my big coat. This lets all your muscles relax – you look up at the sky and do not watch the other competitors jumping – and failing.

What would she have thought of today's pampered superstars with their lycra bodysuits, carefully monitored 'vitamin' intake and personal psychologists?

No modern coach would argue with her view that practising technique is crucially important in sport and she points out that the best athletes, such as the Irish long jumper Peter O'Connor,[3] world record-holder from 1902 to 1921, found it difficult to describe what they did when they ran, jumped or threw. This was because they had practised every movement until it became automatic.

She kept up her interest in athletics that summer, still managing to train and compete regularly, probably inspired by the thought of a trip to Scandinavia at the end of the season. In early June, just days after returning from Prague, she was competing in the first *Daily Mirror* Trophy at Stamford Bridge, an event promoted by her club, Middlesex Ladies, and a month later she was in action at the WAAA Championships at Stamford Bridge, where she managed third place in the high jump and, on a typically busy day, also finished second in the javelin and seventh in the discus. By now, fresh new faces were coming through to replace the ageing pioneers of the sport. After her well-publicised first flight at the opening of the London Aero Club at Stag Lane on 19 August, she had decided to take flying lessons, but still found time for her annual trip to Torquay, where she finished second in the long jump and won the javelin.

Over the next year, Sophie would continue to juggle her two interests, practising her javelin at Stag Lane when she couldn't fly. But as her skill as a pilot increased, her involvement in athletics would inevitably lessen. It had been a short but glorious career and her influence was long-lasting and permanent.

CHAPTER 8

Sophie Takes Flight

On her flight home from the Olympic Congress in Prague in May 1925, an enthralled Sophie got chatting to a pilot, Captain Reid, who told her about the national air club scheme promoted by Sir Sefton Brancker,[1] the director of the Civil Aviation Advisory Board, which had been founded three years earlier in London.

Following World War 1, when flying machines had proved their worth, the British government was determined to see more people flying. To this end, after witnessing the first flight of the de Havilland Moth in 1925, Sir Sefton advised the Air Ministry to sponsor five light aeroplane clubs around the country,[2] with the de Havilland Moth, a small bi-plane with an open cockpit and room for just pilot and passenger, as the approved machine. Coming up soon would be the launch of the London Aeroplane Club at the Stag Lane aerodrome off the Edgware Road and since Sophie had taken to the air with such enthusiasm, Captain Reid suggested that she go along.

She needed little prompting and, on 19 August, was part of a large crowd of attentive listeners when Sir Philip Sassoon, Under Secretary for Air, officially opened the London Aeroplane Club at Stag Lane. In his speech, he emphasised the national importance of such clubs: 'They will help to build up that big reserve of air pilots which we need. They will also develop the air sense we are now looking forward to achieving and bring us nearer our ideal of Britain as a nation of airmen.' Sir Philip then took the first official flight with club instructor F.G.M. Sparkes.

Sophie 'a well-known and forceful sportswoman' was one of the first fifteen members to sign on. Although David Kettel won a ballot for the club's inaugural half-hour flight, he gallantly gave his place to Sophie, and so she became the club's first passenger, taking to the air in the club's dual-control de Havilland Moth. News reporters, by now obsessed with all things aerial, swarmed around her after she returned to earth. If they expected screams and hysteria, they were to be disappointed: 'The machine was beautifully steady. It was not a bit bumpy. It is my ambition after I have qualified as a pilot to own and fly a light aeroplane of my own,' she told the journalists.

It was a busy period for her, coming just over a month after the inaugural meeting of the National Playing Fields Association in the Royal Albert Hall, chaired by the Duke of Sutherland and attended by assorted grandees, many of them also involved in aviation, and with whom Sophie was only too delighted to become associated. The NPFA, which still exists, had emerged in response to the scandalous lack of playing facilities for children, especially in cities, at a time when Britain was becoming increasingly aware of the need to keep fit. For every two to three thousand boys and girls living in crowded urban areas, there was only one acre of playing field. During the 1923/24 season, there had been 973 applications for football pitches to the London County Council alone. Just 205 could be provided. Of the 917 applications for cricket pitches, only 311 were granted. Yet the general health of men and women was declining and, in the previous year, almost two-thirds of army recruits were rejected as unfit.

After the resolution to set up the organisation had been unanimously carried, the Duke of York agreed to become president and Sir Arthur Crosfield chairman. Among the many speakers was Harold Abrahams, the 1924 Olympic 100 metres champion. Lady Astor, the Conservative Member of Parliament for Plymouth, made a specific appeal to women, encouraging their involvement. There was an emotional rendition of 'Land of Hope and Glory' by Harold Williams, while Dame Beatrix Hudson recited a stirring piece of verse:

> Give them a chance for innocent sport
> Give them a chance to run.
> Better a playing field than a court
> Or a gaol when the harm is done.

Three committees were set up. The finance committee was chaired by Sir John Brunner, while Sophie's old friend Brigadier General R.J. Kentish chaired one committee for general organisation and another for 'propaganda'. Sophie was elected to the propaganda committee, along with three others, but although she declared that all profits from her book *Athletics for Women and Girls* should be split between the National Playing Fields Association and the WAAA, she seemed to have little involvement with the new association.

Despite her financial problems, Sophie continued to take flying lessons at Stag Lane during August 1925. Among her instructors were Sir Alan Cobham, one of the best-known aviators in England, and James Milo St John Kearney, later the first instructor with the Shannon Aero Club in Ireland. At the time, her job was described as 'club secretary'. It is easy to see what attracted Sophie to the new and thrilling world of aviation. Not only was it glamorous, attracting only those wealthy enough to support an expensive hobby, but it had an enticing whiff of the daring and the dangerous. Always on the look-out for activities that would bring her notice, Sophie was astute enough to see that a woman pilot could attract enough publicity to generate a steady income.

At Stag Lane, two separate organisations coexisted. The more commercial of the two was the de Havilland School of Flying, run by Geoffrey de Havilland, and catering largely for RAF reservists, with lessons costing £5 an hour. Thanks to its annual government grant of £2,000, the London Aero Club, which leased its land from the canny de Havilland, was able to give lessons for about half that rate. Secretary of the club was the punctilious Lieutenant Commander Harold Perrin, who was also secretary of the Royal Aeronautical Club, the chief authority in Britain when it came to private flying activities.

The Stag Lane aerodrome was nothing fancy. A casual visitor, like Amy Johnson in 1928, would first notice a collection of sheds, holding aeroplanes in various states of construction. There was an open space for taking off, and beside this, more sheds and a pavilion with deck-chairs in front of it. Inside, members could make themselves a cup of tea on a gas ring. The atmosphere was easy-going, with plenty of banter, and Sophie with her background in boarding schools and the army, would have revelled in it.

After seven or eight hours of instruction at the club and a preliminary test for 'nerves', the prospective pilot could apply for an A or private flying licence. Once successful at the various tests, the new pilot could use the club's machines for a fee of £1 per hour and take part in races, displays and stunts. The planes were primitive. Cockpits were open, which meant pilots had no protection from the weather, and instrumentation consisted of a switch to turn on the engine, a throttle, a rudder and little else. With no self-starter, the propeller had to be swung around vigorously by an accomplice on the ground to spark the engine into life. When this happened, the 'chocks' wedged against the wheels were removed and with the help of a rudder, worked by the feet and a stick, the plane was taxied to its start-off position into the wind; hence the expression 'chocks away'. Another handle on the left, usually called the 'cheese cutter', was used to raise the tail at take-off. Providing vital information were the speed and height indicators, fuel gauge, spirit level, rev counter and compass. Perhaps most terrifying from the modern point of view was the absolute lack of any source of communication between aircraft and ground once aloft. If you got into trouble, you were on your own.

Once airborne, it wasn't so difficult, as Sophie herself pointed out:

> In the air, you have only two levers to deal with – a rudder bar for the feet and a control column, the joystick for the hands. There are very few dials – a revolution count, speed indicator, altimeter, oil pressure gauge and petrol gauge. To get the hang of it all, just 20 half hour lessons are enough.

For a lesson, a pupil sat behind the instructor in one of the club's small two-seater planes. After taking off, the instructor, through the movements of his rudder pedals (linked to the pupil's), taught the pupil how to keep the aircraft flying in a straight line. 'Keep your nose on the horizon,' was the customary order. Maintaining speed was also crucial. Verbal guidance came from a speaking tube connected to earpieces in the pupil's helmet. Unlike in a car, a certain delicacy of movement was essential. Even the lightest touch on the control column of a Moth could make it climb, dive or bank.

Next step was learning how to turn the craft. By pressing the left foot on the rudder and moving the stick to the left, the plane's left wing would sink and the right rise in the sky: 'rudder and stick together' was the classic instruction. The plane was now behaving like a bird. Taking off, gliding, side-slipping, taxiing and recovering from a spin: all were techniques that had to be learned. Landing, the most difficult element, had to be practised again and again. A good landing required accurate judgement of speed, height and distance. The engine had to be cut off and the plane allowed to glide earthwards so that wheels and tail-skid hit the ground together. Since no two landing strips were the same, it was always a challenge. Because of a natural sensitivity of touch and co-ordination, born pilots were often compared to an accomplished horse-rider and the pioneering pilots wore jodhpurs because of the perceived links between the two activities.

Sophie took to it all with gusto and proved to be a naturally gifted pilot. Later, she was to remember her first experience of flying: 'It was like learning a new dance. You say to yourself when you start to learn the charleston, my legs will never do this. But after a couple of lessons you begin to master the strange movements, and at the end of half a dozen attempts, you find your legs performing them almost automatically.' It was the same when you learned to fly: 'After a very short time, flying became second nature to me. I fly nearly every day and can remain a long time in the air without feeling fatigued.'

She was still heavily involved in athletics and her 1925 season culminated with the trip to Sweden, where local enthusiasts hoped a visit from the world-famous British squad might help promote athletics for women. The first meet was held in Gothenburg on 20 September, where Sophie finished third in the high jump and won the javelin. Two days later at Falkenberg, she was second in the javelin and third in both the two-handed shot and the discus.

On 18 October 1925, Sophie flew solo for the first time 'and made some excellent landings'. She described it in her book as 'the most thrilling adventure of my life'. Twelve days later, she took a first test for her A licence, flying a DH Moth with a Cirrus engine. Having successfully completed a figure-of-eight, she started climbing skywards for her altitude test. Within minutes, it had become extremely misty and she could see nothing. But although it was impossible to make out the aerodrome below, Sophie did not panic. After making three landings to find out where she was, she eventually came down at Slough where the machine was housed for the night.

Her adventure proved beyond doubt her ability as a pilot. During the flight, she had reached heights of 6,000 feet and, by selecting suitable places for landing and taking off, shown herself thoroughly capable of handling the Moth. A few days later, she undertook her final test, flying to 6,000 feet and then, with the engine cut off, descending and landing within a specified distance at the aerodrome.

On 4 November, less than a week before her 29th birthday, Sophie received her A licence, Certificate Number 7975; it was handed over to her personally on 30 November by Colonel F.C. Shelmerdine of the Air Ministry, who was to feature again in her story, though in less happy circumstances, a decade later. But although now certified to fly privately, she had to wait until she had clocked up over 50 hours of solo flying before she was permitted to carry passengers, even just for fun. That target took her little more than a few weeks to reach. Her licence opened up a new world. In the summer months, every town with an air strip or even a flat racecourse was organising air shows and attracting not only thousands of spectators but pages of press coverage; even the bookmakers, always on the alert for a chance to make easy money, were in attendance. The typical air show included pleasure flights, crazy flying, wing walking, bombing and fighting, as well as air racing, with cash prizes. A competent and fearless pilot could earn a good living touring such shows.

In the meantime, Sophie continued to fly as often as she could over the winter, despite problems finding a plane, with one of the London Aero Club's two Moths out of commission after an accident. She became increasingly immersed in the day-to-day running of the club and a dinner she organised raised nearly £40. In March, she was just one of the club's members who donated £10 towards buying a third Moth, with the fund soon reaching £550. She was now looking further than a menu of stunt flying and racing and had undertaken the technical examination for a B or commercial licence, passing easily on the subjects of navigation and meteorology, as well taking a special test on her ability to manage light machines and engines, such as the DH Moth.

In March, as one of the founding members of the British Private Aircraft Owners' Club, she flew to Yeovil in a DH Moth, registration G-EBKT, with N.H. Jones, an Auxiliary Air Force man. Later in the month, the pair bought the distinctive light blue Moth; it was her first plane. That same month, the Middlesex Women's Athletic Association visited Stag Lane and Sophie gave 22 of them joyrides. By mid-April, she had flown over twenty hours and passed the cross-country test for her B licence. Over the entire month, she flew some 52 hours.

Despite her obvious drive and growing list of achievements, she was not universally popular. Geoffrey de Havilland, whose company not only shared premises at Stag Lane with the London Aero Club while Sophie was there but also supplied the club with its fleet of Moths, makes no mention of her in his book *Sky Fever*, although he writes at length about Lady Bailey, also Irish, though from a distinctly different background and with an influential South African husband, Sir Abe Bailey, who ensured her entrée into the highest levels of British society. Whether she was accepted or not, Sophie had found her life's passion. It gave focus to her considerable energies, as well as providing her with a desperately needed income.

At every opportunity, she argued strenuously that women were meant to fly. In her book *Women and Flying*, co-written with the invalided aviation journalist and lifelong supporter Stella Wolfe Murray and published by John Long in 1929, she somewhat tenuously connects the Queen of Sheba to aviation in a chapter called 'The Story of Women in Aviation':

> Solomon gave unto the Queen of Sheba whatsoever she wished for of splendid things and riches ... a vessel wherein one could traverse the air (or winds), which Solomon had made by the wisdom that God had given unto him.

Manco Huella, founder of the first Peruvian dynasty, was said to have flown from Heaven to Earth with his wife, while in most religions the highest gods and goddesses are gifted with wings; among Christians, only the very best and purest could acquire angel's wings. Sophie continues with a brief history of flying women, from the balloonist Madeline Sophie Blanchard to Raymonde de Laroche, better known as the self-styled Baroness de Laroche, who became the world's first female pilot in 1910 and was followed swiftly by the Americans Harriet Quimby and Mathilde Moisant and by Britain's Hilda Hewlett and Cheridah de Beauvoir Stock.[3] The women pilots had an ambiguous role to play in this new adventure – they became instant heroines when they succeeded, but were proof that women were unfitted to fly, either physically or emotionally, when they failed.

Although it would never be easy for women to get the training, jobs, money or good equipment they needed to become pilots, light aircraft built for one or two, which any woman could fly, had arrived at a very opportune moment in aviation's history. A.V. Roe's Avro Baby, unveiled in 1920, was followed by the hugely successful DH Moth, which became standard equipment for private pilots after its launch in 1925 as the aerial equivalent of a sports car. 'Hops' from London to the country estate or, for the more adventurous, as far as Paris became common among the wealthier, thanks to the advent of the Moth. Only later did Avro catch up with its Avian, powered by the superior Cirrus engines and so capable of travelling farther and faster. It meant that Sophie was soon joined by half-a-dozen other women pilots, all flying from one air show to the next to take part in the popular 'Ladies' Races'.

Sophie's official view was that flying was a skill anyone could master:

> Flying really is absurdly easy – and it is only those who fly themselves who realise this. Just because of necessity, aviation is 'in the air' and … there is a halo of mystery surrounding it. To the uninitiated 'looping the loop' is an achievement and an adventure and the lay mind focuses itself on the moment of being upside down, while looping is merely turning a corner, but doing it in a different direction from the corners we are always turning on the ground and because of the centrifugal force that keeps you on your seat – and your maps on your knee, in a well-done loop, you simply do not realise you are going round until you touch the 'wake' of the air you left behind you when you were going into the corner.

Despite the many sensational accidents, of which the public was all too aware, Sophie was adamant that flying posed no great risks:

> Flying is safe – in 1925 and 1926, Imperial Airways carried 33,000 passengers and not one fare-paying passenger was injured. On the roads, 21 are killed every week from motorcars. Flying is cheap over long distances because you get there so much more quickly than by rail and boat. Your own little machine will cost between £400 and £700, expense two pennies a mile.

To enjoy the pleasant experience of flying, no special clothes were needed – just a loose skirt and a warm coat for cold days and a small, close-fitting felt hat. Sophie, like virtually all women pilots, feels compelled to give her opinion on this subject, one that doesn't interest male pilots. Helmets and goggles were not really necessary, she says, adding: 'You can carry a comfortably large suitcase with you and you can arrive at your destination much cleaner and fresher than if you came on a dusty or muddy road.' Sophie did her best to make leaving *terra firma* in fragile machines made of wood, stretched linen and piano wires, with the most rudimentary of navigational devices and altimeters, sound boring: 'There is no thrill in normal modern aviation – the days of pioneering are over.'

Although in some respects she was right and big business was about to take over the burgeoning industry, she was also somewhat disingenuous. Like most pilots, she had a touch of the daredevil in her and enjoyed the thrill of taking chances and pulling them off. Among the risky activities indulged by almost all pilots was a practice known as 'hedge-hopping', which involved diving at a tree, pulling skywards to safety only at the last minute, and 'shooting up' or flying very low over the house of some friend or relation. Naturally, the authorities frowned on these activities, so they were rarely mentioned in official discourses.

Despite her efforts to downplay her own considerable skill, Sophie quickly gained a reputation for her mechanical prowess. Her years at the Royal College of Science and as a driver during World War 1 had given her a solid knowledge of mechanics which she could call on during her career as a pilot. Yet while she put a brave public face on her efforts, Sophie was struggling hard, first to be accepted as a pilot by her hide-bound male peers and then to be given a commercial licence. Women did not do much of anything in those days, and any woman pilot was taking on centuries of received ideas about her proper place in society. Sophie's battle on behalf of women pilots was described at length in *Women and Flying*:

> When I first flew, I took my pilot's licence, and only afterwards did I discover that I had no right to a commercial one. I needed money very badly, as I had staked my last dollar on flying. I simply hounded the various ministries until they felt at last that if I insisted upon flying and being killed, perhaps it would be a happy release all round. But in the end because the men saw that it was unjust and were sympathetic, I gained my point, and it was agreed between countries that women should fly freely to make a living.

In their jointly written book, Stella Wolfe Murray describes women's struggle for equal opportunities in the air. Initially, women were welcomed in flying circles and a few even ran joyriding companies, she says. A woman's lighter weight and greater ability to resist the cold were recognised as natural advantages; men might be stronger physically, but brute force was not required for piloting the average light machine.

Then in April 1924, the International Commission for Air Navigation passed a resolution that 'women shall be excluded from any employment in the operating crew of an aircraft engaged in public transport', so barring women from working even as flight attendants. This, only hinted at in Sophie's account, was because of the great unmentionable: woman's monthly menstrual cycle. Under resolution No. 146, which dealt with candidates for a pilot's licence, women were excluded even by the wording: 'He must be of the male sex, must have complete use of his four limbs, must not be completely deprived of the use of either eye, must be free from any active or latent, acute or chronic, medical or surgical disability or infection.' Menstruation was clearly considered a disability.

The decision to ban women came to public notice only in 1925 when the highly respected French pilot, Madame Bolland, was stripped of her licence and forced to close down her air transport business at considerable financial loss. In the meantime, Sophie, after successfully taking her A licence tests, was told it would be pointless for her to take the tests for a B licence since, whatever the result, she would not be allowed to carry passengers for hire or reward. This was a decision a woman like Sophie was unlikely to accept and both she and Stella Wolfe Murray wrote to the secretary of the International Commission for Air Navigation in Paris, while Sophie approached Lady Astor, with whom she was already acquainted. She must have been at her persuasive best because Lady Astor agreed to write on her behalf to Sir Samuel Hoare, the Minister responsible for civil aviation.

In her letter to the International Commission for Air Navigation, Sophie clearly explained her position. Thanks to a burgeoning interest in civil aviation, she had abandoned her position as 'an organiser in the world of business' so that she could learn to fly. In researching the subject, she found that most women pilots, especially in the United States of America, had gained recognition by attempting daring feats and stunts. These did nothing to promote flying as a safe and sensible form of transport and so she had decided to train and study for a B licence as a means of demonstrating that women could do a commercial pilot's work.

Her first problems were resolutions Nos. 146 and 147, which barred women commercial pilots: 'I see however in No. 147 that the Medical Sub-Commission was directed to continue its study of the matter, and it is on this account that I venture to write to you.' She points out that because of the scarcity of women pilots, the medical sub-commission had little material to go on, and volunteers herself as a fit subject for examination, even by the Reid indicator, an instrument designed to measure the nervous reactions of intending pilots, at any time of the month.

Meanwhile, in the United States, Stella Wolfe Murray had enlisted the help of the National Aeronautic Association and, while in Washington, was introduced to Majorie Stinson, who not only flew herself but had taught some 83 men how to fly, many of them British, at the family flying school in San Antonio, Texas; by some strange twist of logic, the authorities had no objection to women teaching others to fly. By the spring of 1926, Murray could tell Sir Sefton Brancker, then visiting New York, that Sir Samuel Hoare was now convinced of their arguments and would be asking the international body to rescind the ban on women pilots.

As far as Sir Sefton Brancker, the director of civil aviation, was concerned, women pilots were 'absolutely the equal of men'. All that was holding them back was a lack of training opportunities. 'If ever there is a flood, famine, or pestilence in any part of the world, I think there is no doubt women will be in the forefront in transporting medical stores, food and all the necessaries,' he said during his visit.

He mentioned Sophie specifically: 'I have flown with Mrs Eliott-Lynn, whom I shall describe as the woman flying ace of Great Britain, and her achievements are proof that in small machines at any rate, women are absolutely the equal of men.' He quoted her recent altitude record: 'She rose about four miles high! I don't think that men have much fault to find with that.' He expected more from adventure-loving women. 'I foresee a brilliant future for women in the air, and they have my heartiest support in their efforts to conquer the prejudice which hampers them and which is, as I judge from my experience, without reasonable foundation.'

Some months later, Sophie was suddenly invited by the British aviation authorities to present herself for physical examination 'during a certain period', as it is put tactfully in her book. Despite dancing until 3 a.m. that morning, she went at once to the Air Ministry and had no difficulty passing the 'special' examination, in front of a panel of male examiners, with no mention at all of how outrageously demeaning it must have been for her. Later on, her ability to land a plane was tested and approved. She could now start training for her commercial or B licence. Quitting her secretarial job, Sophie moved into 'digs' near the aerodrome at Stag Lane and for three months did nothing but practise and study, flying by day and night, and immersing herself in such topics as navigation, meteorology, engine-fitting, rigging, and the theory of flight.

Although she passed all her examinations without any problem, though only graded 'fair' for most of them, she still could not carry passengers because the ruling allowing women pilots to fly commercially had yet to come through. To earn a living, she gave exhibitions and indulged in various headline-grabbing stunts. On 3 April, in Hereford, she was the first woman to make a parachute jump from a plane in public. It took two attempts. A day earlier, in a plane piloted by a Captain Lawson, she had been climbing onto the wing at 1,700 feet to make the jump when the plane's engine stuttered and the machine went into freefall. With Sophie clinging on desperately, Lawson narrowly missed the tops of some trees and then grazed the roof of a house with the plane's wheels before landing in the middle of a football pitch, scattering players in every direction. Unshaken, Sophie brushed herself off and took the controls of another plane to give a twenty-minute display of stunt flying for the assembled spectators.

Fortunately, there was no further drama when she tried again after a night's sleep: 'The sensation of landing by parachute was about the same as a jump from a six-foot wall. I could have wished, however, that the ploughed field could have been a little bit softer,' she said.

By May 1926, when the International Commission for Air Navigation was meeting in Paris, and Britain was in the grip of a general strike, she was attracting much attention, owing to 'her courage, beauty and charm', by delivering newspapers from London to Paris. She used several stratagems to get around the ruling forbidding her to take up passengers, one of which she described in a somewhat disingenuous letter to Sir Sefton Brancker:

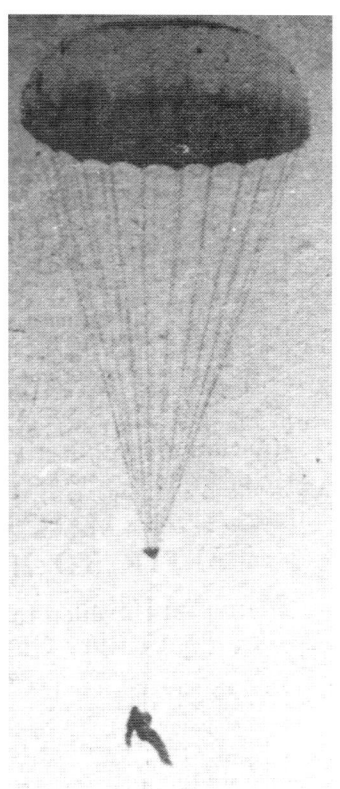

> …as I was unable to get hold of any official to give me permission to take up passengers over the Whitsun weekend, I did not do so in the ordinary way, but only took those who purchased a photograph of a machine at a guinea each. I hope that this is all right?

On 31 May, she successfully completed her night flying test, despite a recently broken wrist, and after a full medical examination a few weeks later, at last was legally entitled to carry passengers and to earn a living as a pilot: 'So the members of the commission who had formerly been unanimous in banning women

Sophie making a safe landing by parachute at a second attempt. (*Cussen Collection*)

After leading members of her Middlesex club on a cross-country run, Sophie explains the art of flying to an attentive group. (*Radio Times Hulton Picture Library*)

from any employment in aircraft, were then unanimous in rescinding the ban on women pilots and deciding in principle that women should be allowed to carry passengers.' Sophie became Britain's first officially recognised female commercial pilot.

Partly to celebrate, Sophie organised an 'Airwoman's At Home' at Stag Lane a few days later. Among the 200 in attendance, for a second time that year, were members of the Middlesex Ladies Athletic Club and other friends. At least half took up the invitation to joyride and afterwards enjoyed an afternoon tea, served by waitresses at tables set up around the planes. Despite the celebrations and the party mood, Sophie was well aware that she had only won the first battle and was already contemplating her future. She would have to earn a good living – or find herself a rich husband – if she was to continue with her new and expensive profession.

CHAPTER 9

Wings over Europe

Sophie's hard work on behalf of women pilots meant that, with backing from Sweden, Norway, Czechoslovakia and France, the ban on women pilots was unanimously rescinded. The only remaining problem was the compulsory medical examination. By July 1926, it was agreed that women should be examined every three months, twice as often as men.

A month earlier, on 7 June, another Irishwoman, Lady Mary Bailey, was given her first joyride by Sophie and was soon under instruction. Lady Bailey, born Mary Westenra in 1890, was the daughter of Baron 'Derry' Rossmore, one of the swinging set that had surrounded the Prince of Wales in Victorian times. At the age of 20, her impoverished family had married her off to 47-year-old Abe Bailey, a wealthy widower, who as founder of the Lonrho company, was the biggest mine owner in South Africa. With five young children, the unassuming Lady Bailey, as unhappy a housewife in her own way as Sophie, flew 'to get away from prams'. Their lives would become inextricably entwined when both opted to fly over Africa at the same time.

Lady Mary Bailey, Sophie's friend and rival.

Already learning to fly was Sicele O'Brien, the third of this celebrated trio of Irish women pilots; her family was based in London but originally from Limerick. O'Brien became the second woman pilot in Britain to receive a commercial licence. She lost a leg in a plane crash in 1928 and died in another crash three years later.

Sophie became the owner of a SE 5a Viper that July. The 'Sopwith Experimental', designed at Farnborough, had been the best-known British scout plane during the Great War. The Viper, G-EBPA, affectionately called 'Pa', proved an erratic performer, but still won its owner a number of prizes.

At Orly Airport, Paris, Lady Mary carefully pulls her wingless DH Moth through the special gate in a dismantling test. (*Flight* Collection)

She had missed the English Women's Athletics Championships held on 19 June at Stamford Bridge; nor did she compete in the 'Olympic Trials' in August because of a clash with a number of overseas flying competitions. Presumably, she had been told that her place on the British team for the Women's World Games was safe since she would be a delegate at the FSFI conference immediately after.

So began a frantic few years of flying literally here, there and everywhere. If a flying display or air show was taking place anywhere in the country, Sophie was likely to be there and hogging much of the publicity. Like any modern celebrity, she was determined to keep her name to the fore and had a nose for a good story.

Late in July, at the first Yorkshire Air Pageant at the Sherburn aerodrome, east of Leeds, her distinctive pale blue DH Moth flew into sight in plenty of time for a disastrous inter-club relay race. After the first four planes landed together, causing hopeless confusion, an over-zealous official had grabbed the tip of the Lancashire club Moth, swinging it into Sophie's machine, which was taxiing alongside. Fortunately there was little damage, and although Sophie suffered a broken wing, she later won the 25-mile Private Owners' Handicap, when she swooped into the lead to beat the only other competitor in a characteristically flamboyant finish.

One of her most notable forays abroad came a couple of weeks later, when Sophie was the only woman competitor in the French Air Association's *Concours d'avions économique* at Orly Airport, just south of Paris. The competition consisted of a number of tests designed to stretch both pilot and machine to the utmost. The stated object of the exercise was to assess the quality of small planes for civil or military training and tests included a fuel consumption trial, as well as landing, climbing and speed tests.

The French were eagerly awaiting the first visit of Sophie: 'a remarkable English athlete who had left the sporting stadiums for the aerodromes and the hurdles for the Channel when she entered the competition'. Flying a DH Moth powered by a 60hp 4-cylinder Cirrus engine, Sophie's most dramatic moment came in the speed trial, thanks to a cracked cylinder head. Forced to cut her speed and fly at less than 400 feet, she landed safely back at base, and with her mechanic close behind her, leapt out of the plane and raced across the airfield to a distant workshop for the tools and materials she needed to repair the damage. In the same test, she improvised a self-starting device, which fortunately she did not have to use – it consisted of a stone dropped into a flying helmet attached to a piece of wood fixed to the propeller. This, in theory, would have forced the propeller to rotate. After finishing seventh of seventeen starters in the competition, and with three wins from the seven tests, she was celebrated in the French press as '*un sport*'.

Her hectic schedule continued after she returned home. At a two-day air festival in Bournemouth, she competed in a number of races, winning the final race on the programme, the Light Aeroplane Club Members' Scratch, for a prize of £20. The competition proved a great success; bookies did a roaring trade and the holiday-makers in attendance were enthralled.

Next up was a long overland journey to a thrilling Women's World Games in Gothenburg, Sweden. Elements of the 'real' Olympics, such as the release of carrier pigeons, added greatly to the atmosphere, with athletes from Belgium, Britain, Czechoslovakia and France joined by Latvia, Poland, Japan and the host nation in the opening parade. Thanks to the quality of the competition, the 3,300 spectators present on the first day of competition swelled to 8,000 a day later, when Sophie was

Members of the Brirish team at the second Women's World Games, Gothenburg, 1926, the British team. Sophie is seated in front beside Major Marchant with Florence Birchenough to his left.

competing in the javelin. She was now a veteran of almost 30 and technique had moved on. Although the Swedes were throwing the javelin by grasping it with just one hand, Sophie and her English team-mate Louise Fawcett stuck to the old two-handed style; Fawcett finished second and Sophie fourth.

At the fourth conference of the FSFI after the games, Sophie was one of the more forceful speakers. With Germany finally being admitted as a member, the seventeen countries represented agreed to standardise rules; in came the metric system for all international competitions and specific weights for the javelin, discus and shot. But the chief subject for discussion was the matter of Olympic acceptance. The proposal to admit women even to a limited degree caused uproar at the IAAF's conference held in The Hague in early August, with vehement opposition from some delegates. Amended to cover only the 1928 Games, the proposal was eventually carried by twelve votes to five. Britain and Ireland both voted against, because they felt that to include just five events was an insult; others remained opposed to women competing at all.

At the FSFI conference, there was considerable anger at the proposed 'experimental' Olympic programme of just five events. Sophie argued that women had nothing to gain from participating in the Olympic Games. The 'women's only'

Pulling her DH Moth, with wings folded back, from a hangar at Stag Lane.

games had been a great success and, in most countries, parents disapproved of mixed meets. Her views, and indeed those of the other British delegates, had little impact. When the International Olympic Committee met in Paris later that year, the British voted against the patronising 'experiment'. The motion to accept women's athletics was passed, but Britain, the sport's strongest nation, would not be present at the 1928 Games.[1]

In September, Sophie's Irish compatriot, Sicele O'Brien, flew solo for the first time and received her pilot's licence a month later. Sophie herself was back in the cockpit that autumn, flying at air shows in Lympne, near Folkestone, Woodford in Lancashire and Sherburn in Yorkshire. She had started giving flying instruction at the London Aero Club, with the first of her pupils, Lieutenant G.H.N. Larden, successfully passing his pilot's exams. Later that month, at an air display to honour the visit of members of the Empire Conference at Croydon, she gave a demonstration of how easy it was to manage a small plane. She wheeled her DH Moth out of a temporary building on the site, unfolded the wings, started up the engine and, after a short flight, rehoused the plane briskly and efficiently.

By now, she was the most prominent female pilot in Britain but her forceful personality and tendency to seek the limelight had earned her the sobriquet 'Lady Hell-of-a-Din', a play on her married name. In late 1926, she was reported somewhat mysteriously by the *Aeroplane* magazine as retiring from aviation 'as quietly as an operatic star making a farewell appearance'; the paper's editor, C.G. Grey, was vehemently anti-Irish and had never liked Sophie anyway. Following a request from the Air Ministry in December for the fee to renew her licence, she had scribbled a note to them saying that since she was leaving for Africa 'almost at once', she would wait until April before she dealt with the matter, a fairly risky stratagem given the trouble she had getting the licence in the first place, although she did send on the fee later. But she had no intention of retiring and when she returned to England, applied to renew both her licences. While in Africa, she had flown a DH 51 Moth belonging to her distant cousin John Carberry, a man as fanatical about flying as she was herself, she told the Air Ministry when making her case.[2]

On 1 May 1927, Sophie's estranged husband Major William Davies Eliott-Lynn was found drowned in the river Thames off Ranelagh sewer with just a single copper penny in his pockets. Aged 52, he had returned from Africa after the failure of the couple's coffee farm a few years earlier and had been living in London, though not at Sophie's Clarges Street address. After his life-threatening bout of malaria in Africa during the final months of his war service, his health had remained poor and he had struggled to find work.

A 'Mrs Mary Eliott-Lynn' appeared as a witness at the inquest held two days later. She told the coroner that her husband had lost his job with Hartley and Company, contractors for road-making, on 23 April. The Coroner, Mr Oddie, asked her whether he had been depressed. She replied that he had been: 'He had worked very hard on the previous Sunday doing his books. He was a most conscientious man and lived for his work. He had most excellent credentials throughout his life.' From 23 to 30 April, Eliott-Lynn, who lived at an address near St Pancras railway station, had answered advertisements and looked for work: 'I saw him last on Saturday. It was the anniversary of my birthday and we had a little dinner. He said he was going to his club to see the papers and to discover if he could get any work.' The implication was that he had walked out of the door and she had not seen him since. Because Sophie had not been living with him and, anyway, her birthday was in November, this statement is puzzling to say the least. There is no evidence that she divorced Eliott-Lynn, allowing him to marry again, but this particular witness sounds most unlike Sophie, and was possibly another woman altogether.

George William Mason, a clerk with Hartley and Company, said that Major Eliott-Lynn had started work with the firm on 10 March as an engineer in road-making. He was discharged on 23 April: 'He did not seem to have enough energy for getting about. There were three or four contracts and he didn't seem to manage.' The coroner asked whether he had been superseded. Mason answered 'yes' to that question and added that he had been paid £7 a week. The coroner returned an open verdict.

A couple of weeks later, on 18 May 1927, Sophie was back in the headlines when she set a new altitude record. For the ambitious woman pilot, anxious to prove her worth, altitude records had the great advantage of being comparatively easy to arrange. So with Lady Bailey as passenger, Sophie had taken off from Hamble aerodrome near Southampton in an Avian Cirrus Mk II and had climbed steadily upwards to a height of 15,748 ft.

Just three days later, Charles Lindbergh in the 'Spirit of St Louis' became the first pilot to fly the Atlantic, a feat many had thought impossible. Even more remarkably, he had done it on his own. Thanks largely to the efforts of the publisher and publicist George Putnam, Lindbergh became a household name, and his book, *We*, published within three months of his flight, proved a phenomenal success. With Lindbergh hysteria putting aviation on the front pages of newspapers worldwide, it was a good time to be a pilot and Sophie was interviewed by the *Daily Mail* on 'The Exhilaration of Flying'.

There was plenty of room for women in the air, she had proclaimed with her Irish eyes twinkling, according to 'F. G. P. W.', the Mail's gushing interviewer. When she was racing or giving demonstrations, Mrs Eliott-Lynn made a point of flying alone, but on ordinary flights, she preferred company, because it could be quite lonely 'upstairs'. She never trained for racing, not even for exploits such as her recent altitude record. Nor did she diet: 'I live very simply and never diet. I eat what I like and plenty of it. Also I have a cigarette whenever I want one and I believe in the advice given by St Paul – to take a little wine for thy stomach's sake.'

To keep fit, she played tennis and continued to make trips to Battersea Park to throw the javelin. She confessed that her narrowest escape in the air had been the result of 'showing off' to some male pilots soon after she had learned to fly: 'I was trying to do a flat turn at high speed. Unfortunately, I got into a "bump" in the air and the nose of my machine turned up when I was only 80 feet above the ground. The plane shot into a spin, but giving her full engine, I managed to pull her out and she staggered over a wood. I have never shown off again!'

The Bournemouth meet on a weekend in early June proved that, despite Sophie's

Sophie's 79-stop trip around England

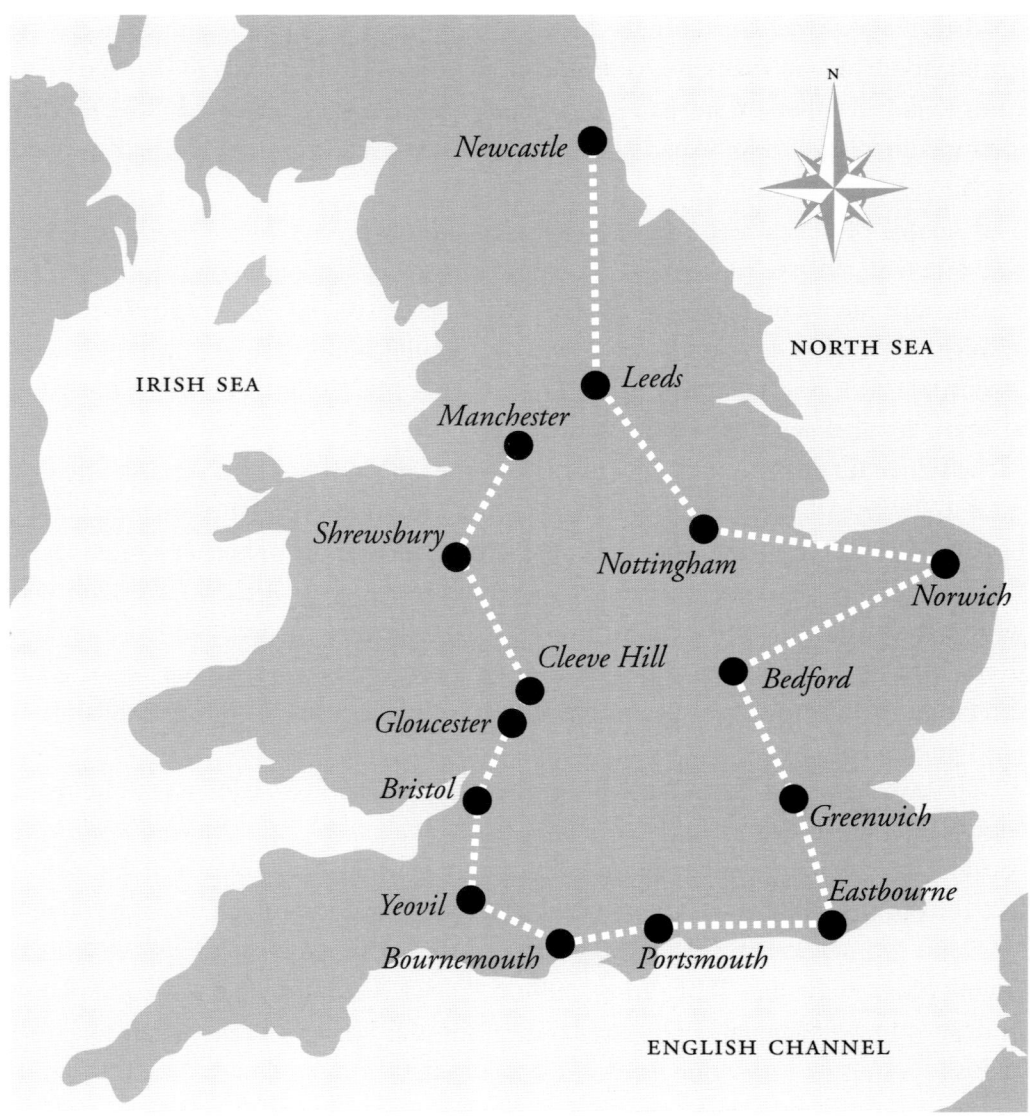

many protestations, flying was far from safe. Before the first race of the day, a Major Harold Hemmings hit a steel number-board and crashed. Both he and his passenger, Claude Plevins, died. A further two pilots were killed two days later. In the meantime, the show went on and, in the ladies' race, Sophie, off scratch, used her superior cornering to beat Sicele O'Brien, with Lady Bailey third. 'All three handled their machines excellently, making very good turns at the aerodrome turning point, those of Mrs Eliott-Lynn being particularly good and practically vertical,' said *Flight* magazine.

As one of the biggest names in British aviation, Sophie was to have been the star attraction at the Newcastle Meet a week later. But since she arrived without a plane and could not borrow one, she was forced to remain earthbound, to the great disappointment of the crowd: 'Mrs Eliott-Lynn had been advertised by the local press as the star attraction of the meet but as she omitted to bring an aeroplane with her and as the other people thought that they would rather like to fly their own machines, the crowd was deprived of the privilege of seeing her in the air.'

An appearance in Birmingham followed, where she did fly, but in early July, it was Sicele O'Brien's turn to capture the limelight when she won what was billed as the first 'Aerial Oaks', a women's only race. Then on 5 July, Lady Bailey, flying Geoffrey de Havilland's own Moth and with his wife, Louie, as a passenger, broke Sophie's altitude record when she reached a reported height of 18,000 ft, later revised down to 17,283 ft but still a world best.

Sophie, while publicly congratulating her sister pilots, was determined to regain her place as Britain's top female pilot. Although a DH Moth G-EBMV was registered to her in early July, Sophie had obviously struck some kind of a deal with the A.V. Roe company, based near Manchester, and grabbed back the headlines later that month when, 'emulating a grasshopper', she flew 1,250 miles around Britain at an average speed of 80 mph, making 79 landings. She was flying an Avro Avian Mk 2 G-ERBS, which had been registered to her name on 19 July, and her purpose was simple: she wanted to prove that a small aeroplane could travel almost anywhere in Britain. As *Flight* magazine put it, an aeroplane 'can fly where it will but it cannot land where it will and this is the only limitation on its freedom'.

With the increase of private flying, and a belief that this was the future, a thorough air survey to determine all existing landing areas was needed. *Flight* praised Sophie for her effort, calling it 'a useful exercise'. She had set off from Woodford, Manchester, at 3.20 am after dozing in the hangar overnight, and following a triangular course over England, stayed mostly airborne for over eighteen hours. Because it had been dark when she had set out, she had steered by the moon until sunrise. By 9 am, she had reached the south coast, following stops at thirty places, including Shrewsbury, Birmingham, Cleeve Hill, Gloucester, Yeovil and Bournemouth. By 2 pm, she had landed at Stag Lane. She then headed north again, stopping at Bedford, Norwich, Nottingham, Leeds, and reaching Newcastle just before 9.30 pm. She had not planned to fly any farther north than Woodford, but with the Avian flying so well, she had decided to carry on.

Sophie pictured with Aunt Cis, Rosie Darcy, Richbel Curling and Robin the dog. *(Cussen Collection)*

On finally landing, she reported that the weather had been perfect and that her new machine had behaved impeccably and was so comfortable that she hardly felt tired. On each of her landings, she had allowed herself ten minutes to fill up with petrol and have a snack. Many landings were made in fields and on roads between aerodromes. An open space at Tewkesbury, between the town and the river, was one of the most perfect natural landing places she had come across. Near Gosport, she had lost her map; fortunately, in Britain at the time, many prominent buildings had their names painted on the roofs to help pilots up above them find their way.

Sophie had always kept in touch with her Irish roots, making at least one annual visit to her Aunt Cis in Ballybunion. Later on in her life, to the joy of the locals, she would land her plane in a place called Larkin's Field, and, for a small fee, take the more intrepid spectators up for short spins. After her new altitude record and flight around Britain, she made a surprise visit to Dublin on 25 July 1927. With mechanic Henry Hollingdrake, she had started off from Manchester at 11 am for Flint, in Wales, from there flown to Kirkcudbright, in Scotland, then over the Irish Sea at its narrowest point and on to Aldergrove in Belfast, where she lunched after landing in mid-afternoon.

Just before six o'clock, she touched down in the broad spaces of the Fifteen Acres at Dublin's Phoenix Park after flying about 500 miles. There, Commandant Fitzmaurice of the Army Air Force welcomed her and, flying an Irish army plane, accompanied her to Baldonnel, about ten miles distant, where she had to land officially in order to clear customs and where she was the honoured guest of the air force. Her Avro Avian, the light aeroplane she had used in her tour of Britain the previous week, was the latest type of flying machine and equipped with folding wings, she told reporters. It could be housed in an ordinary garage and cost only £750.

The flight was her first to Ireland and she had enjoyed every minute of the trip, she said: 'Ireland is an ideal country for flying. It is much better than England because the country is so much more pastoral and there are larger fields. On the way from Belfast to Dublin, I could have taken down my machine at any point with perfect safety had I to do so because of engine trouble.' There was no reason for Dublin not to have its own light aeroplane club: 'The Fifteen Acres is a wonderful place for aeroplanes. If there were a similar park in or near London, it would be an extremely valuable asset to the light aeroplane clubs, which are increasing in membership day after day.' She believed the Irish could fly well – Lady Bailey, Miss O'Brien and herself were just three examples of successful flying Irish women.

Sophie had brought with her a letter from Sir William Letts, chairman of the Avro-Avian company, for Sir James Percy, who was interested in setting up private aeroplane clubs in Ireland. The following day, Sophie was back in the Phoenix Park. She had hoped to start a demonstration at about 3 pm, but gale-force winds forced her to delay her departure from Baldonnel for two hours. A large crowd had gathered in Dublin and gave her a rousing welcome when she finally arrived, accompanied by Commandant Fitzmaurice and Henry Hollingdrake in an army aeroplane. For fifteen minutes after landing, she was kept busy signing autographs. She then thrilled the crowd with an exhibition of stunt flying, including loops, spins, rolls and stills, before returning to Baldonnel. The following day, she was off to Belfast for a similar demonstration.

On the Bank Holiday weekend of 3 August 1927, the annual King's Cup took place at Hucknall in Nottinghamshire and Sophie found herself at the centre of another controversy. According to the notes of the Lancashire club, of which she was by then a member, she and the club's Avian had been entered for the King's Cup, but at the last minute she pulled out 'for some reason of her own'. As it happened, Sophie was just one of seven pilots, including the scratch machine, to withdraw in protest at the new handicap formula. The Lancashire club failed to appreciate the point: 'Our Avian G-EBRR was withdrawn from the King's Cup on publication of the handicaps. Personally, one is all in favour of a joke, but owing to the cost of insurance, coupled with the fact that the machines would have to be off club work for several days, it was felt that this particular joke was one in which the club couldn't share.'

In the end, sixteen of the original 25 planes listed took to the skies, with Lady Bailey the only remaining woman, though a broken valve spring soon forced her out of the race. Strong winds hampered the competition and just six finished, with Captain W.L. Hope in a DH Moth proving the best of them. Sophie went some way towards making up for her boycott of the race when she gave an exhibition of looping in an Avian and later created history by winning the Grosvenor Cup, the chief short race of the day, in a DH Moth prototype with a 60hp Cirrus I engine. With fifteen pilots entered, there were three heats, Sophie winning the third. Despite a handicap of 1 minute 41 seconds, she still beat Colonel the Master of Semphill in the final by a considerable margin. The victory was widely publicised as the first by a woman in an open race against men, though Sophie had beaten men many times before; the record-keeping in aviation was clearly as loose as it had been in athletics, and Sophie was capable of taking full advantage, knowing that hard-pressed journalists rarely check facts presented to them with any degree of authority. That day, Sophie also won the Ladies' Purse for a prize of £20, swooping for the line in typical style to beat Lady Bailey by 'about the length of an engine'. After every race, excited autograph hunters surrounded the two women pilots.

By the middle of August, Sophie was flying the Avian in central Europe, again accompanied by Henry Hollingdrake. At Breslau in Germany, she gave an exhibition of aerobatics, with German pilots particularly impressed by her 'vertical banks'. In Poland, she apparently landed in a field because she needed to post a letter, though the story bears all the marks of one of her well-practised 'tall tales'. Since she had no formal permission to land, she came down in a quiet field outside Lodz, jumped out of the cockpit and set off with letter in hand. Seeing a cartload of local peasants, she attempted to ask them if they could post the letter for her. Suddenly, another group appeared from nowhere, angrily brandishing sticks. Sophie duly posted her letter somehow or other and then sprinted back to the plane, which Hollingdrake had already taxied into the take-off position for a quick getaway.

In Switzerland, Sophie participated at a Flying Club meet in Zurich, with the Avian getting maximum marks for construction, workmanship, accessibility for repairs, and highest points for comfort and luggage capacity, according to later A.V. Roe advertising material. While there, she sold her Avian to three local enthusiasts who hoped to set up a flying club.

By September, Sophie's promotional work with Hollingdrake had taken her to Scotland. The tour, organised by the Scottish Air League, included stops in Perth, Dundee, Aberdeen, Glasgow, Ayr and Edinburgh. In Dundee, a crowd of 8,000 gathered to hear her speak on the history and progress of aviation; while at Aberdeen, the numbers swelled to 10,000. Here, she returned to her athletics roots when she took part in a women's cross-country race to raise funds for athletics in Scotland, ending the day by explaining the controls of the aeroplane to the girls. So anxious was Sophie to help flying clubs that she offered to loan her Avian – at that time, the only plane of its kind equipped for night flying – to any club with members who wished to take their B licence. Whatever the establishment thought of her and her frequent changes of mind and loyalties, at grass roots she could not have been more popular.

On 16 September, back in London at a dinner for 'Women Aviators and Motorists' given by the Women's Engineering Society at the Lyceum Club, Sophie was in typically florid form as she replied to the toast on behalf of women aviators. Britain's first woman pilot, Hilda Hewlett, who had later run her own aircraft factory, had been her inspiration, she proclaimed, before repeating her oft-quoted view that flying was easier than driving or even riding a bike because there was no traffic in the air. She blamed the press, happy to report on every sensational aviation accident, for the biased view of flying as a dangerous occupation.

Over the next few weeks, she was back in the north of England at the Hooton Park meet, organised as part of Liverpool's Civic Week, and at a meet held at the Yorkshire club grounds at Sherburn, winning races at both venues with her customary style. Sadly, the press was able to report on another fatal air accident at Sherburn, when a holidaying Irishwoman called Dorothy Ellison was the victim.

By now, Sophie was looking for a new husband, preferably one who could pay for her flying obsession. She believed quite firmly that ambitious women needed financial security. 'To embark on air-piloting as a career, three things are necessary: youth, health and a modicum of wealth to pay the £30 or so it costs to learn, if not to set up with your own machine and pay insurances thereon with incidental expenses.' In fact, 'you should be prepared to spend at least £1,000 as we have not yet

Sir James Heath.

reached the happy stage when women pilots can get salaries of £1,000 a year.' Stella Wolfe expressed this opinion in the book the pair later wrote, but as a good friend of Sophie's, we can assume that the opinion was shared by her co-author.

Finding a husband required meticulous planning, she was later to tell the young American airwoman Elinor Smith, when describing her pursuit of Sir James Heath, who was to become her second husband: 'My dear, do you think that Sir James wanted to marry me? Of course not! I had to convince him how good it would be for him to have a nurse at his beck and call, and then I had to see to it that he thought the whole thing was his own idea!' To net her wealthy husband, she told Elinor that she had put together a list of the oldest and wealthiest bachelors in the British Empire. After narrowing that down to those needing nursing care, she came up with about five possibles. According to this account, Sir James was then spending most of his time in South Africa, home of his first wife. Exactly where Sophie managed to bump into him, she did not tell the young Elinor. Sir James's version of the story came later: 'We had been real pals for over five years before we were married…we would sometimes dine or lunch together.'

Sophie's choice was eminently practical. The twice-married Sir James Heath, a wealthy colliery owner and former Member of Parliament from Staffordshire, was 75; Sophie, not yet 30, was over 45 years younger, which she did not seem to consider important. Her future husband, an aviation fan, appeared besotted by his glamorous and high-flying wife, but the proposed alliance did nothing for her social standing and confirmed her reputation as a gold-digger.

Sir James's marital history was mixed. His 30-year marriage to Euphemia Celena Vanderbyl, originally from Cape Town, had produced one daughter. After his wife's death, when he was 65, the still grieving widower made a disastrous alliance with Joy Nitch Smyth, which was annulled three years later in 1927. He then fell into the clutches of Sophie, by now calling herself by her second name of Mary. She was to be known publicly as 'Lady Mary' for the rest of her life, clearly relishing the status conferred by a bona fide title.

She told Elinor Smith that the arrangement worked to their mutual satisfaction. She had nursing experience, presumably from her time as a volunteer in World War I, and he was an elderly man who was happy to let her live an independent life, so long as she was kind and paid him occasional visits. Her husband's somewhat divergent views became clear later on. Entirely practical, the future Lady Mary refused to marry Sir James until he had agreed to settle £20,000 on her, bringing in an annual income of between £725 and £925. It meant the wedding, originally planned for 10 October 1927, at Christ Church in London's Mayfair, was delayed by a day.

Since Sophie had written to her aunt on 27 August 1927 that she intended travelling to South Africa on 1 October, just ten days before her marriage, it could be that the wedding was hastily arranged. Few friends knew of her plans and less than a dozen were in the church for the ceremony, summoned at the last minute by telephone calls from the unblushing bride.

When the bride herself finally arrived by taxi at the church, she was wearing a smart black dress trimmed with fur. A Dr Farran performed the ceremony and a cousin of Sophie's, Captain Francis Peirce, gave her away; her name, it was reported, was one of the longest ever seen in the church register. Just minutes after the wedding, Sir James told his new bride that he would be making a will naming the daughter of his first marriage as his principal beneficiary. He thought this was a big joke; she was less than amused. The couple left immediately for Ireland, where no doubt Sophie introduced her new husband to her Aunt Cis. What she thought of the alliance is not on record.

Less than a week before her second marriage, Sophie had made a serious attempt on the altitude record of 17,283 ft, set by Lady Bailey and Louie de Havilland the previous July. With Mrs Williams of the Lancashire club for company, she spent one whole day waiting for ideal conditions before postponing her attempt. So she was glad to get airborne on 8 October, taking off from the Woodford aerodrome, near Manchester, in an Avro Avian with a hand-made 90hp Alpha engine.

Although she had worn extra flying gear for protection, the extreme cold proved to be her biggest problem, particularly since she had set off on a warm autumn day: 'I passed right above the clouds and lost all sight of the earth and when I came through the clouds again, I found I was near Southport, more than thirty miles from my starting point.' Frozen to the bone, she landed without incident in a small field only 250 feet long and lined with forty foot high hedges near Frodsham, Cheshire. Here, she sat tight, waiting for the barograph to be collected by observing officials since a further flight would affect the readings. When the machine was assessed and a height of 19,200 ft announced, it was greeted as a triumph for the A.V. Roe company, which was determined to take on de Havilland and the assortment of records held by the Moth. There are, however, two versions of this story. Contrary to the reports in the national press, *Flight* magazine recorded that Sophie had only equalled Lady Bailey's record.

With her wealthy husband now roped in, the newly minted Lady Mary was financially secure and immediately ordered the latest Avro Avian to add to the two planes still registered in her name.[3] She had ordered the new Avian for her planned trip to South Africa, where a tour of local aero clubs was scheduled. In the meantime, she continued a hectic schedule of flying and lecturing, seeing little of her new husband.

The new Lady Mary was still finding it frustrating to be a woman in a man's world and, as was her wont, sent a flurry of letters to those in authority when she felt that she had been slighted in any way. Although accepted as a full member of the Royal Aeronautical Society, she discovered that, as a woman, she was not entitled to attend meetings. 'The Aero Club is useless to me. I had hoped that when you gave me full membership of your society you would give me the privileges that went with it,' she said in a letter dated 10 November 1927. She told the club that she was going away on 18 November and that when she returned the following March, she hoped to set up her own company. She added that she had given over 50 lectures in the previous year, most recently in Scotland and the north of England. The society fobbed her off as usual.

The Air League of the British Empire, incorporated by the Duke of Sutherland in 1908 to encourage private and civil aviation, had a more open attitude to women pilots; both Lady Bailey and Elsa Mackey were on the advisory committee of pilots, while Sophie was to chair the Ladies' Sub-Committee after her return from South Africa. During her subsequent flight from the Cape to London, she was to write to General P.R.C. Groves, the league's secretary, from Nairobi, reporting that she had distributed several hundred Air League leaflets and had attracted audiences of up to 3,000 to some of her lectures in South Africa. So the link was clearly established before she left England.

CHAPTER 10

At Last a Lady

In her book *Women and Flying*, Lady Mary claims that for some years she had dreamed of flying across Africa: 'It has always been in my mind that I would some day fly over the length of Africa, to me the most fascinating continent of the whole world, for I have lived in Kenya and Tanganyika and love their wild, vast spaces.'

On her three previous trips to Africa, she had visited different areas on her proposed route and gathered important local information on the terrain, the climate and the all-important availability of fuel. She had certainly spent some of the previous winter in East Africa, including Somaliland, when she had visited her distant cousin, John Carberry.

Few would deny the new Lady Heath's fearlessness and sense of adventure, evident since her childhood in Ireland as plain Sophie Peirce. 'When we are very young, we look for adventure and long for it, but it is generally only when we are grown up that we are able to have it, and often then, we do not make use of our opportunities,' she wrote. She quotes with approval Lord Rosebery's advice to his son – 'My boy, live dangerously'– as perhaps the finest advice the youth of any nation could have. 'Fear is a tonic and danger should be something of a stimulant,' she adds, a view not universally held by the women of the time.

But equally, it would be foolish to ignore her opportunistic streak and her ability to change her plans in response to circumstances, in this case the news that Lady Bailey was planning a flight from London to the Cape to visit her husband. Still, in her book she says that she kept her plans to herself in case anyone got to hear of them:

> I did not confide my ambition to fly the continent to anybody, not even to the makers of the machine, as I knew that if I did, some rival firm would organize a similar flight from England.

Her fears were well founded; apart entirely from Lady Bailey's endeavours, on 3 March, when she was well on her way, Lieutenant Pat Murdoch announced an

Lady Mary Bailey with her daughters after her return from Africa in January 1929. *(Associated Press)*

attempt on the air record from Cape Town to London. He hoped to make only two stops on his journey.

On 18 November, just over a month after their marriage, Lady Mary and her new husband had set off on the three-week voyage to Cape Town, with her violet-coloured Avro Avian biplane with its Cirrus engine, 'officially but unromantically described as G-EBUG', carefully boxed and stowed in the liner's hold. The newly-weds duly arrived at the Cape on 5 December after a seventeen-day trip. Judging from her correspondence with the Royal Aeronautical Society, Lady Mary had already scheduled a series of talks in South Africa, but apart from that, her plans were unknown and there had been no mention of a flight back to London when she set off.

Lady Mary was certainly aware that, despite much work by the Air Ministry after World War 1, flying conditions in the least explored of the continents were challenging. To carve out a landing strip, dense jungle had to be cleared, swamps drained and ant hills, often as high as a two-story house, demolished.

Since Colonel Sir Pierre van Rynveld and Dr Chalmers Mitchell had become the first pilots to fly from London to the Cape in 1919, few had followed their example. In early 1926, Sir Alan Cobham made a leisurely three-month journey from London to Cape Town and back with a mechanic and a film-maker in a Shorts seaplane, covering 16,000 miles and winning himself a knighthood when he got back. Later that year, on 7 December, a Dornier Merkur seaplane, piloted by three Swiss aviators set off from Zurich, and after an adventurous trip, arrived in Cape Town on 21 February.

At the end of 1927, Lieutenant (later Captain) Richard Bentley, flying a DH Moth, christened 'Dorys' in honour of his fiancée by his friend Lady Bailey, took just 23 days to travel from London to Cape Town, his trip sponsored by the *Johannesburg Star*. While in South Africa, he duly married Dorys and a few months later, the couple decided to fly back to London, proving themselves useful both to Lady Mary and Lady Bailey.

In January 1928, just after Lady Mary had arrived, the *Rand Daily Mail* announced details of the Chrysler Cape to London motorcar 'speed dash' from Cape Town to Cairo. Emil Millin would drive the car, accompanied by G.S Bouwer, the newspaper's motor editor, and C.F. Noble, a film-maker. Building a road from one end of Africa to the other had been a great ambition of the African pioneer Sir Cecil Rhodes, and his friend and ally, Sir Abe Bailey, husband of Lady Mary, continued to promote the idea of this 'Great North Highway' at every opportunity. The African adventure would have a practical purpose, allowing the drivers to survey roads and to promote the building of tracks where none so far existed. The trip would start in April.

Around the same time, Lady Mary and G-EBUG left Cape Town on a flight that would ultimately see her arriving in Johannesburg; in her book, she claimed that she could find no information on a likely route to Cairo in Cape Town. Along the way she visited flying clubs and gave joyrides for £1 a time; this aspect of the trip had been planned in London months before and the £1,200 she earned was handed back to the clubs later on. As yet, there was no public announcement of a flight back to London, or even one to Cairo, although her every move was widely covered in the local newspapers. Indeed, before she set off, she had been a star attraction at Cape Town's first civil flying meeting, giving joyrides to a succession of excited young women.

The trip to Johannesburg had begun soon after dawn on 5 January 1928, when Lady Mary's tiny craft wobbled into the air at Cape Town, closely followed by the DH Moth of Major Miller, one of the founders of civil aviation in South Africa. After the relatively short hop along the coast to Port Elizabeth, 'one of the windiest places on earth', both gave joyrides, while Lady Mary was an honoured guest when a Westland Widgeon monoplane was presented to the local aero club. This was duly named 'The Lady Heath' and the Monday newspapers carried photographs of her christening it with a bottle, presumably of champagne.

Battling a strong headwind, the two pilots took off again on 9 January with their target the port town of East London, home of the first flying club in South Africa to register an aeroplane. By now, all South Africa was aware of the famous Lady Mary's every move. At Port Alfred, the local mayor had organised a civil ceremony, while a native chief had assembled his warriors for a war-dance and intended presenting Lady Mary with his own assegai (a light spear). Unfortunately, from the air, the small town proved impossible to find.

There were more joyrides and fun at East London before Lady Mary set off for Durban, accompanied by Major Miller and a local Westland Widgeon. The 'extraordinary' early morning light allowed her to see for miles and pick out hundreds of tiny huts, each with its own miniature cultivated patch, on the slanted hills of what she termed 'Kaffirland'. Even with such good visibility, roads were mere dirt tracks and hard to spot, while 'the land was innocent of railways'. With about two hours to go until Durban, they flew over the town of Umtata lying in the foothills of the Drakensburg Mountain. Needing a break, she flew low, with the Wigeon for company, until she found a smooth, ant hill-free road to land on; the Moth had managed to land in a field. The town nearby was Tsolo, where the inhabitants, black and white alike, greeted the aviators with great excitement. A witch-doctor presented Lady Mary with a bead head-dress in token of her 'greater magic'. With fuel proving expensive in this remote town – it had to be brought 160 kilometres in ox-wagons – they backtracked to Umtata to fill their tanks and then resumed their journey to Durban.

She was due to arrive in Durban on 11 January 1928 to lecture on the history and evolution of aviation and to help Durban Light Aeroplane Club in a fund-raising drive. Joining her as a passenger was an aviation enthusiast, Mr Mayers, who had recently travelled from Nairobi to the Cape, and was learning how to fly. Owing to a leak in her petrol tank, Lady Mary took up fewer passengers than usual during two 'Flying Days' in Durban, but she thoroughly enjoyed her stay and, in particular, the hospitality offered by the Durban Country Club, across the road from the aerodrome and just 100 metres from the refreshing waters of the Indian Ocean: 'You can dine, dance, play tennis or golf, or even swim between flights…. The bathing at Durban is world famous…'.

While she was in Durban, news came through of Lady Bailey's award as 'Lady Champion Aviator of the World' by the International Union of Aviators; Lindbergh was the gentleman champion. The woman who had given Lady Bailey her first 'spin', beaten her in races all over Britain and broken her altitude record responded with dignity, expressing her pride and pleasure at the award; it was well-earned and encouraging to all women aviators, she said, although she must have been disappointed that her own pioneering efforts were ignored. Commenting on the rumour that she was contemplating a flight from the Cape to Cairo, Lady Mary replied that she had not entertained the idea of such a feat and did not propose to undertake it.

Next stop was to be Johannesburg, but bad weather delayed her expected arrival at Baragwanath aerodrome on 19 January. Her revised plan was to leave Durban at dawn for Pietermaritzburg, head for Harrisburg a day later and then fly to Johannesburg. Torrential rains damaged her engine and delayed her arrival in Pietermaritzburg, where a flying day and lecture had been arranged. With the engine needing repairs, she decided to 'turn out' her companion, Mr Mayers, leaving him in Durban and, for practical reasons, take Major Miller's mechanic Mr Gillman with her instead. The Major was proving a useful friend: 'Major Miller has educated South Africa towns very well. If you circle the town a couple of times before landing, you find transport and petrol ready for you, almost before you have stopped taxiing across the aerodrome.'

Particularly impressive was the Dundee aerodrome in the centre of a racecourse, with its boundaries clearly marked by white stone and a one-mile runway of billiard-table smoothness. Flying on a compass bearing, they had taken a roundabout route to this oasis after a sighting of the Boer War Memorial had warned them that they had drifted off their course and were close to Ladysmith. Soon after their brief stop in Dundee, Lady Mary knew they were close to Johannesburg, because she could see its gold reef landmark created by the white piles of quartz thrown up from the mines.

Since they were not due to arrive for a couple of days, they decided to make an unscheduled stop at South Africa's administrative capital of Pretoria, just 46 kilometres distant, where they could pay their respects to Colonel Sir Pierre van Rynveld of the South Africa Air Force, the pioneer of the London to Capt Town air route, along with representatives of the Civil Air Board and the Governor General. Although the Avian was running well, doing a steady 80 mph at 7,000 feet, after three hours aloft, Lady Mary was relieved to see the hangars at Robert's Heights; her petrol tank was still leaking and the petrol gauge broken. On the tarmac, where she made 'the world's worst landing', Captain Bentley's DH Moth was being 'titivated'.

While Johannesburg awaited her arrival, Lady Heath was much sought after by journalists and, as opinionated as ever, cheerfully gave her opinions on how to combine home and career to anyone who asked. 'I think that home-running is a whole-time job, but a woman should not allow running a home to absorb all her energy,' she told the *Rand Daily Mail,* and although some of what followed could have been slightly misquoted, much rang true. Women can use their energies for several purposes: to run a house, to have a career, or to express their femininity and personality. But if they took up a career, it should be done wholeheartedly, with everything else taking second place: 'That is why I think that a woman who has to look after a house, a husband and a family and run a home, should do that and nothing else, if she wants her home to be run well.'

Her own energies went mainly into her career, she said – a revelation that can hardly have delighted her new husband, who regarded his wife's aviation as a 'hobby'. Women who wished to pursue a career and had the means should employ help in the home: 'It is much more sensible for a woman who has brains for a career to use them for that and to allow capable people to look after her house.' To keep going, energetic women above all needed plenty of sleep: 'No woman can expect to have poise, self-confidence to carry on her work, whatever it may be – work or play – if she goes without sufficient sleep. Nerves and health suffer.' So strongly did she believe in her own advice that she liked to sleep for ten or eleven hours a night and occasionally spent a whole day in bed. Image-conscious as always, she went on to give a series of fashion tips: 'If a woman wants to be a success and has not got the dress sense, for goodness sake, let her consult a good dress-maker and follow her advice.'

While travelling, Lady Heath favoured silk undergarments and other clothes that would roll up without creasing or showing the dirt: 'When I am flying and likely to be away from home for some days, I have to take the minimum of personal luggage with me.' So she would bring with her a black-beaded evening dress, an embroidered shawl and a pair of evening shoes to ensure that she was fit to be seen. For her flying kit, she had chosen a black leather coat, flying helmet and long leather boots, and she always flew prepared for any social occasion: 'I wear a neat, well-cut tailored navy blue coat and skirt with white silk shirt under my flying kit, so that I can go suitably clad into an hotel dining room after slipping off my jacket and gauntlet gloves.'

Flying, she felt, was an ideal career for a woman. Although it was her passion as well as her job, she never accepted an invitation for a dance or dinner without warning the hostess that she would appear only if the weather was too bad for flying. Her chief relaxations were dancing and tennis, while she was also an excellent shot and her London home was adorned with two 'trophies' – the head of a hartebeest shot in Tanganyika Territory and a leopard-skin rug. She felt everyone had a duty to exploit his or her own talents and at the very least to try flying:

> Physical efficiency is the biggest asset any nation can have – both men and women. Every human being finds some different way of being efficient in finding out in what he or she can excel. It is everybody's duty at any rate to see what flying is like

and to see if he or she is an embryo 'ace'. Flying is a national responsibility as well as being an individual pleasure.

Lady Mary finally arrived in Johannesburg's Baragwanath aerodrome on 22 January, where she received a magnificent welcome. Flying with her from Zwarthopjes was Captain Bentley, with his fiancée Dorys Oldfield and Lady van Ryneveld, wife of Colonel Sir Pierre, as passengers. When the planes approached Johannesburg, the Johannesburg Light Aeroplane Club's Moth, piloted by G.W. Bellin, with the club secretary Mr Douglas as passenger, took off to greet Lady Mary in the air, performing 'some exciting evolutions amid clouds of black smoke'. When Mr Douglas saw Lady Mary's plane, he stood up and leaned out of the Moth, knocking off some of the switches. Only by quick thinking did the pilot avoid an emergency landing and was soon chasing after the two visiting planes with the three then landing in close formation: 'So close indeed were we that Mr Douglas and my passenger were able to converse on their fingers, the new method of communication between machines.' Lady Mary and Captain Bentley had flown from Pretoria in just 35 minutes and when they landed, hundreds of excited spectators broke free from inside the roped enclosure and raced across the aerodrome. Crowding around Lady Mary's green and silver machine, they cheered enthusiastically when she removed her flying cap.

Befitting her celebrity as the first woman pilot ever to visit South Africa, Lady Mary faced a daunting programme in Johannesburg. During her stay, she would give a lecture on aviation at the Carlton Hotel, illustrated by lantern-slides, and find time to discuss with officials the possibility of a municipal aerodrome. A week after her arrival, she was the star attraction of a 'Ladies' Day' which attracted over 6,000 cars and their passengers to Baragwanath, one of the largest crowds ever seen in Johannesburg. Hundreds of women, including her hostess, Mrs Samuel Evans and her daughter, got their first experience of flying thanks to a joyride with Lady Mary. Officials struggled to control the immense crowd during the programme of stunting and aerobatics, and when South Africa's first ever air race was announced, spectators surged on to the runway, surrounding the planes and preventing them from taking off. Only after threatening to call off the meeting did officials force the enthusiastic crowd away from the machines.

With calm restored, the race could begin and, despite being off last as the scratch pilot, Lady Mary in her Avian was favourite to beat Major Miller, Lieutenant Bentley and Lieutenant Bellin, all piloting Moths, over the nine-mile triangular course. For the start, the four machines were lined up together. Major Miller zoomed off first, followed five seconds later by Lieutenant Bentley and Lieutenant Bellin, and eight seconds later by Lady Mary. The first point to be rounded was a belt of trees, but Major Miller, in the lead, missed this and so was disqualified.

The remaining three machines circled the trees and raced off towards a flagpole for the next turn. As Bellin circled the flagpole, he flew so low that the tip of one wing was just six metres above the hangar roof. Bentley was a little higher but took the flagpole at almost the same time before heading for the third landmark on the course – a mine dump. Characteristically, Lady Mary employed an entirely different style, based on her vast experience of air racing. She kept higher and, at the bends, sped upwards, cornering with a great swoop to give her extra speed on the next straight stretch.

By the time the pilots reached the aerodrome on the second lap, Lady Mary was closing rapidly on Bellin in second place and on Bentley who had taken a narrow lead. After the three had passed the flagpole, Bellin, in an effort to overtake Bentley, darted through a small gap barely sixteen metres off the ground in a plantation of gum trees. It was not enough. Within seconds, Lady Mary had overtaken them both and was loudly cheered as her machine flashed past the finishing post. Bentley was second and Bellin third. 'What excellent fun!' said the winner as she climbed from her cockpit.

On 7 February, the full details of the *Rand Daily Mail* and *Sunday Times* Chrysler Cape to London Motorcar Speed Dash 'from end to end of Africa and on to London' were released. The vehicle, with its driver and two passengers, would travel from Cape Town to Johannesburg, then on to Bulawayo in Southern Rhodesia, to Victoria Falls at Livingstone, then Broken Hill in Northern Rhodesia, through Tanganyika Territory at Abercorn and Fife, next diverting to Kenya's capital, Nairobi. After would come a diversion around swamps to Eldueim, then on to Khartoum in the Sudan, and finally, Cairo. Following that, the expedition would sail from Alexandria to Brindisi in the south of Italy and drive up through Europe to London.

Most exciting was the news that Lady Mary would be working with the expedition. She was also set to confirm her own solo flight from South Africa to London, starting on 26 February. At last what she had been broadly hinting was to become a reality; if she were to succeed in such a flight, she would firmly re-establish herself as the foremost woman pilot of her time. Since the motor expedition's starting date had been brought forward by two months and her ambitious flight suddenly announced, negotiations had clearly been going on.

According to the newspapers, the plan was for Lady Mary to see off the motor expedition when they left Johannesburg and link up with them a few days later at Abercorn. Her route would parallel that of the cars all the way to Cairo. Since she would be moving much faster in her plane, she could fly on ahead and reconnoitre the land beyond Abercorn, where few motor vehicles had gone before, and keep in constant touch with the vehicles below through a system of signs. In the Upper Sudan and Egypt, she would fly overhead, 'directing the motorists on the burning sands below on a straight course and towards water'. She would also help in dispatching messages and photographs from the expedition to the nearest telegraph stations and rail heads. In cases of emergency, she would drop food and convey SOS messages. No one underestimated the difficulty of the odyssey – ahead lay swamps, floods, rain, hostile natives and other terrors, but the plan to combine an air and a motor expedition seemed ill-conceived, given the relative speeds of the two forms of transport.

Whatever about the problems of staying in touch with the motor expedition, Lady Mary knew that could she not afford to make any mistakes on her flight: 'I realised I would have many more difficulties to face than the ordinary male pilot, especially in the event of a forced landing in jungle or swamp, or among hostile natives.' Her pragmatic streak meant that she was well capable of getting her hands dirty when necessary but, although she prided herself on knowing every screw and ratchet on her machine, she also knew when to call on expert help. So after her plans were finally announced, she appealed to an old acquaintance, Colonel Henderson of the Henderson Flying School in Brooklands, who was joyriding in South Africa at the time, to reassemble her plane. She then set about the task of finding maps and charts for her route, yet another hint that the decision to fly back to London might have been made on the spur of the moment.

Her task proved almost impossible. Even five years later, the only aviation maps of Africa available were huge in scale at 1/2,000,000. That meant an inch on the map was equal to about 32 miles in the air, whereas on European maps one inch represented four miles. A further nuisance was that towns, villages and other features, marked confidently on maps in large letters, were often invisible from the air. There were also vast tracts bluntly marked 'unsurveyed'. After exhausting every other avenue, Lady Mary appealed to Captain Bentley for help and persuaded him to sell her the set of maps he had used on his flight out to the Cape. Unfortunately, after he decided to fly back to England, Bentley had taken these back and then lost them. With no other maps available, Lady Mary desperately made tracings from borrowed atlases and pieced together what information she could.

Whatever her reasons for setting off on the trip, the logistics of flying over unknown, uncharted and possibly hostile territory would have deterred most pilots, male or female. After she set off, the authorities in the various countries repeatedly placed obstacles in her way. She rarely flew more than a thousand miles without confronting officials adamant that she could go no farther. In one respect, she had no problems. Fearing that she would not find fuel, she negotiated with Sir Charles Wakefield to supply oil at various points along the way. This proved an unnecessary precaution, as motor spirit was available all over Africa for about 5s 6d (30 cent in euro currency) per gallon.

On 8 February in Cape Town, Mrs A.V. Lindbergh sent the Chrysler Cape to London Motor Expedition on its way. The following day in Johannesburg, while she awaited its arrival, Lady Mary, still a vice-president of the *Federation Sportive Feminine Internationale*, or the Women's International Amateur Athletic Federation as it was described in the newspapers, attended an athletics meet at the Police Grounds. There she applauded the 'girl runners' in a special 200m handicap race, held in shocking mud after recent rain. Particularly impressive were the Bennett sisters, Myrtle and Lottie, with Myrtle winning both heat and final. Lady Mary expressed her surprise at the 'sturdiness' and obvious talent of the South African girls, though some needed 'polish'.

After taking a few days rest following their arrival, the Cape to Cairo motor expedition resumed from Johannesburg on 13 February and work began for Lady Mary. The roof of the Chrysler 72 Sedan had been painted white to act as background to a bold black letter 'C' which would be clearly visible from the air. After Sir Julius Jeppe, chairman of the board of the *Rand Daily Mail*, sent the drivers off from the newspaper's offices, a large crowd of enthusiastic spectators pressed and swayed around the car. Ten minutes later, they were at last on their way, after the Mayor bade them farewell on behalf of the city from the town hall steps. Among the gifts they had received were countless boxes of cigars, a Columbia portable gramophone and a waterless cooker.

Flying high above them in the DH Moth of the local flying club was Lady Mary with the club's instructor, G.W. Bellin. Her Avro Avian was still at Robert's Heights having a larger petrol tank fitted so that she could carry up to 60 gallons. As the car moved away from the dense crowd of onlookers, Lady Mary flew as low as regulations permitted and followed the winding course through a maze of traffic. She described the scene from the air: 'The long column of cars made an impressive caravan from the air. At times I flew as low as ten or eleven feet from the ground and had a good look at them.' The car below was aware of her presence as 'an angel up above' and its inhabitants occasionally leaned out of the car windows to greet her.

When the crowd thinned out and there was an open space, she dropped a message for them: 'God speed. Meet you in Abercorn. Don't forget to wear your winter woollies,' it said. She also dropped a glass and a bottle of beer, but the bottle broke, although in Lady Mary's version of the story, she says the motorists got out of their car and drank her health. She was in no hurry to follow them, knowing it would take several weeks before they arrived at Abercorn.

That evening, Lady Mary delivered her third talk on aviation in Johannesburg, giving a vivid description of a novice making his second trip in an aeroplane. Standing at the side of the machine with the instructor, the person about to embark on his second lesson assumes an air of familiarity. The machine takes off and when safely in the air, the learner takes over and is taught how to turn, first to the right and then to the left, by moving the joystick. The earth below seems like a perfectly planned map, while retaining its natural beauty and colour. Towns are clusters, forests are patches and roads are threads. Faint wisps of cloud pass to and fro thousands of feet below.

After nearly half-an-hour, the instructor resumes control and brings the aeroplane back to land. Next time, the beginner is told, he will learn how to take off himself and will practise making really sharp turns. Lady Mary answered a number of queries that had been written on slips of paper. 'Why do you go up to 5,000 feet?' asked a man who signed himself as 'Amateur'. 'I go up there because it is becoming so crowded down here,' she replied, provoking laughter in the hall. Another query concerned the danger to pedestrians of planes falling out of the sky. Lady Heath promised to give this worried individual full details of an aviation insurance scheme.

On 20 February, a week after the departure of the motor expedition, members of the Ladies '89 Pioneer Club honoured Lady Mary with a tea at the Carlton Hotel. She told the women that Lieutenant Bentley, who had married Dorys Oldfield two days earlier, had agreed to accompany her across the forest belt of her journey. He and his new wife were thinking of flying back to Europe as part of their honeymoon. Lady Mary said that she had no plans to hurry over her route; she loved all of Africa and wished to linger, but she must have been frustrated at the Bentley's decision, which would take from her own effort and possibly slow her down, since she would have to keep pace with a DH Moth carrying two people. A day later, she spoke to the Goodwill Luncheon Club at the St James Restaurant on the subject of 'Women's Place in Sport'. There were only two types of women, she said: the one who founds and cares for a family, and the other who helps build social structures in the outside world, like herself. Her words must have had special resonance in a country then debating women's suffrage with some fervour.

The newspapers continued to report on the northward progress of the motor expedition and on Lady Mary's preparations: 'I am taking with me one set of clothes, two changes of blouse and a pair of mosquito boots for when I have to spend a night at a landing place.' To protect her further, she would carry a long length of mosquito netting: 'By draping the netting over the cockpit, I will have a sleeping place.' Later she revealed that 'in case – or for fear', she also carried a tube of morphine: 'It occurred to me before I started that I might crash in one of Africa's dark forests and have my leg broken or something worse. I believe all aviators make some such provision.' For keeping the aeroplane in tune, she would carry a set of tools, including a hacksaw, a jack-knife and plenty of spare parts. She expected to spend most of her non-flying time overhauling the engine, believing that prevention was better than cure.

From Sir Julius Jeppe, of the *Rand Daily Mail*, she had received the gift of a gun for her protection and perhaps to kill game. She believed there was no need to take food, feeling there would be sufficient wherever she landed, but she would carry a few luxuries: 'My luggage in addition will include some pounds of chocolate, a tennis racquet and an evening dress.' She also planned to carry a Bible and a few novels. Lady Mary was expected to fly between 300 and 400 miles at a time and hoped to rejoin the motor expedition 'on the fringes of the wild'. She had already negotiated the first lap of her journey when she flew from Cape Town to Johannesburg, collecting over £1,000 for several light-aeroplane clubs by giving 'flips' and helping with flying days, she reminded reporters.

While the South African Air Force in Pretoria made last-minute adjustments to her Avro Avian, she flew to Johannesburg with G.W. Bellin in the Johannesburg Light Aeroplane Club's DH Moth. There she was greeted by a number of friends, including Mrs Emil Millin, whose husband was part of the motor expedition, and who gave Lady Heath a letter to deliver to her husband when she overtook him somewhere in central Africa. Her machine, she said, was in better shape than when she had left Cape Town, thanks to the help she had received from everyone at Robert's Heights. Converted into a single seater, it had more room for baggage, while the special petrol tank had been fitted successfully.

Leaving Johannesburg, she returned to Pretoria to collect her plane and make final arrangements for an early start the next morning. Fittingly, Sir Pierre van Ryneveld, the pioneer of the Cape to Cairo air route, would escort her for the first few miles. She hoped to be in Bulawayo in plenty of time for a civic luncheon in her honour. In Pretoria, she found time to give one final talk to a packed and enthusiastic crowd in the Town Hall, and ended it by thanking everyone for the warm welcome she had received in South Africa. She then flew her plane back to Johannesburg.

Lady Mary's flight from Cape Town to Catania
5 January to 6 May 1928

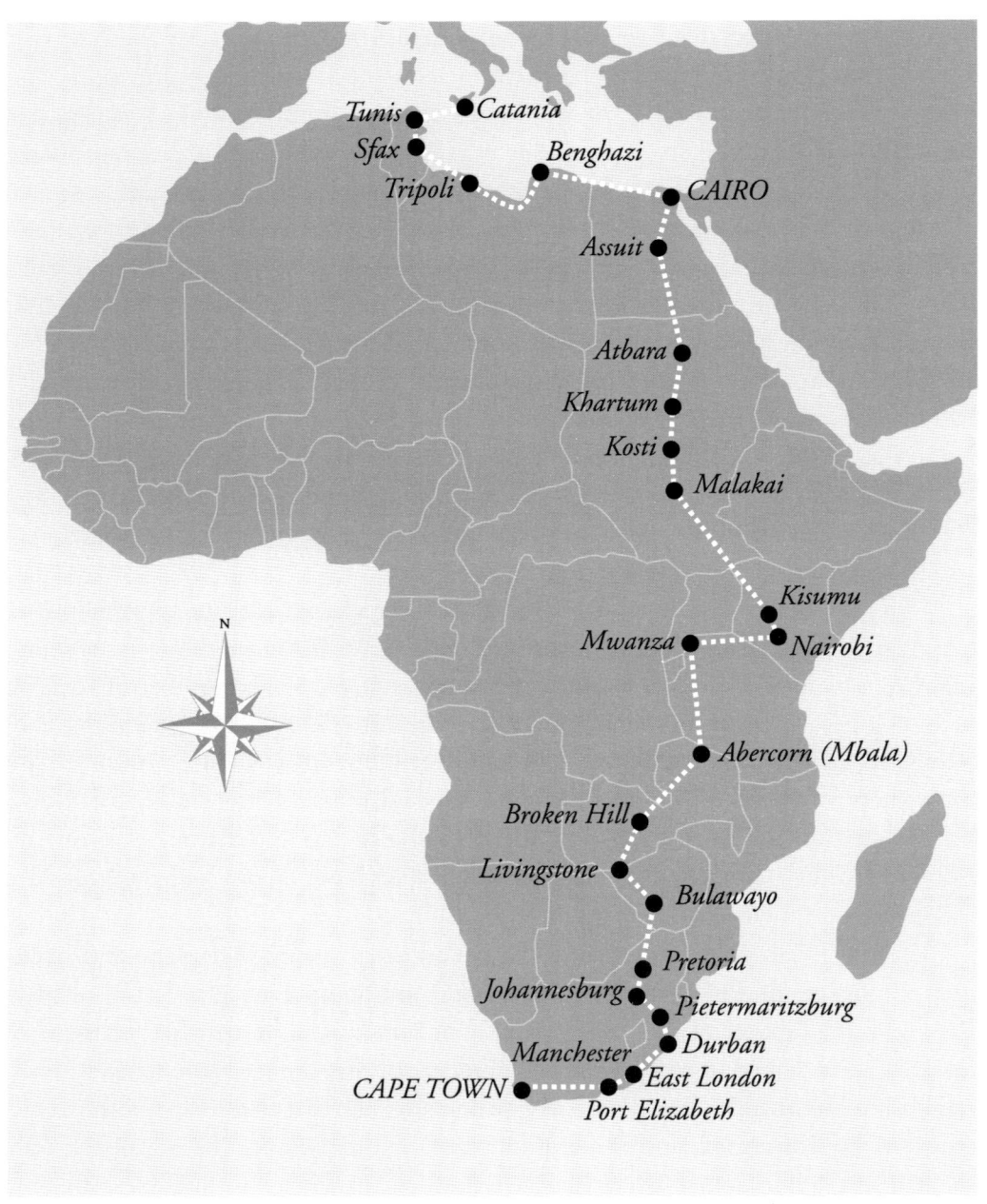

CHAPTER 11

The Flight from the Cape

AT LAST, it was time to leave. On the morning of 25 February, the overloaded Avian wobbled unsteadily into the air from Robert's Heights, after taking 150 yards to lift off. For the 400 mile trip to Bulawayo, Lady Mary was carrying 42 gallons of fuel, and Sir Pierre van Rynveld, who accompanied her for the first hour, had bet her that she wouldn't get off the ground. She proved him wrong. Her trip was still publicly linked with the motor expedition, which earlier that week had managed to cross the Limpopo river only with the help of fourteen donkeys. 'In contrast to the days of weary travel which the land expedition spent in their journey to Bulawayo, Lady Heath, who came to Johannesburg last evening to say good-bye to many friends in the Rand, speaks gaily of being in Bulawayo by noon today,' reported the *Rand Daily Mail*.

The distance from Cape Town to Croydon in South London is between 8,000 and 9,000 miles. Lady Mary would fly about 10,000 miles; like the motor expedition, taking in a deviation from the direct route to visit Nairobi and going the long way along the North African coast because of her fear of flying over water. She had told her husband that the journey would take three weeks. As it turned out, she did not get back to England for three months, all too ready to be distracted along the way by parties in her honour and chances to play tennis or even hunt, when she realised that a record attempt was out of the question.

She was exhilarated to be in the air after all the 'vicissitudes' she had experienced and she reckoned the first day out of Pretoria ranked second only to her first solo flight as the best adventure of her life. Once on her own, she was entranced by a wonderful vista of craggy hills, collections of tiny houses and fleecy clouds. It was warm and bright and she was wearing just her flying helmet, with her head and neck unprotected from the blazing equatorial sun. Six hours into her flight, she had passed the meandering Limpopo and was soon flying over the great quartz hills of Matobo in Zimbabwe, then called Southern Rhodesia, where Sir Cecil Rhodes, the British explorer who had done so much to open up Africa, lay buried.

Thinking idly of how unpleasant it would be to crash-land, she suddenly became aware of a pain in her head, neck and shoulders. She had suffered from sunstroke twice before and knew the signs. Even more ominously, when it had happened before, she had passed out, not an experience she wished to repeat, especially when flying several hundred metres above hard, unforgiving ground. Desperately, she twisted and turned in her tiny seat, trying unsuccessfully to retrieve the special topee, or pith helmet, packed in the back locker of her machine. When the pain in her head and neck got worse and she started to see black blobs dancing in front of her eyes, she pulled off part of her underclothing and wrapped it around her head and shoulders.

With the black blobs turning into waving black feathers, she saw Fort Usher straight ahead. The last thing she remembered was aiming the plane north-east to some clear ground. When she recovered consciousness, she found herself under some thorn bushes, with three native girls 'in various stages of scanty undress, sitting back on their haunches and laughing at me'. They had removed her fur coat and placed it under her, then steeped two of her handkerchiefs in milk and put them on her head, which was very painful. Leaning up woozily on one elbow, she saw her plane a little way off, with one wing drooping but otherwise intact. Mysteriously, her hair was clotted with milk. With the help of the girls, who seemed to understand Swahili, although this was not their language, she staggered to the plane to discover the time. She had been unconscious for about four hours.

So little damaged was the machine that had she been at all well, she could have flown it away. But she could hardly see straight and the effort of making it to the plane made her sick again:

> So I sat on the ground and told the girls to collect stones and earth for my sandbags to secure the machine for the night…. They thought it a tremendous joke and in spite of feeling as ill as I did, I could not help seeing the amusing side of it too. A great silver bird comes out of the sky and lands beside their huts and a strange white woman is found in it unconscious, and flops to the ground even after she has come to!

Lady Mary had landed – or as she put it, the plane landed itself, since she remembered nothing of it – just ten miles from her target of Bulawayo. Her expertise as a pilot had undoubtedly saved her life, since she had headed the plane into the wind and not hit any of the trees or thorn bushes dotting the veldt. After helping her to their hut about a quarter of a mile away, one of her new friends, Makula, who spoke a little English, told Lady Mary that in her delirium she had written a note to be delivered to white people and had asked for milk. Of this she had absolutely no recollection and when she saw the note a few days later, she realised why no help had come: 'It was a confused scrawl of what looked like Egyptian hieroglyphics and I was unable to read it myself!'

Lying on her fur coat with a 'tiny silver fitted dressing case which the Johannesburg Light Aeroplane had given me' as a pillow, Lady Mary realised she was in a harem hut and that the owner of the kraal had five wives. They looked after her in an entirely matter-of-fact way, feeding her gourds of milk and a whole boiled chicken, complete with innards: 'At dusk, they lit the fire close to my head and, with their youngest children, undressed entirely and covered themselves with blankets.' The small, round hut was swarming with mosquitoes and flies and, although still in a state of coma, Lady Mary stirred occasionally because she had been badly bitten, despite covering herself with mosquito netting.

The next morning, after Makula had woken and washed her, a white woman, Mrs Pat Fletcher, was motoring past the encampment with her husband in search of grass for their cattle. To her astonishment, she found an emotional Lady Mary, still feeling dizzy and ill, though the pains in her head and back had eased. She immediately bundled her into the car and drove her back to their farm, where the patient, 'weeping like a kid', was put to bed. In the evening, Captain Douglas Mail of the Rhodesian Aviation Syndicate agreed to rescue Lady Mary's machine. Reporting back, he told her that there was not too much damage, although the machine was bone dry of oil and 'owing to a bend in the undercarriage fitting, the port forward flying wire was loose'.

Her disappearance had made front-page headlines in the South African press. 'The absence of any news in any of the newspapers published on Saturday night and Sunday morning of the arrival in Bulawayo of Lady Heath, who set out in her Avro Avian from Pretoria on Saturday morning, caused intense excitement throughout the union,' said the *Rand Daily Mail*. The newspaper had received hundreds of calls from concerned members of the public. Prominent members of the South African air force had been planning to start a search.

They speculated that she might have been blown off course. Air force members had escorted her as far as Warmbaths, along a route that followed the railway line. From this point, she had left the railway and would have been relying entirely on compass bearings. There was a strong wind blowing from the north-west, which meant that she could have drifted several degrees to the east and been forced to land in an unknown part of the veldt. As it happens, she was not far off her course when forced to land.

When it left Pretoria a day earlier, the Avro Avian was carrying enough petrol for over ten hours' flying, the consumption of the engine being four and a half gallons per hour and the average cruising speed 80 mph. Lady Mary had passed Warmbaths at 8.45 am and so should have appeared in Bulawayo at 2pm or soon after. News that she was safe came though at 7.30pm the following day from the newspaper's Bulawayo correspondent. After she had spent the night in a native hut, a party of motorists had discovered an exhausted Lady Heath earlier that day, he reported, adding that oil trouble appeared to have been the cause of the forced landing.

The Avian was now in Bulawayo and, when she awoke from a long sleep, Lady Mary was flown there by Captain Mail in his own DH Moth and taken to Sister Rigby's Maternity Home because all the nursing homes were full. Placed in a room with a tiny white cot at its foot, she slept for a further eighteen hours. A few days later, her temperature was back to normal. She could continue with her adventure.

While Lady Mary travelled on after her adventure near Bulawayo, reports on her progress became sparse. Later, she would express her annoyance when accused of failing to keep in touch with the outside world. This, after all, was a woman relying on the power of the media to keep her exploits in the public eye and very aware of it. But communicating from the depths of Africa had proved a frustrating task and what telegraph wires there were rarely worked. It was one reason why she failed to link up with the motor expedition as planned.

On 28 February 1928, after recovering from her sunstroke, she was collected from the nursing home and delivered by Captain Mail to Bulawayo aerodrome. Soon she was airborne again, heading for Livingstone in Northern Rhodesia (now Zambia), the town nearest the mighty Victoria Falls, or 'Smoke Falls' in the local language. With the rainy season now well advanced, she found herself flying between two rainstorms at the Umgassa (Umguza) river, but used the railway as a navigational aid. After an hour and a half in the air, she saw her first game, a band of eland, near Malindi. Flying down for a closer look, she disturbed a mother rhino, which she noted had no qualms about abandoning her baby to save herself. Next, she 'went down to worry' a train chugging along below and, at Wankie, dropped off a copy of the *Bulawayo Chronicle* for the mine manager. A few minutes later, the distinctive white 'smoke' raised by the thundering waters of Victoria Falls was visible, forming an excellent landmark, and she landed in the nearby town after an enjoyable three-hour flight.

At Livingstone, Lady Mary was reunited with Dick Bentley and his new wife, Dorys, along with Major Cochrane Patrick and, somewhat dubiously, professed herself 'delighted'. Her main worry was the Avian's bent undercarriage fitting: 'When I was non compos mentis, I must have side-slipped on the ground, for the fitting was bent at a 45 degree angle and the two bolts through it were sheared.' It meant that the Avian was not safe to land, but after much discussion with Major Patrick, she decided to pin her faith on 'luck and other wheel landings', rather than return to Bulawayo for repairs, and spent the following afternoon working on the Avian's engine.

There was a dawn wake-up call on 1 March, and soon after, weighed down with 227 litres of petrol, the Avian staggered into the air only with the greatest of difficulty. Having it even worse were the Bentleys: 'I cannot speak too highly of Captain Bentley's Moth, which with Mrs Bentley, two large suitcases, 30 gallons of petrol and spares took off in 200 yards,' says Lady Mary, plainly exasperated with having to fly in convoy with the pair, who were bound to be much slower. Comparing the two aircraft, Lady Mary believed that while the Moth's petrol consumption was better, the Avian had a heavy Fairey Reid propeller, 'without which I would not be for worlds'.

After setting a course of 49 degrees east, the two planes flew towards Broken Hill (now Kabwe) in pleasant conditions. They were cruising at over almost 2,000 metres, but even from that height could spot herds of impala and a trio of rhinoceros below. The first sign of habitation they saw was a little village called Maoanza, followed by a number of European farms and then what Lady Mary described as the fine alluvial plains of the Kafue river: 'It looked like a most wonderful farming district.' The railway proved a good navigational guide, especially after a 20 mile cloud no higher than 300 feet off the ground started spilling out rain, forcing both planes to dive under the cloud-bank and fly low: 'We were obliged to sit on the railway line for nearly ten miles through this downpour, before it cleared again and we were able to climb again to a safe and respectable height.'

After the rain cleared, the smoke from the zinc and lead mines guided them into the 'extraordinarily fine' aerodrome at Broken Hill where, after five hours in the air, they touched down at exactly midday. Among those waiting to greet them was Mrs Moffat Thompson, wife of the resident manager. Lady Mary landed safely despite the problems with her plane and quickly enlisted the help of an ex-Air Force mechanic called Howell ('such a nice lad') to make a new undercarriage with 'a bit of mild steel' at the local mine's workshops.

The rain broke with a vengeance that afternoon, persuading both fliers to rest for a day or two. By now, provided Dorys's mother approved, the Bentleys had decided that they would fly on back to England, although they were without passports, clothing, money or maps, and Dorys would have to spend the trip squeezed into the front cockpit along with a spare petrol tank. Lady Mary continued to have mixed feelings about their decision which 'took from the credit of a solo flight'; it would also slow her down, since Dorys Bentley was to find flying in a small plane with her husband an arduous business and needed frequent rests. 'It was most interesting making things stretch for them,' she says enigmatically, no doubt comparing her own meticulous preparations with their slap-happy ways. Later on, Lady Mary said she had been glad of their company 'because I do not think the part of Africa we flew over is fit for any human being alone, man or woman'.

From a rain-saturated, boggy runway, the two small planes left Broken Hill on 4 March, taking off in light rain and heading northwards into what looked like more bad weather. They were now over forest country, with 'open vleis' (marshes) of long swampy grass providing the only relief; in the air, high-flying eagles 'treating us with lordly disdain' swooped around the planes. After two and a half hours, they reached Ndola, where the Bwana Mkubwa copper mine, as well as the large X-shaped aerodrome, stood out clearly.

The whole population of the town had turned out to greet the visitors, with local residents vying with each other to put them up for the night. Lady Mary's eventual host was Mrs Sanford, wife of the Resident Magistrate, but she admits to not being much of a house guest – 'lunch, sleep, work on the machine till dark, and then sleep again was the order of the day'. The next morning, she was back at the aerodrome and had both machines prepared when the Bentleys arrived. Despite the 'absurdly' early hour, the town's residents turned out to send them on their way. An hour later when taking off from a small runway, an altitude of 4,500 feet proved a little difficult; with less oxygen in the air at these heights, a long runway is essential. After take off, Lady Mary worried briefly about a strong smell of petrol in the cockpit, but decided that this came from the overflow.

With more rain to endure, they faced a day of flying above and below nasty, bumpy clouds; these were so dense that, at one point, Lady Mary entirely lost sight of her companions. She was flying blind on a compass bearing when she spotted a gleam of water below through a break in the clouds. After she 'gingerly' spiralled down, she found herself about 100 feet above the shores of Lake Kampolombo and she skirted the lake, badly scaring some hippos. Just then, she caught sight of the Bentley's DH Moth, and the two small planes were reunited. Three hours of unpleasant flying in damp, rainy weather over 'vicious-looking swamps' followed. Over the high ridge to the south of Lake Tanganyika, the rain was so heavy that it descended like a waterfall, drenching them. Fortunately, the visibility was good, and they easily found their target town of Abercorn (now Mbala), on the southern tip of the lake, small though it was.

Just an hour later the Chrysler expedition drove into town and Lady Mary was reunited with them, just as she had planned almost three weeks earlier in Johannesburg. With the Bentleys, she opted to stay in the town for an extra few days as guests of the Resident Magistrate, since their supplies had not yet arrived. Although a small town, Abercorn was prosperous, with many rich settlers growing coffee in the hinterland: 'There are only two cars in the town, and while we were there, only one was available, that of Mrs Jelfe, who very kindly drove us everywhere.' As far as Lady Mary was concerned, all that was holding the area back was its 'rotten postal facilities': with telegraph wires on both side of the town down, no contact was possible with the outside world: 'We could have been lost for a fortnight on either side of Abercorn without anybody being any the wiser'.

After their few days' rest, the two planes set off again, with no further mention of the motor expedition in her own account, although Lady Mary had agreed to remain in particularly close contact with the car after Abercorn. Quite why the collaboration broke down is unknown, although the simple logistics of staying in touch with a land-bound vehicle from a speedy, high-flying plane was one likely reason. The decision of the Bentleys to fly with Lady Mary was another, since she knew that she would be delayed more often:

> Looking back on my flight, I realise how my preliminary idea of attending on the Chrysler Cape to London Motor Expedition was impossible. These gallant people struggled along on the ground, and it took me all my time and plenty of hard work to get through by air. We met certainly at various points, but the wonderful system of signals we had arranged to communicate by were useless, and it was only the pleasant feeling that we were thinking about each other that gave us both some small moral support....

No sooner had Lady Mary and Captain Bentley left Abercorn than they had to contend with a foul downdraught over the nearby hills, forcing the engines to labour hard; Lady Mary's speedometer read zero miles per hour, but she didn't seem too worried as long as the engine kept revving away. Such downdraughts were a common problem near mountains, which tended to create their own wind systems. Since they were unable to fly over the hills, they circled the high ground, giving them the chance to examine a huge extinct crater, full of game sheltering in the reeds. There were more surprises when they reached the Rungwa Swamp, north of Lake Rukwa. This Lady

Mary described as 'one of the most beautiful sights I have ever seen, with the winding rivers flowing into it, and the flecks of cloud above'.

To the northeast were the alluvial gold claims of the Luba valley, a combination of forest and impassable swamps. The few villages they saw were abandoned, their inhabitants ravaged by sleeping sickness. At the Ungalla river, an enchanted Lady Mary dropped down to inspect a herd of 15 to 20 small elephants feeding on the riverbank. By now the hard work of the day was over and for the final 100 miles, the two planes followed a straight road through the bush to Tabora, a railway junction town in Tanganyika Territory, which she knew from her first visit to Africa several years earlier: 'Flying low over the town, we attracted the attention of the inhabitants, who came rushing out. It was lovely to hear Swahili again and to realise that we were once more in East Africa.'

Among the town's inhabitants were the Wyatts, Lady Mary's 'oldest friends in Tanganyika'. She was delighted to discover that they were now 'Mr and Mrs Provincial Commissioner'. Despite the usual routine work on tappets and filters taking longer than usual and an enjoyable dinner party, the three adventurers were airborne again by 8.30 the following morning; an attempt to take off even earlier had failed when the car designated to pick up the Bentleys 'overslept', leaving Lady Mary forced to wait on her companions yet again. Their next port of call was to be the port of Mwanza on the southern shores of Lake Victoria, because both Kisumu and Nairobi were probably 'a little difficult', especially for the Bentleys, whose plane could carry only a limited amount of fuel; Lady Mary just about concealed her impatience. Shortly after taking off, she went low to have a look at a small herd of giraffe. She then lost sight of Bentley, only to find out later that he had spent two hours amusing himself by playing cat-and-mouse behind her; this time, she was happy to join in the joke.

After flying over the black soil used for cotton growing, they soon landed at the picturesque town of Mwanza, where they were welcomed on the runway by laughing local residents carrying glasses of beer. They were relieved to find that the aerodrome was fine and spacious and had a hundred tins of petrol on hand. After refreshments and a few hours' work on her engine, Lady Mary accepted an invitation to play a game of tennis with their hosts, District Commissioner Captain Sturridge and his wife, since another delay seemed likely: 'poor Dorys Bentley looked a bit fagged'. During their second set of tennis, members of the King's Royal Rifles in attendance offered to arrange a buffalo shoot on the other side of the lake for the next day. By now the Bentleys wanted a few days' rest from flying and Lady Mary had decided to make the best of any enforced delays. So with their new friends, the three visitors rushed off to talk to a wealthy Italian trader, Signor Bonini, who immediately offered the loan of his boat, *The Otter*.

The following morning, the small party set off, 'full of high hopes and clad in "the shirt and the shorts of safari"'. The trip across Lake Victoria took a tedious ten hours, during which time Lady Mary was very ill. *The Otter* cruised into a shaded bay on the Busoga coast, soon after passing the long island of Kome, full 'of missionaries and crocodiles'. After a wonderful dinner and good Italian wine, it was an early night for all. Next morning, they were up an hour before dawn 'and away into the bush, with two hunting boys ahead and a trail of half a hundred behind'. Two hours later, thrilled to come upon the fresh footmarks of wild animals not an hour old, they dropped to the ground and crawled on. After a quarter of an hour's tracking, 'the grass woke into sound about us like waves of the sea breaking' and the hunters could hear, smell and almost feel a big herd of buffalo, stampeding in panic within half a dozen metres of them. Lady Mary, who had none of the modern squeamishness about hunting, was thrilled: 'The best moment of my life, I think, as far as the poor old earth is concerned.'

Back on their knees, they approached the herd of 60 buffalo grazing in a glade nearby and watching out warily for the hunters. A whiff of human scent and they were off. Three times this happened; the third time, it had started raining and, with the sounds of their movements muffled, the hunters got close enough to fire off a few shots before the herd took flight. Back on the trail, following a single spoor, 'natives' helped Lady Mary to within 70 yards of a fine bull. She raised her rifle, aimed carefully and shot twice, hitting it in the back and the head. After leaving some of her escorts to cut up the dead animal, Lady Mary and the hunting party crawled to the top of a ridge through close vegetation and found the herd again: 'I got a standing tail-shot at a young bull, the best I could see. The first shot broke his leg and he had to be finished with a head shot, as he swung round towards us.'

After many more miles of careful stalking 'over ridges, down through cruel, close dongas in the rain', they came upon a particularly steep donga or gully, filled with a heavy, beefy scent. Suddenly, right in front of them, rose a black, horned head. When the buffalo charged, Lady Mary's shot 'got him in the boss' and all but jolted him off his feet. The wounded animal changed direction and the herd scattered, but the drama was not over, as two great black shadows attacked the hunting party, sending the local boys bolting up nearby trees with terrified screams. Two shots rang out and the buffalo lay dead. Also killed by a ricochet was a young calf. Lady Mary showed no remorse:

This calf we did not declare, as it was an accidental death, but we opened him up and traced the path of the bullet, and then ate his liver fried deliciously between layers of fat over a big fire built in the rain.

They left Busoga the next day, steaming back into Mwanza tired and happy after feasting on buffalo steak, buffalo brains, buffalo soup and buffalo tongue, as well as their other 'bag': lots of guinea fowl. The buffalo heads, black and gory, were strapped to the prow, the mastheads and the davits (cranes), as they hooted their way into the port.

With Dorys Bentley now suffering both from the sun and a stomach problem, Lady Mary's departure was delayed again, and so the next day, she set off with the hunting party to track kudu, speckled leopard and sable for many miles off the Mwanza Gulf: 'When we got in at 2, we felt completely finished, but after sleep and food, we woke up again and steamed, after a heavy tropical deluge, tired but happy, back to beloved Mwanza.' Lady Mary's physical fitness was impressive – in four days, they had walked almost 80 miles, including one 27 mile trek before breakfast.

After six days' rest, the far less fit Dorys Bentley had practically recovered her strength, and so on 14 March the two planes set off for Nairobi. Among those waving goodbye was Signor Bonini, who insisted that Lady Mary visit Mussolini when she got to Italy, an offer she would remember later in her trip. Lady Mary was particularly relieved to get safely off the ground and back into the air: not only was her engine leaking, but the heavy, waterlogged grounds at Mwanza had bent the Avian's fragile undercarriage and main spar fittings again. After an hour or so of flying, the two small planes passed over the fabled Serengeti Plain, where they saw their first lions, slinking along beside a herd of topi and eland in full flight. All the local villages were built 'boma-wise' with a high stockade to keep out lions, and with many entrances, or exits, the cattle being guarded in the centre. Lady Mary was enchanted.

Flying conditions were bumpy, with downdraughts again a problem, and Nairobi, with its large aerodrome ten kilometres south of the city, was a welcome sight. Thanks to a regular flight schedule, this was now as good as any aerodrome in Europe; the days of holes on the runway, wandering zebra and oil flares for lighting had long gone. To their alarm, they saw a crashed aeroplane near the aerodrome. After they landed, they were told to their horror that it was the plane of Maïa Carberry, 'our dear little friend who had so pluckily flown from Mombasa to Nairobi only a week or two before'.

Maïa Carberry had met Lady Mary at Stag Lane a year earlier in August 1927, when she came to London with her husband, John, originally from Castle Freke in

Maïa Carberry, the first person to fly non-stop from Mombasa to Nairobi.

County Cork. Within a fortnight, she had passed flight, landing and altitude tests for her pilot's licence and soon after, competed in her first international air race, attracting much media attention. After flying back to East Africa in January 1928, she set herself the target of becoming the first person to fly non-stop from Mombasa to Nairobi. This she did in just three and a half hours on 16 February 1928, bringing the first Coast-Highland mail with her.

Just a fortnight later, Carberry attended Kenya's first air fair, taking friends up for joyrides. With a budding young aviator Dudley Cowie as passenger, the plane had begun circling to descend at 500 feet when it appeared to lose speed. To the horror of those watching, it then spun out of control before diving to earth with a sickening crash. The two occupants were killed instantly; Maïa was just 24; her passenger 22.

The Nairobi community was still in shock after the accident, the colony's first flying tragedy. After laying a wreath on Maïa's grave, a deeply affected Lady Mary sent a letter to the *East Africa Standard* asking that an aerodrome be built at Mombasa and called after Mrs Carberry: 'I am sure that those who had the privilege of knowing her and, if I may say so, of loving her and admiring her, would be only too glad of a suggestion whereby her feelings could find tangible form.'[1]

While she was in Nairobi, Lady Mary asked a local garage to remake the Avian's undercarriage and repair the petrol tank. She was annoyed to find that few of the telegrams she had sent at considerable personal cost to let the authorities know where they were, 'and what we were trying to do for aviation and the British Empire', had even been delivered and those that did get to their destination were mutilated and virtually unreadable. Yet she still got the blame for communication problems, as an official file revealed: 'Owing to her slackness in letting us know her movements, we are unable to keep pace with the vagaries of Lady Heath,' it said.

This seems unfair; copies of telegrams she sent while in Nairobi to the authorities in Khartoum and Cairo as well as in Kisumu and Entebbe still exist and most of her delays were not her fault. Additionally, she was well aware that staying in touch with the aerodromes and the various officials along the way greatly lessened the dangers on such a long and arduous trip: 'All aviators agree that the system of wiring one's departure, thus advising the next aerodrome to expect one, is a great safeguard,' she said in her book *Women and Flying*. Her telegram to the Civil Secretary in Khartoum states that she will leave Nairobi about 21 March, that she requests all facilities, will wire in advance if possible and does not require smoke fire 'until machine over town'. But in Africa, a combination of storms, giraffe damage and sabotage by locals, who stripped the wires to make copper bracelets, meant that telegraph lines rarely worked. There was also the problem of local politics: 'From Abercorn to Tabora, there is no line because it would interfere with some contract of one of the cable companies.'

Despite the hospitality she had received from Sir Edward Grigg, the Governor General of Kenya, Lady Mary was in no mood to be placated: 'We British are supposed to be the best colonists in the world and yet we permit this terrible state of affairs to go on.' Italian and French authorities in North Africa and in countries like the Sudan and the Belgian Congo communicated by wireless, which removed the problem of maintaining overhead wires. 'Flying up the whole length of the vast African continent, my chief impression was the amount of land that was under British control and the way we had barely scratched the surface,' she writes, implying that when it came to running a colony, the French and Italians made a much better job of it. Nowhere does she even question the policy of these European nations in taking over large parts of the globe, though when she arrives in Uganda, she remarks not only on the beauty of the local women but on the men, who mostly travel by bicycle and seem 'very civilised'.

In Nairobi, Lady Mary confessed that she and her two travelling companions were so downhearted, 'we could have sat down and howled!' although she hinted that perhaps Captain Bentley was not quite so depressed. The lack of publicity for her adventure was undoubtedly one cause of her despondency; the enforced company of the Bentleys another. As if that were not enough, an intruder broke into her room while she was asleep, making off with £50 and a gold cigarette case. She had woken briefly, thinking that she had carelessly left her door unlocked and that someone had come in by mistake. Only the next morning did she discover her loss.

On 22 March, the dispirited trio were off again. With the Avian heavily loaded, it took nearly 250 yards for the craft to become airborne, the longest run yet. There were further difficulties to overcome. Ahead lay the 10,000 foot Kijabe escarpment, an intimidating height for a small and overloaded plane to surmount in thin air. After a fruitless attempt to gain altitude, Lady Mary decided to make an 50 mile detour, following the railway line in hopes of finding an easier way over the top. Even when she did, she scraped over the hills by a mere 20 feet after lightening her load by throwing overboard her tennis racquet, some books and a pair of shoes: 'It was one of the most exciting moments of the trip and only achieved by an earnest prayer', she says laconically.

Despite her problems, she reached Kisumu, 270 miles distant on the north-east shore of Lake Victoria, ahead of Captain Bentley, who had taken another route. Making the most of it, she stopped only to refuel, before continuing on for another 200 miles, sticking to the northern shore of the lake until she reached Jinja, then the only aerodrome in Uganda. It meant she became the first woman pilot to fly over the equator, a fact she fails to mention in her book, but a feat widely publicised at the time by the world's press.

When Dick Bentley arrived at Jinja, he got to work on his engine, while Lady Mary, after finishing up with her own engine and putting in new gaskets, motored to Entebbe, just south of the capital, Kampala, and to this day the location of the country's main airport. There she spent a couple of days at Government House with Sir William Gowers, the Governor of Uganda and a renowned aviation enthusiast whom she wished to consult about the next stage of her journey.

At the time, no woman was allowed to fly solo between Juba, just north of the border with the Sudan, and Wadi Halfa, close to the border with Egypt, without the permission of the Royal Air Force headquarters at Khartoum. The edict was understandable enough – a forced landing in the area's 700 square miles of oozing swamp, a by-product of the Nile, could be fatal. To add to the problems, the Sudd, as the area was called, looked flat and green from the air. But land on it and the plane would immediately sink into the decomposing vegetation, often four metres thick and lying on a sluice of black water. Farther on, local tribes could prove less than welcoming hosts. A British district commissioner had been murdered just three months earlier and there had been skirmishes since then between Sudanese rebels and the authorities. [2]

To appease the Air Force, Lady Mary proposed paying Captain Bentley £5 an hour to see her safely over the treacherous swamp; at last he was proving his worth. The deal was agreed. On 28 March they set off for Mongalla in the Sudan from a specially extended runway. After about 30 miles, the winding Blue Nile had just appeared through the mist when Lady Mary noticed Captain Bentley turning back. Worried, she chased after him. He leaned out of his cockpit and indicated that he had an oil problem but that she should go on alone if she wished. She decided she had no option but to return to Jinja with him.

The following day, they were back on the same course, observing great herds of elephant on the banks of the Nile and a rare white rhino 'that is really a dirty grey'. Over Lake Kyoga, just north of Jinja, small black beetles, carried up by an air current, invaded the cockpit. They reminded Lady Mary of the butterflies she had found in her cockpit at 5000 feet while flying over mountains between Breslau in Poland and the Czech border the previous year. Soon, they struck a bend on the Nile; they had reached Nimule, just inside the Sudanese border and the official start of the no-go area. Here, Lady Mary found it impossible to stay with Bentley, who had slowed drastically: 'I was flying 2,000 feet above him, and must have had a more favourable air current, because throttled down to 1,600 revolutions and with an indicated air speed of 50mph, I had to keep turning and twisting to keep pace with him.'

Afraid that her engine would overheat, she pushed on, disregarding the warnings that she must not travel alone over this dangerous area. Following the course of the Nile, she took the opportunity to dive down on the houses of various district commissioners she had met while studying the route on the ground the previous year. A few appeared to wave her on, while others later jokingly protested later that they were very cross that she had not landed in their back gardens to say hello. On landing at Mongalla, the Avian was surrounded by natives carrying water, marshalled by an officer of the Sudan Defence Force, who had arrived on a bicycle. To them, the arrival of an aeroplane was synonymous with water, since most engines then were water-cooled. Not so the Avian, and it was all Lady Mary could do to persuade them to keep their water in their buckets and give her what she really wanted – stones and sand to fill her sandbags and help her weigh down the machine. This system, she had discovered, could resist the strongest winds, unlike pegs, which could be pulled out of the ground with disastrous consequences.

Mongalla was sweltering in a 108 to 112 degrees fahrenheit heat and even chairs and tables were burning to the touch. As she anxiously awaited the Bentleys, cabling when she could for news, Lady Mary worked on her engine and quickly learned that placing a spanner or wrench directly in sunlight could be a blistering experience. As evening approached, there was still no sign of her travelling companions. Finally, to her great relief, they arrived safely; the delay had been caused by a forced landing at Nimule. Despite her anxious wait, the Sudan, then largely self-sufficient because of its cotton industry, proved best of all the British territories for organisation, probably because of the recent troubles: 'Every station wires you out to the next one, and if you do not turn up, search parties are sent out to look for you.'

The take-off from Mongalla for Malakal on 30 March provided more drama when Lady Mary taxied into an unmarked ditch. It took the combined force of the Bentleys, along with ten local troops and their commanding officer, to pull her out. Once airborne, the two planes flew in close formation over the forbidding terrain below. For Lady Mary flying over wild desert 'populated mainly by honey-badgers, ants, hornets and hostile natives' was the worst part of the entire trip. Happily, a following wind helped them along, and with the Nile as a guide, they had no navigational problems.

Once safely over the Sudd, they experienced another short delay at Malakal when Lady Mary hit one of many cracks on the sun-baked airstrip and burst a tyre on landing. Since she always carried a spare, it took only a moment or two to change and then to refuel. Although it was now midday and she preferred to fly in the cool of the morning to spare her engine, Lady Mary decided to press on alone for Khartoum, using the Nile as a guide; clearly she had tolerated the Bentleys' company for just long enough. Despite the blazing sun, she was so relaxed that she spent some of her time reading a novel, glancing out from her cockpit occasionally to check that her 'beloved' Nile was still below.

She soon regretted her decision when the thermometer rose to 120 degrees fahrenheit and higher. Forced to fly fairly low at 3,000 feet and dressed in her fur coat to protect her neck and shoulders, she began to feel queasy from the combination of the scorching sun and air 'bumps'. The engine was also suffering 'and I felt that my wings were like the tired wings of a bird, giving me little support'.

The sight of the bridge at Kosti, with a well-marked aerodrome right beside it, proved too tempting and, abandoning plans to make it all the way to Khartoum, she touched down, just avoiding a couple of wandering camels running about loose. Alerted by the noise of the engine, the District Commissioner, Mr Arkel, came 'tearing down' to meet her, providing two Arab ponies for transport back to his house. The Bentleys arrived later, but the next morning, Lady Mary rode her 'lovely little Arab pony' to the aerodrome and flew off early and alone, clearly determined to avoid their company. Despite poor visibility and a couple of sandstorms that caused her to swerve westwards, she made the 185 miles journey to Khartoum in just two and a half hours, landing to a heartening welcome from the Air Force and opting for a few days rest, during which time she particularly enjoyed luxuriating in the local swimming baths.

On 1 April, Lady Bailey arrived in Khartoum in her DH 60 Moth after setting off from Croydon on 9 March, just a fortnight after Lady Mary had left Johannesburg, in an attempt to fly to the Cape; just as Lady Mary had predicted, 'a rival" company had organised a flight around the same time as her own. Neither woman can have been too pleased, but while we know nothing of Lady Bailey's reaction, Lady Mary is all barbed sweetness: 'I cannot speak too highly of Lady Bailey's gallant and plucky attitude in making this flight when she had never flown outside England before and when she had always been accustomed to the marvellous care and attention which de Havillands give their machine and engine, making it unnecessary for you ever to work on them yourself.' Lady Bailey began her flight from London to Cape Town in a DH Moth 'without any real knowledge of her engine or of Africa conditions' says Lady Mary waspishly.

According to Lady Mary, Lady Bailey had limited navigational skills and had already made one forced landing in the desert with engine problems: 'It hurt me to see her looking tired and weary after it.'[3] That evening, a dinner was given in honour of the two Irishwomen. The contrast in style was marked. While Lady Mary appeared in an elegant evening dress, the ever-diffident Lady Bailey wore her dusty, tweed flying-suit, clearly unconcerned that Lady Mary might be attempting to score points at her expense. But then Lady Bailey, with her aristocratic background, never felt the need to prove anything to anyone, and when she ran into trouble, she had her fabulously wealthy husband on hand to bail her out. The two could not have been more different in personality, personal circumstances and ambition.

What they shared was a love of flying and the two Marys undoubtedly exchanged stories of their experiences. In Cairo, Lady Bailey had faced the same difficulty as Lady Mary in getting permission to fly over southern Sudan. Her plane was impounded for several days as telegrams flew to and fro, but she was eventually allowed to fly on as far as Khartoum. Fortunately, Captain Bentley, who by then had arrived in Khartoum, agreed to interrupt his own flight and escort Lady Bailey southwards as far as Nimule; his travel-weary wife consented to the plan, delighted to have a break from flying.

To appease a still nervous Sudanese government, unused to women doing much of anything on their own, let alone flying solo, Lady Mary set off the next morning in tandem with a Fairey service aeroplane heading for Wadi Halfa. She soon left the slower machine in her slipstream. Landing at Atbara a couple of hours later, she accepted an invitation to play tennis and stay the night. The next day, she put down on the banks of the Nile, having failed to find an aerodrome at 'Station 10'. There she dabbled her feet in the river, had a drink and took some photographs. Airborne again, she took five hours to reach Wadi Halfa, following a railway line through the desert. An inspection of her propellers after she landed showed that the bolts had loosened, and, alarmingly, she found she could tighten them two full turns each.

On 4 April, she made a marathon nine-hour trip all the way to Cairo, about 700 miles away, using a page torn from an atlas as a very rough guide. She had intended stopping at Assuit but, with the Nile as her guide, pushed on, planning to pass the time by reopening her novel and eat chocolates; even when flying yourself, long-distance flights could be just as tedious then as they are now. The novel got little attention, however, as she flew low to gaze at the amazing sights below – the old palaces and temples of Luxor, the cultivated banks of the majestic Nile, the vast nothingness of the desert. Finally came the Sphinx, whose paws had been unburied only two years earlier in 1926, and then the breathtaking sight of the giant Pyramids.

Soon she could see the houses, domes and minarets of what she described as 'Africa's greatest city' in the distance. Because of the heat, Lady Mary had worn no stockings on her flight. For an important city such as Cairo, the largest she had visited since leaving Johannesburg, she felt she had to make an effort. Poking around her back locker in mid-air, she found a pair of silk stockings, which she managed to pull on, keeping one foot on the rudder bar as balance: 'not very difficult, my machine has tow-straps in the rudder bar'.

Coming into Cairo proved an emotional experience: 'I do not think in all my life I have ever seen anything which to me seemed so beautiful as Cairo from the air that day.' In arriving there, she had achieved her first goal, which was to cross the continent of Africa safely: 'In spite of the ten hours work I had done, I could not resist coming down to the aerodrome at Heliopolis in a series of long and enthusiastic loops!' As it happens, she had landed at the wrong aerodrome – there were two at Heliopolis, one for single-engined aeroplanes and the other, larger one, for multi-engined machines.

She was soon forgiven and the adjutant of the aerodrome, Mr Emerson, whisked her off for a late but very welcome lunch. Group Captain McLean and Flight Sergeant Lord then looked after her engine, still running 'like a sewing machine' and better than when she had started out. This she attributed largely to her own diligence:

One of the Pyramids; 'a breathtaking sight'. The Sphinx, seen by Lady Mary from the air.

'I did the tappet clearances every day, no matter how short the flight was, and cleaned the petrol and oil filters. Only once did I fly in the heat of the day and I never flew at less than 7,000 feet to get the cool air. I ran my engine at 1,700 rpm [revolutions per minute] throughout and did one to three hours' routine work daily.'

After sending off cables to A.V. Roe, to the Aircraft Disposal Company, makers of her Cirrus engine, and to KLG Plugs, she went to bed and slept solidly for fifteen hours. She had taken thirty-eight days to fly from Pretoria to Cairo, a distance of 5,132 miles, flying on sixteen of those days and spending just over seventy-two hours in the air: 'I had come safely through the heart of Africa and I felt my machine was a live entity and a very faithful one to have brought me so well and truly over mountain ranges and swamps, over forests and deserts, without ever faltering.'

CHAPTER 12

A World-Famous Flyer

LIKE LADY BAILEY before her, Lady Mary ran into difficulties in Cairo. She woke from her long sleep to find that the local authorities had impounded her aeroplane and locked it up in a hangar at Heliopolis. Although she had proved her skill as a pilot by flying over some of the most inhospitable territories in the world, they were worried that she would not be able to find her way safely across the Mediterranean; this was a time when flying across water was considered particularly perilous.

Lady Mary's fear of flying over water should have been enough to reassure them; unlike other pilots, such as the Swiss, who flew their seaplane from Athens to Alexandria, not seeing land for 400 miles after they passed Crete, Lady Mary planned on making her traverse of the Mediterranean as short as possible. She would fly along the North African coast from Egypt to Tunisia and then make the relatively short hop across the sea to Sicily from the port of Tunis: 'Tunis to Sicily was the shorter sea journey, but a longer land one; the more direct route being via Malta across the Mediterranean. But then Africa is a big continent and you are practically bound to see it, whereas flying … from Homs, on the north coast of Africa, you might easily not find Malta if visibility was not good.' Even when she pointed out that Lady Bailey had flown the north coast of Africa solo only a few weeks earlier and swore that she had no plans to cross 230 miles of sea alone, the Cairo authorities insisted she ask the RAF to provide an escort. The RAF refused 'since it might be quoted as a precedent'.

Not until Lady Mary wired Mussolini, addressing him as 'Mussolini, Italy', was the next stage of her flight assured. Lady Mary had already promised her Mwanza host, Signor Bonini, that she would visit Mussolini when in Italy and, at a dance hosted by Lord and Lady Lloyd, the High Commissioner for Egypt, had remembered her promise when discussing her plight with a sympathetic dance partner. He not only encouraged her to ask the Italian leader for help, but also, at dance Number 16 of the planned 25, whisked her off in his car to a telegraph office. The staff there

[143]

proved more than willing to help, having come to the rescue of Lady Bailey a few weeks earlier. When the pair got back to the Residency, the house was shrouded in darkness and two irate people were awaiting them – her new-found friend's wife and the RAF officer delegated to escort Lady Mary back to her Heliopolis hotel. The pair were placated over a quiet drink.

The following morning, she was delighted to find a reply from Mussolini; he had put a seaplane at her disposal and she would meet up with the pilots in Tunisia. Although thoroughly enjoying her stay in Cairo, where she played tennis, attended parties and was the centre of attention, Lady Mary was relieved to set off for the frontier port of Sollum (Salum) on 15 April, especially since, for the first time on her trip, she now had a set of decent maps, sent to her from London. As she flew over the Egyptian desert, she could recognise Bedouin encampments by their characteristic black tents, and she passed over Mersa Matruh, set between two lagoons and the location of Cleopatra's country villa 'in the old Roman days'.

Just over six hours later, she reached the Sollum aerodrome, perched high on a cliff behind the town, a place of great antiquity, used as a port by the ancient Romans and indeed the point from which they had left Africa. Uncertain of what lay below, she circled a couple of times before an attendant at the aerodrome lit a fire to give her an idea of the wind direction. As it was, the runway was less than ideal, the surface consisting of boulders set in loose sand. The town, mainly occupied by the army, had a few shops that were supported by Arabs coming in from the desert to buy food and clothing: 'The Arabs in this part of the desert live mainly on their barley farming, and a very sparse crop indeed do they get.'

Although the one Englishman in the area, Colonel Green of the Frontier Administration, was away on a journey, she was brought to the Rest House, where she enjoyed a typically Egyptian lunch, including a 'thin long vegetable like a cucumber stuffed with hash [minced meat] and rice' that she could have gone on eating indefinitely. That evening, after an afternoon nap and a ride up to the aerodrome to do some work on her engine, she returned to the Rest House to find that Colonel Green was back from his trip. Over dinner, he entertained her with tales of battles between the Italian army and the Senussi Arabs across the nearby border: 'The Italian, of course is one of the bravest men made and the Arab a splendid enemy who would always fight to the finish, so their battles are really rather bloodthirsty,' says his impressed guest.

Disaster struck the next morning as Lady Mary attempted to take off from the boulder-strewn runway: 'I felt, as I thought, my wheels come up against some stones and I gave a big burst of engine to press the machine over them.' The plane jerked forward with a bump but then continued to rattle along the stoney aerodrome, so she looked behind to find out what was the problem. Caught between two rocks, the rear quarter of the machine was pulled right off and was trailing forlornly in the dirt: 'I got out of the machine and laughed before I could be angry.' It turned out that such accidents were a regular occurrence at the airfield; a plane carrying Sir Sefton Brancker and others had broken a wheel on landing and, as for light planes, Captain Bentley's was the only one Lady Mary knew of to have landed without breaking at least a tailskid. With four longerons 'quite done in', she would need to replace the entire rear quarter of the Avian.

There followed a frantic dash 'over rocks and ravines, bushes and pot-holes' in 'a screenless Ford' to the Italian fortress at Amsiate for help. It being early in the morning and with Italian time an hour before British, no one was yet up and they headed for the mess, where they were offered an assortment of liqueurs: 'It was the first time I had drunk them before breakfast!' When the commanidng officer, Capitane Matoni, finally surfaced, he was all help and kindness and immediately set off to another fortress five miles distant, where the armoured car division was situated and there was plenty of material available for repairs.

After an hour he was back, bringing with him a mechanic along with his tools and spare bits of wood and metal. Back at the aerodrome, work finally began on the Avian, with the additional help of an Egyptian carpenter and for three days, they worked away, using an assortment of soap-boxes, petrol tins and odd scraps of wood in an attempt to make the Avian airworthy again. Then came a small miracle: Lady Mary's persistent complaints about the condition of the aerodrome had resulted in a full complement of RAF personnel, including a squadron leader, a flight-Lieutenant, a Flight-Sergeant, a corporal and a couple of mechanics, arriving to inspect the set-up and repair her plane.

After they had rigged up a couple of tents on the sandy waste by the aerodrome, they set to work and, finding she was getting in their way, Lady Mary spend most of the next few days enjoying 'the lovely pools of the gulf' while they worked, although their labours were interrupted by three nights spent holding down the aeroplanes after the *ghibli*, a storm wind from the south, 'hot and strong and fierce', hit the small station. The attention of the Italian officers, always careful of their appearance and equipped with spotless white gloves, even when driving their heavy armoured cars, proved welcome: 'I retaliated by digging out my best frocks...and traipsing about the Libyan desert in high-heeled shoes and black silk when I was not working – a horrible sight!'

She was also given 'lovely pots of cold cream' to stave off sunburn by the wife of the man in charge of the nearby Egyptian station, who took an interest in Lady Mary's progress: 'The Egyptian woman is becoming very advanced…'.

Not until 23 April, and after a thick fog had cleared was Lady Mary airborne again, flying over the little Italian fort at Amsiate to drop in a message bag and 'thank-you' note and asking them to wireless ahead for her: 'we had rigged the wings and the empannage more by guesswork and the light of nature than by any knowledge we had of them, but she flew very well'.

She then headed towards the coast, worrying slightly about the mountains straight ahead. Passing over Arab encampments and Italian fortresses, and noting the good quality of the Italian-built roads below, she made it to Derna (Darnah), about 160 miles away, in two hours, thanks to a following wind. A fire at the aerodrome showed her the way down, but she ignored it: 'I dipped in greeting and waved and went on.' What had been a tailwind was now against her, thanks to the *ghibli*, and approaching Benghazi, she experienced her first North Africa rain. When she attempted to land, she was tossed about 'like a feather' but eventually made it without damaging anything: 'I could have sworn that my machine dropped 25 feet and only a lightning-burst of engine saved her from bumping to earth.' There was a further fright on the ground, when the machine was tipped first onto one wing and then the other in the heavy wind, bouncing Lady Mary around in the cockpit. Fortunately, no damage was done.

After she had climbed out of her plane, Lady Mary's camera was seized by the local Italian army authorities and then carefully sealed and labelled; she does not mention why or whether she ever got it back, but her book contains striking photographs of the Pyramids and other sights along her route, so presumably, she was allowed to keep her films. She endured a routine that had become familiar when she had met the Egyptians and French – walking into a roomful of men and having to shake hands with them all 'like a bad imitation of Princess Pat reviewing the Connaught Rangers'.

A stiff vermouth helped cheer her up, as her new acquaintances taught her how to eat what she called macaroni (most likely spaghetti) properly, 'a difficult and delicate operation'. After lunch, she began to feel very tired. A fever she had felt coming on at Sollum took full hold and she slept for the rest of the afternoon in the commanding officer's bedroom: 'I do not know where he slept – perhaps a bathroom. Frankly, I felt too ill to care.' Pulling herself together after teatime, she returned to the aerodrome to work on her machine. But following a visit to the beautiful palace of Cyrene, where she met the governor, Attilio Teruzzi, her teeth were again chattering and her head 'going round', and a trip into Benghazi town left no clear impression 'save of white houses and well stocked shops, and hundreds of curiously gaping Arabs'.

Back in her room, she fell into bed with a raging fever; the squadron doctor found she had a temperature of 103 degrees fahrenheit. Although she was excused the public dinner that night, the fever did not stop her staggering from her bed early the next morning and, after some work on the Avian, which was reacting to the cold temperature, she took off two hours later, some of the planes from the squadron flying with her. Along the coast, she could see fine aerodromes every 50 or 60 miles, with people waving at her and clearly prepared to help if she decided to land. Feeling weak with the fever, she gave into temptation and came down at Aghaila (Al Joaylah) just in time for lunch, renewing her acquaintance with an Italian officer, the elegantly monocled Colonel Garelli, whom she had met the previous year in the Italian Somaliland. To her surprise, she also met a number of Italians who had been to the USA and spoke English with an American accent. After a lunch of poached eggs and asparagus, washed down by a bottle of champagne opened in her honour, she took off again in good spirits. The entire garrison had signed their names on her machine and presented her with a green Italian Camel Corps scarf: 'The nicest remark I collected on my wings was the Italian proverb which being translated means: "It is better to travel alone than badly accompanied".' This was a philosophy with which she could heartily concur.

High above the land, she hugged the Libyan coast so she wouldn't get lost and kept herself amused by flicking through an out-of-date *Pearson's Magazine* before arriving at Sirte (Surt). There, a swarm of mechanics swept her aside every time she tried to do any work on her engine, apart from her usual ritual of cleaning the plugs, magnetos and tappets, and wrote nice messages on the wings of the Avian. Put up in the mess and finding it hard to sleep, possibly because of the fever, she raided the kitchen for a little more of the wine they had drunk at dinner. With the room swimming about her and the moon 'dancing about the window', she eventually dozed off, only to wake the next morning with two empty glasses sitting by her bed and a headache so dreadful she wondered had she drunk neat brandy in error. She admitted that her farewells were not as hearty as she would have wished, thanks to the combination of hangover and fever.

Once she was airborne, the headache vanished and she savoured the beauties of the coastline below, despite reaching a speed of 100 miles per hour. After an hour and a half, she could see the long lines of date palms leading into the town of Misurata, the mid-point of her journey, and was soon touching down in the Libyan capital of Tripoli, with its harbour in the centre of town, including a large hangar for seaplanes,

Lady Mary's flight from Tunis to Croydon South London
6 – 17 May 1928

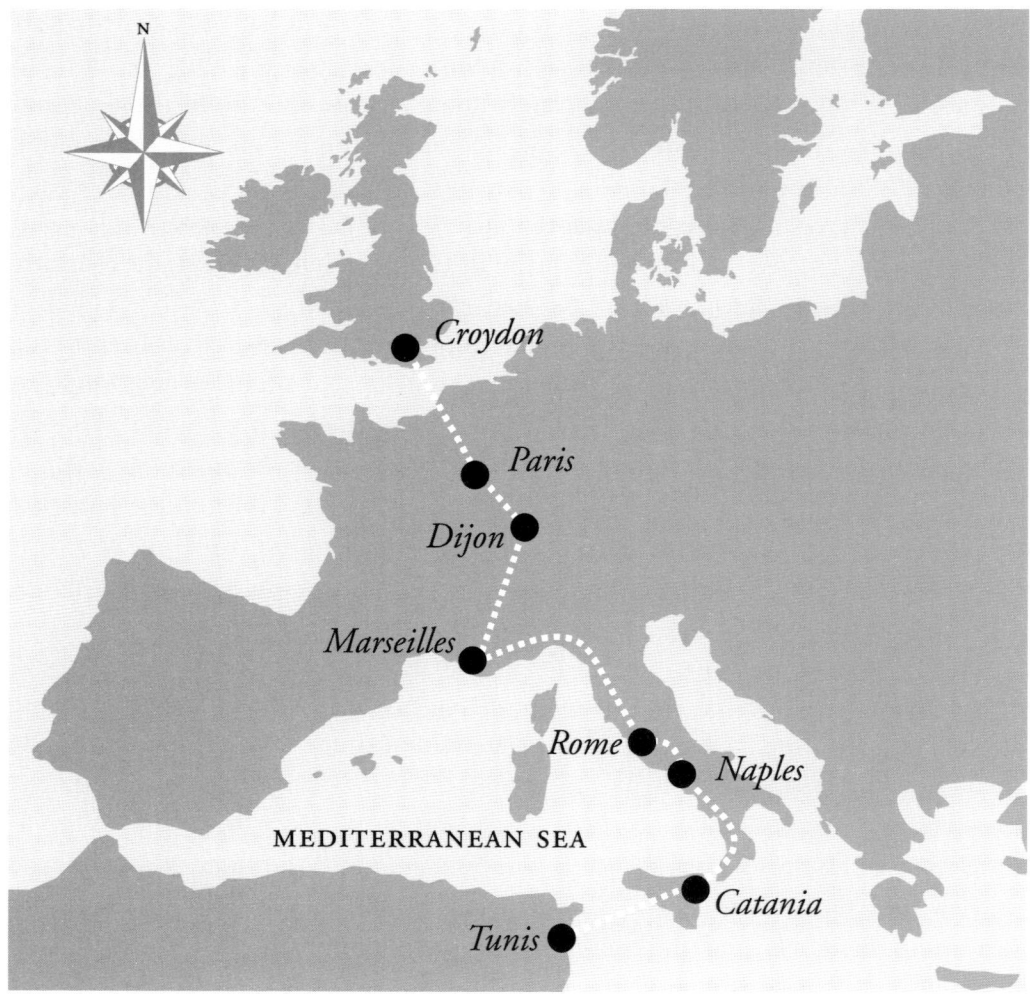

and aerodrome about ten kilometres to the west. There she expected to meet her seaplane escort, because she had telegraphed from Sirte to say that she was on her way.

At Tripoli, she heard dreadful news. The seaplane that had set out on 26 April from Syracuse had been less lucky than Lady Mary when it ran into the *ghibli* and had been forced down about 40 miles off the coast. A full search involving seaplanes and destroyers was underway, with the British base in Malta also alerted. Booked into her hotel, Lady Mary succumbed to a 'tiresome' dose of rheumatic fever, which only added to her worries about the fate of the seaplane: 'I think I went through perhaps the worst days of my life, lying in the Grand Hotel, trying to be polite and gracious to the people who were so wonderful and polite to me, bringing me fruit and flowers and things, and thinking all the time of the three brave men whose death I might have caused.'

To her great relief, the seaplane was found on the fifth day with all its crew alive and well. But it meant she would be forced to face the terrors of the Mediterranean on her own, since the crew of a second seaplane designated to escort her had stayed back to help rescue their friends. After all the drama, she spared a thought for her 'poor husband, who did not know all the details of the various delays'; presumably she had been keeping in touch with him during her trip. With Captain Bentley also planning to cross the Mediterranean, she reluctantly decided to meet up with him in Tunis and offer him the fee of £5 an hour she had paid him before for escort duties: 'I think I am rather foolish about water, but the experiences of those gallant officers from Italy...had made me more than ever scared of tackling water in a land machine.'

She finally left Tripoli on 6 May, ten days later than planned. Because the Grand Hotel had refused a request for an early breakfast, she sent the night porter off to find a taxi and then raided the pantry for fruit and sandwiches before she left: 'I am terribly glad I stole these because they were the only thing I had to eat until seven o'clock that evening.' While she was taking off and waving to a group of new friends, her left wheel hit a pile of stones. The shock reverberated through the small craft, loosening the flying wire on that side, but she made it into the air and decided to worry about possible problems later on.

On the way past the port of Zougha, she saw the stricken seaplane being towed towards Tripoli by a destroyer and greeted the two vessels with a 'dip'. She flew on, and using a succession of distinctive salt lakes and a road map to guide her, soon crossed over into the French territory of Tunisia, where immediately the ground became very fertile and thickly cultivated and towns seemed closer together and more prosperous than in Libya. She found the locals considerably less efficient than the Italians, never thinking of wiring ahead her movements, though still very kind. Unable to find the promised aerodrome at Sfax, she landed on the local racecourse, after which she refuelled unnecessarily, took some photographs and examined her 'rather dicky-looking' left main spar, deciding that the only thing to do was to fly on. The enthusiastic crowd that greeted her proved so large that she needed help to clear the runway before taking off again for Tunis. Soon she was enjoying her flight. Below her the little towns 'like jewels in their lovely setting' had probably changed little since the time of the Romans thousands of years earlier. Although close to Tunis, she delayed her arrival to detour over the ruins of the ancient city of Carthage, home to the fabled Queen Dido. She then landed at the wrong aerodrome and had to take off again.

On finally making it to her destination, she found three planes already on the runway. Captain Bentley's DH Moth she was certainly familiar with, but there was also a Westland Widgeon belonging to Wing Commander Manning, who was en route to Australia, and an Avian like her own, owned by Captain Stack and E.C. Bowyer of the *Daily News*, who were on a tour of the north-west coast of Africa and about to take off for Sicily. She would gladly have gone with them, but was afraid her damaged plane would not stand another landing.

After seeing them off, Lady Mary's main concern was to repair the undercarriage and main spar damaged earlier in the day. This was not easy. Even after passing out bribes to get the French mechanics started 'out of hours', she was less than impressed and, in the end, had to complete the repair work herself, including painting the underside of the wings: 'There was none of the enthusiasm and pride in a good job well done that I had met on all the English and Italian aerodromes.' Later she was to give the mechanics more credit when they reported that they had found a bullet hole in one of the Avian's wings. Despite this extraordinary discovery, Lady Mary had noticed nothing threatening during her 600 mile flight from Tripoli, although the local Arabs had a reputation for taking pot-shots at planes flying overhead, particularly if they were Italian. She could only express relief that they had missed her petrol tank 'or I might not have been here to tell the tale'.

On 6 May, Lady Mary finally left Africa behind, flying again with the Bentleys across the Mediterranean from Cape Bon, near Tunis, to Sicily, a distance of 95 miles: 'It was a little thrilling to fly over this wonderful cape in the same machine that a couple of months before had circled the Cape of Good Hope, at the furthermost end of the Continent.' Thanks to her fear of water, she slept little the night before the ocean crossing and devised her own version of a lifebelt: 'I had obtained a couple of motor-cycle tyres, and having blown them up, had wrapped them round my waist as a life-belt if I came down in the sea.' This was a tale she was to relate many times, with the number of tyres increasing from two to six over the years.

To increase her chances of reaching land in case of trouble, she ascended as high as she could: 'the higher I went the safer I felt'. As she reached 7,000 feet, the tyres burst with a loud pop in the thin air and she was left with shreds of rubber hanging around her neck: 'My heart was thumping and bumping. The blue sea looked frightfully wet and deep. Shreds of red rubber may have looked decorative, bizarre. But they lacked buoyancy.'

Flying even higher at two miles above the earth and with excellent visibility, she was able to see both Europe and Africa. Indeed, Europe was now within gliding range and knowing that while she could still crash, there was little possibility of her drowning, she could relax and enjoy the extraordinary views. Ahead, Mount Etna pierced the clouds, making a perfect landmark on the way to the aerodrome at Catania on the east coast of Sicily. She landed in mid-morning, with the Bentleys following half an hour later. After a hasty lunch and running repairs by the Italian mechanics, who even repainted portions of the machine 'which the French had scamped', she was soon airborne again, flying alone and enduring a bumpy ride as she headed over the Straits of Messina to Naples.

Thanks to the hospitality and help she had received in North Africa, Lady Mary was by now a confirmed fan of Italy and the Italians. She was particularly impressed when, from high above, she could pick up emergency landing grounds, all with their names cut out in white chalk and clearly visible from the air: 'Only one of the forced landing grounds did I find to be useless. It is a very tiny one and perched on the side of a hill. As there was nothing else one could have possibly landed on for twenty miles on either side, even that was pleasing.' It was growing dark as she approached Naples, clouded by the volcanic outpourings of Vesuvius drifting gently downwind. So thick was the smoke that she was forced to descend almost to ground level, crawling along and using the roads below as a guide: 'I had got into bad habits flying at altitude in Africa, and found it a little difficult to land slowly enough to get in gracefully.' Although it was Sunday, she was welcomed by a duty officer at the aerodrome and, after eight and a half hours flying, was grateful for an invitation to stay overnight with Commandant Cancianotti and his wife: 'They were very kind and understanding and let me go to bed early, a thing which I found very difficult to do at most places where I landed.'

Her take-off from the small aerodrome the next morning was delayed for two hours until the officer who took payments appeared. After her overloaded machine just cleared the trees beside the runway, which she found 'rather exciting', she followed the wind to Rome, and was then guided by the Via Appia into Rome's 'vast' new aerodrome, where it took a full ten minutes to taxi to the sheds. She stayed for a week in Rome, partly to convalesce from her rheumatic fever, partly because of the Italians' 'wonderful hospitality', and partly because General Balbo, head of the Italian air force, offered her a free overhaul of her engine so that she could be certain of 'a strong finish' to her adventure. While in Rome, she was invited to meet Mussolini and, like many more of the time, was enchanted by the dictator, describing him as 'that great man who is more of a national monument than an individual'. He had a good knowledge of aviation and 'seemed interested to hear my experiences, and glad of what I was conscientiously able to say about Italian hospitality and efficiency'.

The night before she left Rome, the Marquis de Pinedo, one of Italy's best-known aviators, hosted a dinner in Lady Mary's honour, an occasion she particularly relished because she had read translations of his books while flying over Africa's north coast. The harmonious mixture of old and new in the Eternal City made it 'surely the most beautiful city in the world' and she found it difficult to tear herself away. But London was now just a few days distant and, early on 14 May, she left Rome for Marseilles, and following the coast, arrived there in the late afternoon. 'The Riviera coast looked more beautiful than I had ever seen it before,' she commented in her book, adding that she had only known it 'on the ground' before, when she had come to Monte Carlo to gamble 'as one does', or for the Women's Olympic Games, first held there six years earlier: 'On the ground in these Riviera towns, there is an atmosphere of fever and unrest, but from the air they look like peaceful and beautiful villages.'

In Marseilles, she met her friend and the co-author of *Women and Flying*, Stella Wolfe Murray. 'When Lady Heath arrived after eight hours' non-stop flight from Rome, she looked as if she had stepped out of a bandbox, having changed her flying helmet for a little black cloche straw hat,' reported an admiring Wolfe in the book they later wrote together. For luggage, she had just a soft leather duffel bag 'that would screw in anywhere', in which she carried her eight frocks, and the dressing-case presented to her by the Johannesburg Flying Club: 'I have never seen anyone unpack and pack so quickly, or undress and dress so quickly as she did, contriving to look like a fashion plate all the same.' After tea and sandwiches, she donned a cretonne overall and set to work on her engine, while an admiring group of mechanics looked on open-mouthed. When Murray brought her back to her hotel, Lady Mary took the opportunity 'to devour' the latest aviation magazines.

Low clouds and driving rain hampered her progress as she flew northwards along the Rhône valley to Lyons the next day. After months in warmer climates, she had lost the habit of manoeuvring through fog and clouds and, forced to stay no more than 500 feet above the river, picking her way between the hills, decided that she might as well press on in case the weather got even worse. So she settled for a height of less than 60 feet, found a railway line to follow, and 'groped' her way as far as Dijon, feeling more shattered after her four-hour flight than on even her longest stint over Africa. Delighted to plunder a library of English books at the aerodrome's library, she retired to bed at teatime, still slightly affected by rheumatic fever.

Le Bourget airport, Paris, on her way home to England after her epic flight from Cape Town. *(Cussen Collection)*

With a bouquet of flowers after arriving back in Croydon on 17 May 1928. (Flight *Collection*)

The next morning, though damp, was beautiful and clear and she flew as high as 2,000 feet on her way to Paris. As she got close to the city, she was battered by thunder and lightning, with hail cutting her face and beating her plane almost down to ground level. Following a safe landing at Le Bourget, she was an honoured guest at a party hosted by Clifford Harmon, president of the International League of Aviators, to celebrate the second birthday of the League. Next morning, Harmon drove her from Claridges Hotel on the Champs Elysées to Le Bourget, from where she set off on the last lap of her long journey.

Flying over the English Channel in stormy conditions, she was blown northwards as far as the coastal town of Deal in Kent. This left her so annoyed and cold that she landed for a cup of tea at the Lympne aerodrome near Folkestone before continuing on for Croydon. By now, her arrival was eagerly anticipated and two circling aeroplanes greeted her in mid-air. Despite a warning that her make-shift tail could fall off, she could not resist exuberantly looping the loop over the aerodrome. She finally landed, to be surrounded by a crowd of cheering mechanics. It was 17 May 1928 and her long adventure was over.

She had become the first woman to fly solo from South Africa to London. It was also the first solo flight from any of Britain's overseas colonies to London. Greeting

Journalists and supporters greet Lady Mary on her return home after her epic flight. (Flight *Collection*)

her as she stepped from her aeroplane was her husband, Sir James Heath, while Dorys Bentley was also there, along with a throng of journalists.

Her feat was to make headline news in newspapers all over the world. Few reports, however, did justice to her achievements and her mechanical ability, with newspapers preferring to report on her glamorous appearance. If she wanted to be taken seriously, she hardly helped her cause: 'There is one thing I want to emphasise again which will show what a fine thing flying is. You can powder in the air and as long as you can do that, it will forever be popular with the ladies.'

This theme was repeated in many other newspapers: 'When my powder blew off, I simply clamped the joy stick between my knees, held my mirror with one hand and powdered with the other and I did it many a time with a lion, a giraffe or a herd of elephants gazing up at me.' Lady Mary was clearly terrified of being considered anything other than the most conventionally feminine of women.

On 23 May at the Mayfair Hotel in London, a luncheon in her honour was hosted

Irish Independent 18 May 1928.

The letter to the Editor of *The Times* from Frederick Guest on 11 April 1928.

by the Air League of the British Empire, in co-operation with the Royal Aeronautical Society, Royal Aero Club and Society of British Aircraft Constructors. Some journalists described it conventionally as a lunch of 'mass-produced chicken and over-long speeches'.

Presiding was the Duke of Sutherland, one of the founding fathers of aviation in Britain, who referred first of all to the many telegrams of congratulation they had received for Lady Mary, mentioning one in particular from the Women's Amateur Athletic Association. Among those attending were some of the best-known names in British aviation, including Sir Sefton Brancker, Sir Charles Wakefield, A.V. Roe and Tommy Sopwith. The Bentleys were also honoured, Dick Bentley being presented with the Britannia Trophy for his return flight to the Cape and effusively compared to both Don Quixote and Don Juan.

The Duke then moved on to the main reason for the celebration. Before Lady Heath's flight, he said, the world had not thought it possible for a woman to fly alone from Cape Town to London. Her flight had proved the safety and reliability of the British aeroplane and the British engine. In her reply, Lady Mary emphasised that her flight had been done in a slow time over a roundabout route, and after describing her adventures briefly, she suggested that the firms that had supplied her might like to subscribe to a fund to allow the Air League establish four flying scholarships annually. Sir Charles Wakefield, the oil magnate, enthusiastically backed her idea.

Amid the universal adulation, there was one sour note. After she returned from her epic trip, a letter was awaiting Lady Mary from the Colonial Secretary in Nairobi, seeking payment of 418.90 shillings (£20 18s 12d sterling) for six telegrams sent on her behalf while in Kenya. Lady Mary was indignant: she had already spent over £100 on telegrams, and since the other colonies had been good enough to send telegrams for her without charge, she had no idea that she would be asked to foot this bill herself, she claimed.

This was slightly disingenuous. 'I feel sure I owe you something for those wires,' she had plainly stated in a letter dated 21 March, giving her London address as a contact.

In response to a further letter, Lady Mary send a cheque for £14 but refused to pay the remaining £6 18s. This produced a flurry of communications between the Colonial Office and Government House in Nairobi, including suggestions that she be 'blacklisted' and threats of legal action, until it was sensibly decided to drop the entire matter.

'Lady Heath regards herself as a pioneer of Imperial air development, and if she cared to, she would not find it difficult to persuade the Press to take the same view,' dryly pointed out a Mr Eastwood of the Colonial Office in a note.

Soon after her return, a ladies' committee of the Air League of the British Empire was formed, with Lady Mary elected its first chairman and top pilots, such as Lady Bailey, Sicele O'Brien, Winifrid Spooner and the Duchess of Bedford, as well as wealthy and influential wives and daughters, like Lady Cobham, wife of Sir Alan, also involved. Determined to cash in on her fame, Lady Mary began a hectic schedule of personal appearances all over Britain. So busy did she find herself that she kept deferring her obligatory attendance at an Air Ministry medical examination:

> I have two secretaries working at full pressure on letters etc, at present and the only chance to get through the correspondence, newspaper articles, etc., is to slog at the dictation all the morning and for the girls to work on it all the afternoon and evening.

Amelia Earhart, the first woman to fly across the Atlantic.

Everything seemed to be going her way until 18 June 1928 when Amelia Earhart became the first woman to fly across the Atlantic. Earhart may not have piloted the plane, but her fearlessness in flying over an expanse of water far vaster than the Mediterranean effectively eclipsed the achievements of every other woman pilot, including Lady Mary.

The 'Friendship', a three-engined Fokker owned by a wealthy socialite, Amy Guest, had taken off from Newfoundland on 17 June 1928, piloted by Wilmer Stultz, with Lou Gordon as co-pilot and mechanic. A day later, it touched down in Burry Port, near Llanelli in south Wales. Earhart may have remarked that she had been 'as useful as a sack of potatoes', but when the 'Friendship' landed, the press clamoured for interviews with 'the girl'; indeed the whole point of the flight was that it had carried a woman. Not all the publicity was kind. 'Well the first lady passenger has crossed the Atlantic by air although what special merit there is in that is not altogether easy to see. In these ages [sic] of sex equality, such a feat should not arouse any particular comment. Compared with the solo flights of such lady pilots as Lady Bailey and Lady Heath, the crossing of the Atlantic as a passenger does not seem to us to prove anything in particular,' commented *Flight* magazine.

Air-minded women were more generous and Lady Mary wrote Earhart a supportive note promising to 'throw down whatever I'm doing' if she wanted to go flying or simply needed someone to talk to. She struck a chord: Earhart was feeling the pressure of her instant celebrity and wanted more than anything to spend a few hours in the air. A week later, Lady Mary organised a 'secret' rendezvous at Croydon for her new friend, who left the London home of her host Amy Guest at dawn. After finding out where Earhart had gone, Guest arrived in Croydon in time to see Earhart landing a DH Gypsy Moth following a short flight to Northolt with Captain A.H. White. Later, with a few reporters now present, Earhart flew a few circuits in Lady Mary's Avro Avian, still in good shape despite its long journey.

Earhart, smarting from the insinuation that she was not a 'real' pilot, was secretly happy that her flight in the Avian had been noticed. On landing, she declared that she was so impressed by the Avian that she wanted to buy one and take it home so that she could fly it on a planned 12,000-mile lecture tour of the USA. Perhaps carried away by the moment, Lady Mary immediately offered to sell. The little Avian was subsequently dismantled, put in a crate, and shipped back to the USA with the 'Friendship'; quite where the cash-strapped Earhart got the money is not known. On the fuselage, Lady Mary had inscribed: 'To Amelia Earhart from Mary Heath. Always think with your stick forward.' Earhart had little subsequent luck with the plane. Attempting to fly from Rye in New York to California, she was to smash the undercarriage and the left wing on landing at Pittsburgh. Subsequently, she had forced landings in Utah and at Utica, New York, when the engine failed. A year later, she sold it. So ended the known story of G-EBUG, and of the flight from the Cape to London. Both the small plane and its pilot had been eclipsed by larger events and ambitions.

CHAPTER 13

After Earhart

THE IMPULSIVE SALE of her Avian caused problems for Lady Mary. At the Blackpool air pageant organised by the Lancashire Aero Club on the weekend of 6 July, she was disqualified from competing because she had not produced a plane in time. She lodged a protest but it was dismissed.

Four days later, she was back in the headlines when she took a 30-horse power all-metal British light seaplane to a height of 13,400 feet, or nearly three miles above the earth's surface, taking off from the Medway at Rochester in Kent. The seaplane, called the Mussel and built by Shorts Brothers at Rochester, had been used by Sir Alan Cobham on his 16,000 mile tour of Africa. Fitted with water rudders, it gave Britain the first world record in a new class created by the French-based *Fédération Aéronatique International* (FAI). Some technical details had to be sorted out before the record was attempted, which Lady Mary herself explained in an article for *Flight* magazine:

> The FAI regulations for light seaplanes, necessitate, according to the bulletin of the Aero Club, March 30, 1927, a total maximum weight of 400 kg, but they were kind enough to consider a proposition which I put directly to them in the summer of that year and they raised the weight to 500 kg.

The Mussel, fitted with a super-efficient Cirrus II engine, was even heavier at 530 kg, but Lady Mary opted to go ahead with her attempt anyway in the hope, she said, that it would inspire others to raise the record to 30,000 feet or higher.

With Sicele O'Brien as passenger, she took 1 hour 32 minutes to reach the record height. The time taken was not surprising, as seaplanes were bulkier and heavier than ordinary machines. That Lady Mary could manage one without any apparent difficulty, despite her fear of water was a tribute to her considerable ability as a pilot: 'The climb was not steady owing to some peculiar wind currents which, directly over Rochester and heading towards the north-west, gave no climb whatever,' she said in her *Flight* article. As the plane continued to ascend, the rate of climb slowed down

and it took about five minutes for each hundred feet after 13,000 feet. Given time, she felt the machine could have gone higher, perhaps to 1,500 feet, but owing to the thickness of the ink, the barograph ceased to record.

Almost every attempt at an altitude record at this time was shrouded in controversy. 'There are no really good barographs available at either the Royal Aero Club or any of the firms in this country,' Lady Mary wrote in frustration. 'It was a particularly lovely day; the higher up we went the clearer everything got, and we could see 30-40 miles with ease.' So thrilled with the flight was Sicele O'Brien that she stayed on at Rochester to learn how to fly one of these extraordinary machines.

By now, Lady Mary was again immersed in the various committees and societies organising aviation in England. In a letter to the Royal Aeronautical Society, dated 26 June 1928, she encloses a receipt for £2. For the luncheon given for 'Friendship' crew, including Amelia Earhart, she had distributed 900 copies of a special leaflet to the members of the Society at her own expense. She next became embroiled in a dispute over a lunch in honour of the aviator Sir George Wilkins. Wilkins, born in Australia and a superb aerial photographer, had made two unsuccessful attempts to fly across the North Pole before finally succeeding in 1928 with his pilot Carl Eielson. 'It is one of the biggest scandals of modern aviation that he should have been compelled to go outside this country for his backing for his record-making flight,' she said in the second of a series of letters to the Society, provoked by the fact that no notice had been sent to any of the women members of the three bodies giving the lunch to honour Wilkins, although all were licensed commercial pilots. These included Winifred Spooner of the London Aero Club and Sicele O'Brien, also a member of the Royal Engineering Society.

The reply agreed in broad terms with her argument, but made it clear that a formal letter should come from the general secretary of the Air League and not from a sub-committee, such as the one run by Lady Mary. The letter was written in a tone of scarcely concealed exasperation and, dripping with condescension, stated that women were as welcome as men in the society. The Society did have its better moments. Following her altitude record, Lady Mary received a congratulatory letter: 'The council are all the more glad to be able to congratulate you as you are the only woman pilot who is a technical member of the society,' it said.

[160]

In mid-July, she was an honoured guest at the English Women's Track and Field Championships held at Stamford Bridge, where the forthcoming Amsterdam Olympics cast a long shadow. The WAAA's decision not to send a team because of the restricted programme on offer had not won universal approval, but at least this competition gave the British women a chance to compete against some of the best women athletes in the world. Star of the show was Kinue Hitomi of Japan who competed in six events, equalling the world record in the 220 yards and winning Lady Mary's old event, the javelin.

Although it was the biggest day on the British aviation calendar, Lady Mary made only a brief appearance at Brooklands for the King's Cup, where Winifred Spooner's third place, the best ever result by a woman, saw her installed as the nation's latest female aviation darling. Since her flight over Africa, Lady Mary had become increasingly determined to find herself a job as a pilot with a commercial airline, preferably flying long-haul. In England, the first commercial flight to India was already being discussed[1], but when she approached Imperial Airways, she was rebuffed.

At the same time, Royal Dutch Airlines, or KLM, was planning a regular commercial flight to Jakarta, then called Batavia, the capital of Indonesia, which was still a Dutch colony; a charter flight, with J.B. Scholte as second pilot, had already been made. Hearing of the Waalhaven Aviation Festival, organised by Rotterdam Aero Club in conjunction with KLM, Lady Mary flew to the Netherlands in her new DH Moth, seizing the opportunity to combine pitching for a job with showing off her flying skills. Her arrival, with an unnamed secretary as passenger, was greeted with awe by the Dutch 'because a woman flying alone was a novelty for our country' reported *Het Vliegveld* (The Airfield), a specialist aviation magazine. An older woman tut-tutted: 'It should not be allowed to happen, a woman flying on her own.' A few hours later, Sicele O'Brien arrived with her passenger, Miss Leith, in another Moth; she, like Lady Mary, was prepared to miss out on the King's Cup for this opportunity. Over the two days of competition, Lady Mary finished first overall, with O'Brien seventh. In take-off and landing tests, she underlined her skill by clearing a string of flags placed three metres (10 feet) above the ground. There was also a 20 km (12.2 miles) speed test consisting of two laps of a triangular route, where she clocked 158 kph (98 mph).

The competition had begun with an altitude test, with the reporter from *Het Vliegveld* allowing himself to be piloted by a woman for the first time in his life when he agreed to accompany Lady Mary. All went well on the ascent, with Lady Mary 'following the ascending lines of the clouds perfectly'. Having climbed to 1,650 metres (5,414 feet), Lady Mary shouted a warning to her passenger and then turned

At the King's Cup in Brooklands on 26 July 1928; a stylish Lady Mary to the right. (Flight *Collection*)

the plane earthwards: '…suddenly the Moth made an aggressive sideways dive and we corkscrewed in the direction of the Moerdijk bridge, far beneath us over the Hollands Diep river. Next, the Moth straightened out, according to the book. We arrived back at Waalhaven intact.' A few minutes later, Lady Mary was back in the air to reconnoitre the course for the relay event and the speed contest: 'Flying low, the Moth jumped over farms and ditches for forty minutes. Madame's turns were impeccable…this British woman, when taking part in competitions, leaves nothing to chance, but prepares seriously and thoroughly.'

Watching the competition were some of the most eminent authorities in European aviation at the time. Sir Sefton Branker arrived during the second afternoon, while General Snijders, commander-in-chief of the Dutch Army in World War 1, made a short flight with Lady Mary. For her victory, she received a thousand guilders and the compliments of Albert Plesman, managing director of KLM and one of the founding fathers of Dutch aviation; Lady Mary not only won many prizes, but

Lady Mary with an unknown companion in a DH Moth at the King's Cup in Brooklands on 26 July 1928. (Flight *Collection*)

also many hearts, he said. Not everyone agreed; a column by Edgar Fuld, a member of the KLM board of directors, in the August 1929 issue of *Het Vliegveld*, begrudgingly praises Lady Mary, but worries about her influence on local women: '…one is in good hands with her and for KLM, it is nice publicity (for the Lady as well!)'. He hopes airline flying will not become fashionable with women: '…I love to see women participating with the men…. But there are things I would rather see a man doing than a woman, for instance, boxing and [commercial] airline flying.'

Three days later came an urgent request from the Air Ministry in London for her to renew both her A and B licences. Because Lady Mary had failed to fit in the mandatory medical test as requested, these had now lapsed; she clearly chaffed at having to undergo a medical test every three months. In reply, she proposed taking a test while in Rotterdam, where she had been awarded a Dutch commercial license, allowing her to act as a 'second pilot'.

Whether she would be allowed to fly to Batavia or not, she had by now persuaded

ABOVE: Beside her new DH Moth at Rotterdam. Her secretary is standing beside her; the other four people are unknown, though the two other women are probably Sicele O'Brien and her passenger, Miss Leith. (Flight *Collection*)

RIGHT: Trying out one of the small planes used by the Rotterdam Aero Club, with unidentifiable admirers looking on. (Flight *Collection*)

KLM to allow her fly the big Fokker planes on their European routes. On 27 July, she flew as second pilot on a Fokker Jupiter from Amsterdam to London, carrying eighteen passengers, and was photographed arriving at Croydon with J.B. Scholte, the pilot who was later to pioneer the first Irish 'air mail' service from Baldonnel to Berlin with Captain Paddy Armstrong. She told reporters that KLM was planning to expand its services to the Dutch colonies in the East Indies, and that initially, four Fokker planes would fly the route. When a fifth was proposed, Lady Mary was asked to join as second pilot; or so she claimed. In her attempt to persuade KLM that she was capable of handling a large plane, she spent the next few weeks carrying passengers all over Europe, flying several times each day and accumulating thirty hours experience.

She learned much and wrote about her experience in Air, the journal of the Air League: 'On some of my later journeys, the pilot, beyond ensuring that the landing and taking off should be as comfortable as possible for the passengers, did not touch the machine at all.' She observed that the passengers were always a priority on the Dutch flights, with the numbers suffering from airsickness counted after every journey. If this was too high, the pilot got a letter of advice and warning.

Piloting the bigger planes took practice: 'Coming in too high at Brussels

Wearing her leopard-skin coat and smoking one of her foul Turkish cigarettes, Lady Mary is surrounded by admirers in Rotterdam. On the extreme left is Frederick Koolhoven, the aircraft designer; third from left is Albert Plesman. (Flight *Collection*)

aerodrome one day, I attempted a very gentle side-slip to lose the speed of the machine. The controls were immediately taken over by the first pilot, who gave me an anguished look as the door between pilot and passengers were open.' Blind flying through cloud and fog she found wonderful but most difficult of all. The compass needle and the altimeter had to be watched carefully, which she discovered when she came out of cloud 11,000 feet too high and facing the wrong direction after attempting a gentle turn.

She was due to set off for Batavia on 11 October 1928. It was not to be. Some of the publicity she got was extraordinarily negative and underlined the deep prejudices facing the pioneering women pilots of the time. The eccentric C.G. Grey, editor of *Aeroplane*, was among the most vituperative. Reacting to the publicity surrounding 'a woman pilot' who had flown from Amsterdam to Croydon and her apparent statement that she hoped to fly one of the Imperial Airline Argosies, he feared that this may have given the impression that women might soon be employed piloting commercial airlines. He made his opinion quite clear. 'Few women would trust themselves in an air-line machine piloted by a woman,' he said, quoting Albert Plesman as stating that KLM would never employ women pilots. Neither would

Lady Mary with KLM managing director Albert Plesman, left, and aircraft designer and manufacturer, Frederick Koolman, right. (*Ed Nolte, Aviodrome Documentation Centre, Lelystad, the Netherlands*)

Imperial Airways nor any serious airline, since there was an assortment of physical reasons why women were unfitted to pilot airline machines. The 'woman concerned' perhaps might take part in a long-distance flight, with no passengers, he said, adding that the phrase 'second pilot' usually meant a mechanic who could hold the controls and give the pilot a rest. 'This paper is by no means hostile to women pilots as such but merely to the way in which publicity of an undesirable kind has been obtained,' he concluded.

The 1928 annual report of the KLM station managers at Schiphol airport puts it equally plainly: 'At the end of July and the beginning of August, Lady Heath made some flights as second pilot on the KLM lines; the public reacted in a negative fashion though.'

Lady Mary never flew to Batavia and was not to become the world's first official female commercial pilot; as was so often the case, she was ahead of her time and failed to anticipate the opposition she faced. But although it all turned sour, she was still the first woman to have flown a commercial aircraft and she held on to her KLM 'wings', displaying them with pride when she returned to Dublin in the 1930s. She had come very close indeed to flying full-time with a major airline and her life may well have turned out differently had she got the chance she deserved. But even today, less than one in a hundred commercial pilots are women.

AFTER EARHART

Two days after her flight from Rotterdam to London on 29 July, the track and field programme at Amsterdam Olympics began and there are reports that Lady Mary was there, despite the British women's boycott. Still involved with the FSFI, she was expected to officiate in Amsterdam, but when the British team withdrew, her name was removed from the list.

Unaware of this, she reportedly presented herself at the gate, after flying back to the Netherlands from her London base in the DH Moth. Her plan was to do whatever job she was given at the games and then attend the conference immediately afterwards. When refused entry, she found a unique method of pressing her case. After heading back to the airfield where she had left her plane, she returned by air and was soon seen circling the stadium. A note fluttered to the ground stating her intentions: 'I shall continue circling around until tickets of admission are left at the front office. When these arrangements are made, place coats in the shape of a cross in the centre of the stadium and I will immediately make a landing and come along.'

Tickets were hastily found and, persuaded not to land in the middle of the stadium by some means that is not recorded, Lady Mary shortly after returned to the stadium by car and took up her place in the stands. With no report in any of the local newspapers and nothing in the Olympic Committee report on the games, there is little corroborative evidence for this story, although it has become very much part of the Lady Mary legend. But much of what women did went without notice in those days and a report on the incident later appeared in F.A.M. Webster's book on women's athletics.

At the fifth congress of the FSFI, held after the games, the continuation of women's athletics as part of the Olympic Games schedule was top of the agenda. The motion to retain women's athletics was passed, but the request for a fuller programme rejected. Britain, along with Ireland, Canada, Finland, Hungary and Italy, later voted to abstain from the next games if the women's programme was not expanded.

Ireland, meanwhile, had gone aviation mad, particularly after Commandant (later Colonel) James Fitzmaurice's pioneering flight across the Atlantic the previous April when Lady Mary was still in Africa. While fighting in World War I, Fitzmaurice developed a keen interest in flying. By 1926, he was commanding officer of the Irish Air Corps and when offered a place on the proposed Atlantic flight by German aviators Herman Kohl and Gunther von Hunefeld, he jumped at the chance. On 12 April, a large crowd gathered at Baldonnel to see off the *Bremen,* including the President, W. T. Cosgrave. A day later, the Junkers monoplane landed on Greenly

Commandant James Fitzmaurice (centre) with Herman Kohl and Gunther von Hunefeld. *(Independent Newspapers)*

Island off Labrador, becoming the first plane to cross the Atlantic on the more difficult route from west to east.

During the following summer, in mid-August, the Irish Aero Club, largely instigated by Colonel Charles Russell, held its first meeting in Dublin, with some 100 members enrolling that night alone, a large number of them from the upper circles of Dublin life. Colonel Fitzmaurice presided and, along with Charles Russell, Oliver St John Gogarty, and Osmond Grattan Esmonde, was elected to look after the club's business. Soon after, the club bought an Avro Avian for £700; it was Ireland's first civil aircraft, with the registration number EI-AAA. Lady Mary's promotional work for A.V. Roe the previous year had not been in vain.

Just a week later, on 22 August, Lady Mary returned to Ireland for a fortnight's visit at the invitation of Gogarty, who described her as 'an intrepid, charming and accomplished daughter of the West'. With Molly McGovern as her passenger, she set off from Stag Lane in her DH Moth, leaving her husband to follow her by ferry. She flew north from London, preferring to cross the short channel of water from Scotland to Northern Ireland than risk the 56 miles of sea between Holyhead and Dublin.

At Blackpool, the pair called into the Lancashire School of Aviation at Woodford. The thick fog and drizzle made Lady Mary wary of crossing even the short distance from Stranraer to Aldergrove that evening, so they whiled away a couple of happy hours at Woodford before taking to the air again and setting course for Scotland. After crawling around the coast just above sea level at Stranraer, they finally landed on the side of what Lady Mary called 'a Scottish Alp' in an article she wrote about her Irish trip for *Flight*. Tying the Moth to the fence, they left it in wind and rain for the night.

The next morning, they made an uneventful flight to Belfast, where a new aero club signed up a hundred members during the week of their visit; just a month earlier, the first air races had been held in the province. Flying south, they passed Drogheda, and with the clouds as low as Lady Mary had ever seen, were forced to fly with wheels a few feet off the sea and the body of the plane touching cloud. Carefully they wound their way round the coast, passing the towns of Balbriggan, Skerries and Malahide before reaching the modest height of Howth Head, a few miles from Dublin. After being forced to skirt around the hill rather than fly over it, Lady Mary realised it would be impossible to get to the aerodrome at Baldonnel as planned. Instead, she landed on Dollymount strand, just north of Dublin's city centre, and then, seeking a sheltered spot, pulled the plane along the beach for a full half-mile with the wings folded, protecting the delicate tail with a contraption on wheels she called the 'Heath Patent Tailskid Trolley'.

By the next day, word had spread that the famous Lady Heath had arrived in town and aviation enthusiasts and dignitaries flocked to Dollymount to see her in action. By now the plane was stuck in the sand, and only after much digging could it be taxied into a suitable position for take-off. With Colonel Fitzmaurice clinging to a strut, the plane made it into the air; Lady Mary then landed again and before heading for Baldonnel, gave joyrides to thrilled members of the Irish Aero Club. Next morning, she set off to visit her Aunt Cis in Ballybunion. Travelling with her was an RAF pilot, J.S. Shepherd, whom she had agreed to drop off at his home in Rathangan, County Kildare, a village Lady Mary described bizarrely as 'nestling in the curve of the highlands'. When they arrived, she found that the largest field available was filled with haycocks and so she landed in a much smaller one, less than 200 yards wide and surrounded by high trees.

After taking to the air again and flying over the mountains of north Tipperary, she spied the lakes of the Shannon valley, with Lough Derg as beautiful as any Swiss lake as far as she was concerned. Shortly after, the high-tension cable of the Shannon power station warned her that she was approaching her native County Limerick. As she flew over it, the 'great city' of her childhood seemed to her to have shrunk. Using the Shannon estuary as a guide, she flew on to Foynes and Ballylongford until she

Lady Mary (centre back) on a flying visit to Ballybunion. Aunt Cis (with dog) is seated in front. *(Cussen Collection)*

reached Ballybunion: 'We played about in the air for a long time diving down on the long bathing beaches where, being Ireland, the sexes are separated, and there is a men's and a ladies' beach. High on the cliff, we found the world's most wonderful field, 600 yards every way, waiting for our landing.' Her 'very air-minded' Aunt Cis had let her house to Mr Reid, 'of Reid Turn Indicator fame', for the summer and the Reids and auntie arrived within ten minutes of her landing.

A few days later, she left Ballybunion, and heading north for the Clare coast, amused herself by flying low into Doon Bay, a beach surround by steep cliffs that was reserved for nuns. When she continued north by Slieve Elva to Galway, she could see the fish swimming in the clear blue waters below. Lady Mary had planned to land in Oranmore, where an aerodrome had operated since 1918, but when she spied the flat open space of South Park, just south of the city centre, she put down there. According to an account in the *Connacht Tribune*, Lady Mary thought she had landed on Galway Golf Course. She pronounced herself delighted with the Claddagh swamp where she had landed; with an investment of even £1,000, it could be made into an aerodrome for Galway, she said which on the west of the country, and with docks nearby, would form an ideal base for liners, seaplanes and aeroplanes, she declared.

Her arrival meant that an increasing stream of curious onlookers were arriving at

South Park to view her aircraft and at the request of the gardaí, Lady Mary took off again for Oranmore, carrying local man Willie Naughton as a passenger. At Oranmore she had to abort her first attempt at landing because of sheep on the runway, but after circling the aerodrome, made it down safely at the second attempt. The wings of her small plane were then folded and a garda assigned to look after it for the night.

The following morning, she set off to meet her husband at Renvyle in Connemara, the home of Oliver St John Gogarty: 'I sallied forth next morning to find somewhere to come down near Senator Gogarty's house, Renvyle, built on an island in the most westerly lake that Ireland owns [sic].'² Like many other visitors before and since, she found the high

Oliver St John Gogarty, photographed here as a young man, and Lady Mary had a mutual interest in aviation

purple peaks of Connemara almost too beautiful for description, while the shifting and sinister bogs made her reflect with appreciation on the historic transatlantic flight of Alcock and Brown just nine years earlier; what progress aviation had made since then. Flying over Clifden, she saw the very place they had landed, as well as the open space the Irish Air Force had used as a base when flying to help stranded French trawlers the previous winter.

Landing close to Senator Gogarty's house proved a problem, since all the fields were 'smallholdings of the impoverished Irish peasants' and, even with a stiff wind blowing in from the sea to act as a brake, she was not prepared to risk landing in any of them. So for the second time on her trip, she was forced to land on a beach, which she described as being 'in a curve of the bold headland of the extreme northeast'. Getting her small plane down safely, she half-taxied and half-pushed the machine up the steep slopes of the shore and fastened it down with sacks of stones tied to its wings and tail; later the tide was to rise within a metre and a half of the tail.

Lady Mary had struck up a friendship with Gogarty through their mutual interest in aviation. The surgeon and man of letters, although now over fifty, was constantly seeking outlets for his physical energy. Since returning to Ireland after some years in England, Gogarty had added flying to his long list of interests and had begun taking flying lessons at Baldonnel. Later, he would fly to England to perform operations. His literary friends were not immune to his new enthusiasm – W. B. Yeats and AE were both taken up for spins.

In Connemara, Lady Mary got a warm welcome from the senator and was reunited with her husband. After an enjoyable few days, Gogarty and Lady Mary decided to fly back to Dublin, with Sir James making the trip by car. Diverting off course, they decided to land at Tullabawn Strand for a swim, but discovered too late that the sand was wet. Once on the ground, the plane quickly started to sink and, the pair found themselves deep in seawater, she told an *Irish Independant* reporter:

> It was a pretty thrilling moment. Immediately the plane began to sink, Dr Oliver nobly said to me, 'You jump out and get clear first'. Fishermen rowed to our aid, ropes were obtained and after strenuous efforts, we got the plane clear and safe on a patch of solid strand 100 yards away. The only damage done was to the tip of the propeller where it stuck in the quicksand. I have left the plane in the charge of some kindly cottagers who promised to look after it for me and Dr Gogarty and I are motoring to Dublin tonight to get the tip of the propeller repaired. This is only a minor job. I shall then be able to take off again from the sands of Mweelrea.

Since she was reluctant to embark on a tedious ten-hour return trip to Dublin, some 170 miles distant, Lady Mary tried another option. She found a phone box and made a call to London: 'A long distance trunk call at 10pm from a remote box in Ireland woke the watch man at Stag Lane; DH had [the] spare propeller on Irish Mail at Euston at 8.30 the next morning and it was fitted within 24 hours. It was impossible to take off that night as sea fog covered the islands only 200 yards off. The next morning, we got back to Baldonnel.'

Gogarty used the incident as an opportunity to promote flying in Ireland, writing an enthusiastic article in the *Irish Independent*:

> By demonstrating how easily the beauty spots of the South-West and West coasts could be reached, Lady Heath has done a work of national importance. When she flew from the road-less and unreachable coast of Mayo, where the quicksand detained her, to Dublin in two hours without effort or fatigue, she became the pioneer of what must undoubtedly be a considerable factor in tourist development in Ireland – tours in light aeroplanes.

He quotes Lady Mary:

> To appreciate Galway properly, one must see it from the air. It was magnificent – the bay and the mountains. The day was one of the clearest on which I have ever been up and, by flying low, it was possible to see the rocks on the bottom of the sea.

Back in London, Lady Mary faced a hectic schedule. Of the 60 applicants for the

ABOVE: Lady Mary gets her plane moving again on Tullabawn Strand.

RIGHT: Examining the damaged propeller of her plane on Tullabawn Strand.

Heath Flying Scholarships, fifteen had been accepted. This figure was later reduced to six, with one going to the Irish Aero Club. Dates for her October lecture tour were announced, with visits to Bournemouth, Epsom, Newcastle, Folkestone, Southampton and Birmingham, as well as London, to take place in the space of a fortnight.

By October 1928, she knew she would not be flying to Indonesia with KLM as she had hoped. Though bitterly disappointed, she quickly formulated an alternative plan. She decided to accept an invitation to visit the USA and, before travelling, would make an attempt to regain the world altitude record. The previous July, Geoffrey de Havilland had soared to 21,000 feet in a DH Moth with his wife Louie as passenger; without her extra weight, he could possibly have gone higher. There was also an unofficial record of about 30,000 feet set by a Captain N. Lang in a big bombing plane just after World War I.

'It occurred to me that it might be quite amusing for me to try and beat this record in a Moth, solo and carefully streamlined, and so raise the British altitude record a little, although an international record could also be touched on,' she said. She made her opinion of the various planes she had flown quite clear:

> I am lucky at the moment in possessing the best light aeroplane I have ever flown. I have flown beautiful Avians and Avians which were not so good, lovely Moths and

Moths with none too good a performance, but by some happy combination of circumstances, a Moth bought from de Havilland last July, turned out to be the best that to my mind they have turned out. With a Mk II Cirrus engine, a passenger and a full load, it averaged 98.8 mph at Rotterdam around a triangular course and climbed like a scout to 5,000 feet in seven minutes, so I persuaded Messrs. Aircraft Disposal Company to take my machine in hand, loan me a Mk III Cirrus engine which had 10 extra hp, cover in my front cockpit, take off my jury struts and everything that might make extra weight and resistance and let me have a shot at the altitude record.

The morning of 4 October dawned brightly – 'the gods who have always been so good to me in flying were better to me than usual'. She and Harold Perrin, secretary of the Royal Aero Club, who was to be the official observer, then drove to Croydon 'armed with many barographs'. There, Captain Stack, test pilot at the Aircraft Disposal Company, was waiting with some last-minute advice, while she donned her furry boots and a thick coat. At 11.55 am, she took off 'with nose pointed to heaven' and took just eight minutes to climb to 10,000 feet and another seven minutes to reach 16,000 feet: 'As we circled and turned over Croydon with everything beneath us clear and brilliant, I could not help marvelling at the little aeroplane which, with a total weight of 805lb, could lift a big woman like me with all her kit so rapidly.'

Ever higher she went, with a private plane, which had taken off with her, now a tiny dot below. Soon she could see the French coast and was able to pick out towns. But while the visibility was exceptional to the east, it was less so to the west and north, although some green stretches were visible through the haze over London. In her tiny craft, the altimeter stopped working at 19,000 feet: 'Beyond that, I just had to guess; I estimated that I had got beyond 23,000 feet [7,000 metres] when the climbing became a little slow.' So high was she by then that frost formed on her goggles.

Now, at least five miles above the earth's surface, the engine of her small plane cut out. Her own account is phlegmatic: 'Here I boobed and managed to stop my engine by forgetting to close the altitude control with the throttle.' Fortunately, she remembered the advice of a Mr Brown from the Lancashire club, who had shown her how to restart an Avian with a Cirrus engine by diving at 200 mph and pulling up sharply. Keeping calm, she pointed the plane downwards and let it pick up speed; the engine duly fired, although spluttering from the cold.

Over an hour had passed while she ascended ever higher; it took just ten minutes after her engine had re-fired to descend. Unusually, she had no physical after-effects from her time at high altitude – she did not have to blow hard or try and clear her ears in any way and she put this down to her fast return to earth. Now came the problem of ratifying her record, since the two barographs did not agree. To the untrained observer, the one in the back of the plane appeared to register 26,000 feet, but because every altitude record had to be examined for temperature and pressure before it was accepted, the pilot herself was doubtful that this figure would pass close examination.

Both barographs were sent to the National Physical Laboratory where, after correction, one read 24,000 feet and the second just 19,000 feet. Despite this discrepancy, and somewhat inexplicably Lady Mary was given a new record height of 24,700 feet, higher even than the better reading. The figure caused an outcry, with Lady Mary's detractors accusing her of attempting to fake the record, although barographs were acknowledged to be exceptionally unreliable. The Royal Aeronautical Association announced that her record 'was entirely without justification', so possibly its observer, Harold Perrin, never a fan of the forthright Lady Mary, harboured doubts about the various readings. Lady Mary was philosophical and resolved to try again before sailing for the United States, or failing that, while she was over there.

CHAPTER 14

The New World

Her feat had made the front pages of the American newspapers and, a few days later, the announcement that she planned to visit the United States in December was greeted with great excitement. As a British Empire Air League delegate, she would attend the International Conference on Civil Aviation in Washington on 9 December and as the only woman delegate at the conference and later, on a country-wide lecture tour, hoped to interest American women in flying. One report said that Lady Mary would fly an Avro Avian biplane, equipped with the Handley Page slotted wings; in another account, it was a Gypsy Moth, powered with a new 4-cylinder-in-line air-cooled engine to be assembled at Hadley Field in New Jersey. Judging from later reports, she appears to have flown both planes while in the United States.

'I am embarking on a campaign to start a new British industry,' she declared at a farewell party held in London's Ladies Army and Navy Club. 'We lost our colonial car trade owing to the fact that we let other people slip in and sell cars in South Africa, Australia and all our colonies. Every nation has its speciality and in Great Britain, we have the best light aeroplanes in the world.' On her visit, she would meet female pilots such as Amelia Earhart and Ruth Nichols and hoped to help set up light aeroplane clubs.

Lady Mary set sail from Southampton on board the *Leviathan* on 2 November 1928. She had invited her husband to come with her but he had refused, for reasons that would become clear later on. Two planes from the Hampshire Air Club escorted the liner down Southampton water, with the pilots dropping flowers to Lady Mary as she stood on deck waving farewell. On arrival in New York a week later, she immediately made the headlines when customs officials seized and poured into the harbour a bottle of champagne she had brought with her to name her new DH Moth. Under the notorious Eighteenth Amendment, America was in the full fervour of Prohibition and all alcohol was banned. 'Now I shan't christen the plane at all. You see, there's a superstition among aviators that a plane without a name is luckier. I don't know why because I wanted to christen mine anyway,' said Lady Mary cheerfully.

In the afternoon, she made her first flight in the United States, a fifteen-minute 'flip' at Hadley Field in New Jersey that was widely reported. Reading her audience with her customary canniness, she made it clear to the Irish-loving Americans that she was Irish and not English, and said that she was in the USA because American women had contributed 'very wonderful work' towards the advancement of aviation. While the main reason for her visit was the International Conference on Civil Aviation in Washington, she hoped to give lectures and might make an attempt on her own altitude record during her stay, although her plans were not definite. One confirmed date was with President and Mrs Coolidge in Washington; C.V. Bob, a mining expert and aviation enthusiast, would fly her there in the Bellanca plane he had just bought from the celebrated if sometimes controversial pilot Commander Byrd.[1]

In early December, she arrived in Washington, where she was photographed wearing her cold-weather flying gear – a leather greatcoat and hat with ear-flaps – after a flight in a Curtiss Falcon, lent to her by the American Army Air Corps. She continued to make typically effusive statements:

> America is far in advance of England in many ways aerial, especially with regard to its airmail lines. America certainly excels there, while Holland and Germany are famous for their national transport systems, and England for light aeroplane development and use. I am primarily interested in commercial aviation and I am over here to learn what you can teach me, and in return for any new knowledge I acquire, I want to let American women know more about flying as a profession so more of them may have the intense pleasure I have experienced in the air.

Women would have to start taking aviation seriously: 'This is a business, a sport, a recreation – whatever you choose to term it – which does not permit of dilettantism. If women will only give to it the same concentrated and determined serious attention that men do, they will accomplish wonders in aviation. For there is no reason why women should not be as successful as men in this field.' Aviation, she believed, helped break down boundaries between nations and could be used to promote peace, happiness and prosperity all over the globe. It also gave hard-pressed urban men and women an outlet. In a revealing insight into her own love-affair with flying, she described how many a temperamental woman pilot, herself included, wanted nothing more than to soar skywards, away from the crowds and congestion of the city:

> How can I describe the splendid tonic effect of flying? To be up there alone, in the air, free and in space, is like being alone in a vast cathedral. There is something awe-inspiring and solemn about it. To fly is an adventure, and at the same moment a

time of spirit renewal and refreshment. At such times, I always climb out of my plane when I land feeling rested and soothed.

While Lady Mary was enjoying the attention and the accolades she was receiving in the United States, trouble was brewing for her in London where she had left a very unhappy husband. On 17 November 1928, a letter from Sir James appeared in a number of British newspapers, announcing that he would be taking the drastic action of repudiating her considerable debts:

> Hereby give notice that I expressly withdraw all and every authority which my wife Lady Sophia Catherine Mary Heath may have at any time, either expressly or by implication or otherwise acquired to contract for me or in my name or as my agent or in any way pledge my credit and that she has been since the 11th day of October 1927 (the day of our marriage) and still is in receipt of sufficient allowance from me for the purpose of providing herself with all sustainable necessaries and that I will not be responsible for her debts, whensoever or howsoever incurred, dated this 15th day of November 1928.

There is little doubt that Lady Mary had a weakness for high fashion and not much taste for the conventions of marriage; her first husband had found her spending and her independent habits equally difficult to control. But the publication of the letter was at best tactless and Lady Mary was deeply hurt. In a statement from New York, she emphasised that she was financially independent and that there was no question of a separation:

> Sir James has seen fit to commit a breach of etiquette by making public a matter which should be private. I am therefore reluctantly constrained to reply publicly. My husband's attitude is probably due to the fact that he is not aware of the courtesy and consideration which prevail in American business circles and of which I have had such happy experiences during the past week. Immediately upon receipt of my husband's action this morning, I deposited $1,000 [£200] with each house with which I am transacting business. This is a guarantee of good faith.

Clearly, this was a carefully coded message to her new American friends concerning her solvency. No where does she admit any responsibility for the problem: that she had left her husband to pay a large bill when apparently forbidden to pledge his credit. Sir James was later to defend himself:

> My wife is a marvellous creature, but what can a man say under the circumstances?

> She has a way of making the money fly as well as the machines, and I have been obliged to take action for her protection as well as my own. She says that I am making private matters public in saying I won't be responsible for her debts. But there is nothing private about owing money. If I allowed my credit to be pledged and I was unable to pay, the matter would soon be made public. I am a reasonable man and I told my wife that I would spend all my income to advance her career in flying, politics or almost anything else she might choose. No man could offer more than that. She considered that flying was her own independent business, and I allowed her five thousand a year for it. But as far as I knew, she never paid for anything, but sent all the bills to me.

Her first husband had complained that his wife, then with the excuse of youth, had seen husbands as little more than cash cows. Sir James seems to have experienced the same problem. Although she had often consulted him about her flying plans before they married, all that ceased once he became her husband: 'As a husband, I was not even allowed to know of Lady Heath's flying plans…. Politeness is essential between married couples and it is only common courtesy between human beings in any case, to allow those that will be affected by one's arrangements to become aware of one's plans.'

Lady Mary's American friends felt that Sir James was exaggerating just a little. Although he had promised that he would fully back her career, he balked at paying bills and described her flying as a 'hobby'. Nor did they consider her annual allowance of £5,000 particularly lavish.

The day the story broke, she was guest of honour at a luncheon given by Isaac Liberman, president of Arnold Constable and Company. Others attending the influential gathering included Mrs Clarence Chamberlain, wife of the transatlantic pilot who had followed Lindbergh across 'The Big Jump', and a number of journalists. 'The least said about such matters, the better, don't you think?' she replied when asked by a journalist for a comment on her husband's action. If she ever had any plans to return to Britain, she certainly shelved them now. Later her husband was to complain that she had not written him one letter while she was away.

For any ambitious aviator, the United States was the place to be during the 1920s. When Orville Wright staggered into the air for twelve seconds near Kitty Hawk, North Carolina, in September 1903, Americans took a while to understand that the Wright brothers' motor-powered, heavier-than-air flying machine was not another sophisticated balloon buoyed aloft by gas. Once they appreciated fully that it could move under its own power, their enthusiasm was unqualified, and thousands flocked to follow them into the air. It was an exhilarating period for the air-minded: anyone could attempt to fly at the start of the twentieth century, as Amelia Earhart points out in her 1932 book, *The Fun of It* : '…it wasn't really necessary to have any licence at this period. There were no regulations such as exist today. People just flew, when and if they could.'

Such a country inevitably exerted a magnetic attraction on a forceful and ambitious woman like Lady Mary. By the time she arrived in the United States in late 1928, she was a vastly experienced pilot, with more than 1,500 solo hours to her credit. She created a stir right from the start and her programme in the United States included talks to political groups, aviation clubs and social clubs, for which, presumably, she was paid. Late in November, she was speaking to the Philadelphia Congress, while a week later, she was in New York at a luncheon of the Eclectic Club at the Waldorf Hotel, paying tribute to Catherine Wright, Katherine Stinson and Ruth Nichols and other American female pilots; the British regarded Amelia Earhart as one of their own, Lady Mary claimed effusively, because she had landed in the United Kingdom with the 'Friendship'. During that month, she also spoke to the Amateur Athletic Union convention as vice president of the FSFI. The Redpath Chautauqua Circuit, an immensely popular touring lecture circuit that visited cities and towns in the United States over the summer, signed her up as one of their celebrity speakers and she also found time to make a 'talkie' film on flying, which was used by flying clubs to promote their activities.

Her high profile meant that she was consulted on all sorts of topics concerning women, among them athletics. Following an effort by Dr Frederick Rand Rogers, director of the New York State Department of Health and Physical Education, to bar women from the 1932 Olympic Games in Los Angeles, she spoke out on behalf of women, supporting the more progressive views of the Amateur Athletic Union in a speech to their annual congress which was widely reported.

On 1 December, her hectic schedule continued with a luncheon given by the National Women's Party at the Town Hall Club in New York. In proportion to its population, England was ahead of America when it came to women aviators, with twelve licensed pilots, compared to just twenty in the much vaster United States, she proclaimed. She left the luncheon early for the Long Island airfield at Curtiss Field[2] where she planned to make another attempt on the controversial altitude record. In the *Daily News,* the precocious 16-year-old pilot Elinor Smith had publicly challenged Lady Mary to an altitude contest: 'As we are the holders of separate altitude records in our own countries, I suggest an altitude race in any type of ship Lady Heath would care to use, provided, naturally, that I be furnished with one of exactly the same type and motor,' said the cheeky young pretender.

ABOVE: Lady Mary and an unknown gentleman during her travels around the USA.

RIGHT: Elinor Smith, the young aviator Lady Mary befriended.

After first soloing when aged just 15, Smith, the daughter of a vaudeville star, Tom Smith, had achieved some notoriety earlier that year when she had flown – illegally – under New York's four East River bridges in a tiny Waco machine.

Lady Mary had decided to ignore Smith and go it alone, but her initial attempt was postponed for a day because of low cloud. The following morning, she climbed into the cockpit warmly dressed and pointed the plane into a fresh north-easterly wind. She was soon climbing at a rate of 500 feet a minute and watchers on the ground saw her circling higher and higher. The hum of the engine was clearly audible even when she reached 10,000 feet, but then grew fainter and began to miss and stutter. When she knew she had a problem, Lady Mary pointed the nose downwards and made a perfect landing midfield. The altimeter indicated that she had reached a height of 19,300 feet and the barograph was sent to Washington to be checked. It was to be her last attempt at an altitude record.

After she had handed over the barograph and got warm again, she set off from Long Island for Hartford to lunch with Governor Trumbull of Connecticut; later she flew on to Boston. Through an old friend, the British pilot Bill Lancaster, and his companion Chubbie Miller, who the previous year had flown an Avian to Australia together, and her connection with the Aircraft Disposal Company in London, she had found herself a job. At the end of November, Lancaster, backed by a firm of New York bankers, had won a contract to manufacture the Cirrus engine in the United States and after the deal was confirmed, he was appointed chief test and demonstration pilot. Two demonstration Avro Avians, with the British-made engines, were bought by the American company and Lady Mary joined the fledgling enterprise, promoting the engines wherever she could, though her appointment was not made official until the following March.

In January 1929, Lady Mary had been planning to fly her DH Moth to an air meeting in Miami when the American Cirrus company decided Lancaster should travel also to show off the Avian. Lancaster's romance with Chubbie Miller was widely acknowledged by this stage, but for some reason, his wife, Kiki, had come to the United States from England to spend Christmas with her husband. Kiki struck up an immediate friendship with Lady Mary and the pair arranged to fly down to Miami from Washington together. A flight of such length by two women was a novelty and it got extensive press coverage.

The two planes left New York at midday on 2 January. Joining Lancaster in the Avian was Elinor Smith, who had already met Lady Mary by then. Although just six years younger than Smith's mother, Lady Mary seemed older to the young pilot, possibly because her hair had started to turn grey. She found her impressively regal in bearing and appearance, towering over most other women and not a few men. 'Though not a great beauty, her flawless complexion, commanding carriage and always impeccable wardrobe made her the centre of attention wherever she went,' Smith remembered.

After that first meeting, Lady Mary had insisted on taking the young daredevil to tea at the Garden City Hotel on Long Island, where she immediately created a stir by ordering high tea with fresh strawberries, whipped cream, tea with lemon and cream, and 'some of those little iced cakes over there'. The staff rose to the occasion and, with only a short delay, served the tea and even found some off-season strawberries.

Once she had confirmed that the young pilot was indeed as young as she claimed, Lady Mary proved a good friend to Smith. With their shared passion for every aspect of flying, they had a lot in common: 'Lady Mary and I were not intimate friends – there was too much of an age gap for that – but we were good friends, the kind you count on no matter what.'

Lady Mary talked the Canadian Avro Company into hiring Smith to demonstrate aircraft for visiting VIPs, arguing that if a 16-year-old could fly planes, anyone could.

The pair flew cross-country several times, always in separate planes, with the flight to Florida just one instance. She also supported her young friend in her battles with George Putnam, whose machinations on behalf of Amelia Earhart were making it difficult for any other women pilot to earn a living in the United States.[3]

Lady Mary liked to upbraid her young friend for her naïvely romantic approach to marriage and motherhood. For women, independence was not possible, she told her; it was 'all a mirage, my dear'. A woman aiming to make her way in the world needed a rich husband who could hire staff to handle the details of her career. She gently ridiculed Smith's wish for a family and children: since there were already too many people in this depressing world, why on earth would anyone wish to add to their number? Because of her recent spats with the British aviation establishment over her attempts to fly with KLM and her altitude record, and her troubled marriage, Lady Mary's jaundiced view of the world at that time was probably excusable.

Smith, like many other Americans, considered Lady Mary to be a member of the British nobility, largely because of her accent: 'It never occurred to me that Lady Mary wasn't blue blood, or at least as well-born as her titled husband.' According to Smith, Lady Mary would say that Sir James controlled all the coffee exports from South Africa, which was patently not true; she and Eliott-Lynn, her first husband, certainly grew coffee, but in East Africa. As for Sir James, his first wife had been South African, but there is no evidence that he had any major business interests in Africa. She seems either to have been the victim of Lady Mary's yarns or, looking back after half a century, to have mixed up some of her stories.

The young Elinor noted with admiration Lady Mary's ability to court publicity; for much of 1929, no newsworthy aviation story in the United States was complete without either a quote from or a picture of the 'British Lady Lindy'. More than to anyone else, Lady Mary seems to have revealed something of her true self to her young acolyte. Behind her well-cultivated 'feminine' image and the occasional bluster of her public statements, Lady Mary took her flying very seriously indeed, practising constantly and working hard on her skills, and Smith followed her example. 'We both knew that flying (in those days) was a skill that depended on time spent practising. Not that either of us ever admitted this publicly. It was just a shared and deeply guarded secret.'

In her book, Lady Mary had admitted that in aviation, 'many lives have been lost in the past' but added that 'there is no need to run foolish risks'. Despite her public statements that flying was a perfectly safe occupation, Smith felt that Lady Mary tacitly accepted the risks every pilot took and suspected that this outwardly self-assured woman might have been superstitious, although she was certainly not religious: 'A large pair of wings was always in evidence, either on her attire or even in her handbag, but she would never tell me whose they were or why they were always with her.' These were possibly the wings she received during her brief period with KLM when she was so tantalisingly close to becoming the world's first female commercial pilot.

Although she was one of the best pilots, male or female, of her era, Lady Mary had problems being accepted: 'She didn't seem to "fit" with the other ladies then flying. Her manner was as close to regal as you could get. It didn't bother me, probably because I'd been exposed as a child to theatrical figures with the same manufactured air of grandeur. I could always see the insecure person behind the cardboard façade,' said Elinor Smith.

On the trip to Miami, Lady Mary and Kiki Lancaster soon left the Avian of Lancaster and Smith behind, although a combination of headwinds and severe cold reduced their range and, with the engine forced to work harder than usual, they kept running out of fuel. The first time this happened, they came down in a farm; the owner obligingly fetched them some gasoline. At Washington, still in intense cold, it took four hours and much help from the US Navy to get the engine restarted. Later, after leaving Fayetteville, North Carolina, the thirsty DH Moth was yet again forced down. After setting off from Charleston on 4 January, they missed the flying field at Savannah and came down in a field of crops; this time, the farmer needed some mollifying before providing them with fuel.

When they finally landed in Jacksonville, Florida, in mid-afternoon, an awed crowd watched her every move: 'She made the wings fast in flying position, climbing around the plane like a great cat. She was clad in a colourful cretonne smock and wore high, soft leather boots.... She spun the propeller and started the engine herself while a score of men and boys stood open-mouthed in a semi-circles,' reported the *Jackonsville Journal*. At Daytona, they landed on the beach with the tide coming in rapidly and the wingtip only inches from a dune. Sympathetic onlookers rushed into town to get fuel while the sea crept ever closer to the plane. For Lady Mary, such panics were routine; her passenger, a flying novice, found the trip exhausting but exhilarating.

Lancaster caught up with them at various points on the journey and when they finally reached Florida, the two small planes joined 150 others at the air spectacular. Lady Mary's Moth won two races and was second in a third, while Lancaster gave

Chubbie Miller (centre) and Bill Lancaster right with an admirer.

demonstrations in the Avian. After they all returned to New York, Kiki sailed for home, leaving Lancaster to continue his ill-starred affair with Chubbie.[4]

Lancaster's salary with American Cirrus Engines Incorporated began at $500 a month and was soon raised to $800; Lady Mary was paid about the same and did well financially from her first few months in the United States, using her 'ladyship' to good effect. Elinor Smith remarked on her ability to make money, a gift that had not struck many of her earlier acquaintances. According to Smith, she 'pyramided' her funds and dabbled in British and Canadian aircraft stocks. Wherever she stayed, she looked for a suite with a telephone in the bathroom: 'One must be in touch with one's broker at all times, m'deah!'

By now she had begun a 3,000-mile tour of the continent, selling Cirrus engines and acting as her own mechanic. Her job as aeronautical advisor to American Cirrus Engines involved making test flights of American light planes, as well as selling engines to manufacturing companies such as the Great Lakes Company. The Cirrus Mark III engine, in production from 1929 at Belleville, New Jersey, was publicised as 'the world's most famous 4-cylinder in-line air-cooled engine, so simple in its design that it requires no greater skill for its maintenance than the ordinary automobile engine'. She was to claim that she sold a hundred engines, earning £10,000, that year.

She continued to court publicity and was quite happy to write articles for the aviation press whenever asked. In a January edition of *Aviation* magazine, her opinions on 'Short Distance Racing and Handicaps' were spelt out. Describing herself as one who had 'suffered' much from 'the loss of an odd second in short distance races', she admits that the handicapper is bound to be 'everyone's whipping post' and praised Goodman Crouch, the official Royal Aero Club handicapper, who was then visiting the United States: 'It has always amazed us racing pilots how he can ferret out our humble efforts in hoodwinking him….'

In late January, it was reported that Lady Mary had called at the Naturalisation Bureau in New York's Federal Court Building to apply for American citizenship. Although she had clearly given up on her marriage, this highly publicised move could have been a ruse to avoid visa problems. When told she might lose her title as a 'Lady' if she became an American, she replied that she could not lose it as long as her husband was alive; she did not care anyway whether she was called 'Mrs' or 'Lady' (clearly untrue) and claimed that she had decided during World War I to become American (unlikely). She would be eligible for citizenship after four years' residence, officials told her.

She continued to attract attention wherever she went. Elinor Smith remembers flying into Chicago with her on a bitterly cold winter's day, where a rush of photographers and reporters greeted them on landing. Smith was eager to escape into the warmth of the airport lounge, but Lady Mary was in no hurry, showing off her leopardskin coat and beret with a pirouette for a female reporter: 'It is smart isn't it? I shot it – in Kenya, you know,' she said, leaving the reporter speechless.

Around this period, she started to speculate about her family's origins and sent identical letters, dated 29 January 1929, to her Aunt Cis in Ballybunion and to a cousin, Jane Langford Glenville, living in Ardagh, County Limerick: 'I hate to be a nuisance to you, but I have found a genealogist in this country who has written a book on our family with its collateral branches, and I am anxious to compile for the next edition some account of our family. I wonder if I could trouble you to let me have some little account of the Peirces and the Evans for the last three or four generations if you know of their inter-marriages.' Revealingly, she does not enquire at all about her mother's roots.

In late January, she was among the honoured guests of the League of American Penwomen's New York branch at its aviation dinner. At this, she read a poem and gave her views on the safety of current aircraft. Accidents in aviation made 'good stories', but most accidents occurred in military or experimental planes, she said, ignoring the considerable number of accidents she herself had come across at air shows in Britain and elsewhere.

Although she had been flying aeroplanes since her arrival in the United States, she now faced a small problem – she was not licensed under American aviation laws. In early February, she reluctantly took an examination for a transport flier's licence at the Curtiss Field aerodrome. After she was failed because of her sketchy knowledge of American aviation traffic law and procedures, she immediately telegraphed the Department of Commerce, pointing out that she had 1,300 hours of flying experience and was the holder of an international pilot's licence recognised in thirty-six countries. She had not been told that if failed a test on American aviation regulations, her application would be deferred for a further three months. By then, she claimed, she would be attending an international aviation conference in Europe, which may or may not have been true. She asked permission to retake the examination immediately.

Her request kept the Air Regulations division of the Department busy for an entire day, division chief Edward P. Howard reported afterwards. They were conscious of Lady Heath's undoubted flying ability and recognised that she had failed the examination purely because of her ignorance of the American air traffic regulations. Meanwhile, the centre of the controversy was on her way to the Yale Junior Prom with Bill Lancaster. When they landed at Bethany Field after flying from Newark, she was questioned about the controversy: 'I feel foolish for flunking the Federal examination. I am not at all sore at Uncle Sam. I'm sore at myself for falling down on such simple questions. I feel boobish. I am going to try again tomorrow. Two questions I know I fell down on were how old must a person be before he or she applies for a licence and, after one fails an exam, how long must he or she wait to try again.' Her request to take the test again was granted and this time she made no mistakes. While she was at it, she passed a test qualifying as an aeroplane mechanic, the first woman to do so in the United States.

The New York Aviation Show was due to take place in Grand Central Station from 6 to 13 February, with Lady Mary joining many celebrated American pilots, such as Amelia Earhart and Clarence Chamberlain, in presenting prizes. At the show, forty aircraft manufacturers, as well as scores of engine and accessory makers, displayed their wares. Underlining the general attitude to women pilots, Lady Heath and Amelia Earhart were in charge of a booth dedicated to clothing for the well-dressed aviatrix and 'what milady has accomplished in the field of aeronautics'. The

Lady Mary is nominated for election as a fellow of the Royal Geographical Society.

American *Aviation* magazine criticised the show in its 16 February edition, commenting that some of the best-known companies were absent.

Elsewhere in the weekly magazine, Lady Mary praises the Aristocrat, 'America's finest small plane' in a special advertisement. A letter dated 19 December 1928 and addressed to G. McLean Gardner of the General Aeroplane Corporation in Buffalo, New York, is quoted. In the letter, 'Britain's Lady Lindy' describes how she flew to Toronto and back in a borrowed Aristocrat on 18 December, braving a snowstorm. She describes the monoplane's 'saloon car interior', fitting three people comfortably, and praises the low landing speed and lateral control at low speeds.

In February, she announced that she was settling in the United States; since

January, she had been giving her address as 112 Central Park South, New York. In a letter home, she told her Aunt Cis how she had met Rose Moyland from the post office in Newcastle West: 'Everywhere one goes in New York one finds the Irish accent. I may get you over eventually!' Although she admitted to working very hard to make ends meet, she had ordered her bank to send her aunt a pound a week: 'If I find that I am doing very well I may be able to make it a little more later on'. She was clearly in touch with all four aunts: 'I am sending the same amount to Auntie Lou, and do not think that Auntie Margaret or Auntie Effie need it.' She is delighted that her aunt is going to get 'a new little dog', and, later on in the letter, wishes she would get someone to live with her and asks how much that might cost. 'Loneliness is very bad,' she says baldly.

Life in the United States was treating her well, she reports: 'I am doing much better than I expected in this country. America has received me with open arms and is giving me a good livelihood in spite of my poor husband's efforts to trample me down.'

In March, she announced the formation of a new company called Aerial Activities, to represent all her activities and handle the American rights she held on foreign planes. Lady Mary was company president, with Arthur von Briesen Menken vice president and Gertrude M. Shreiber the secretary and treasurer.

Around the same time, P.J. Cox nominated her for election as a fellow of the Royal Geographical Society in London, with Maurice de Hansen as seconder, most likely at her own behest. In her application, she had described herself as an aeronautical expert and traveller, and made sure to append the initials ARCSc. I (Associate Royal College of Science for Ireland) and MRAe. S (Member Royal Aeronautical Society) to her name. She was duly elected on 18 March. It gave her one more set of initials for her letterhead; indeed she appears to have been using this even before her election was announced.

CHAPTER 15

The Women's Air Derby

ALL OVER North America that year, the aviation business was booming. In Canada, de Havilland had sold 28 DH Moths since March 1928 and the Canadian Vickers company at Montreal was also expanding. Cities from one side of the continent to the other were organising air shows, and Lady Mary made a point of attending most of them.

In March came the first hint of her association with the Great Lakes Aircraft Corporation, with Lady Mary photographed for *Aviation* in her trademark leopard-skin coat beside a small plane called 'Miss Great Lakes', the first commercial plane produced by the Cleveland-based corporation, until then best known for the Martin bomber. With a Cirrus engine capable of reaching 125 mph and a cruising speed of 110 mph, 'Miss Great Lakes' was a lot faster than the Moths and Avians Lady Mary generally flew.

Her role with Cirrus expanded after Bill Lancaster was involved in a disastrous accident. To publicise the reliability of the first American-built engine, Cirrus had ordered Lancaster to compete for a gold medal on offer for the first successful return flight from New York to Mexico City. Lancaster left New York on 4 March and, after a brief stop in Miami, carried on to Havana, Haiti, Puerto Rico, Guadeloupe, Martinique and Barbados. A month later, he was the first pilot to carry mail from Barbados to Trinidad, but on taking off from Port of Spain, he crashed badly. He was to spend three months in a Trinidad hospital, returning to New York by stretcher in late June. By then, he had lost his job with Cirrus, and Lady Mary was swiftly into the breach, describing herself to supporters, such as Elizabeth 'Queenie' McQueen of the Women's Aeronautic Association, as 'technical advisor and chief test pilot' with the company. Bill Lancaster remained a loyal friend for the rest of her stay in the USA.

In late May came news of the first ever Women's Air Derby, due to take place in August to coincide with the annual National Air Show, the biggest air show in the country. Starting from Santa Monica, California on 18 August and touching down in fifteen cities along the way, it would arrive in Cleveland in time for the show's

Lady Mary with Mrs Ulysses Grant McQueen.

opening eight days later. The race was the brainchild of Cliff Henderson, who had turned the National Air Races into the country's most spectacular aviation carnival. A gifted showman, Henderson had staged an International Aeronautics Exposition in conjunction with the National Air Races in Los Angeles the previous year. When this proved a huge success, he was asked to organise the entire event for 1929.

The women's derby had clearly been in the planning stages for some months, with Elizabeth McQueen delegated to approach suitably qualified women pilots and see if they were interested. In April, Lady Mary wrote an enthusiastic letter to Mrs McQueen from her New York address, signalling her intention to enter the Women's Air Derby. 'I think it sounds tremendous fun,' she says, asking for further details so that she could find a suitable machine. Above all, she wants to know if the race would be a handicap or a free-for-all; in a free-for-all, the smaller machines better suited to women aviators would have no chance of winning.

When Mrs McQueen wrote back, she invited Lady Mary to become president of the proposed International Aeronautic Association. The letter belatedly caught up with Lady Mary in Little Rock, Arkansas, a town she was visiting as part of her Cirrus sales tour. She replied on 16 May, fully endorsing the idea and offering to give Mrs

McQueen a list of influential women in aviation from Europe and the British Empire. She mentions, somewhat mysteriously, that 'when Detroit formed a national body', they had made her an honorary member. She had also been the guest 'of the Wichita branch' for almost a week, where June Harrison, 'a splendid little businesswoman', seemed to be the chief inspiration and 'worked closely with the industry'. Perhaps another women's organisation existed already?

Her views on the proposed Women's Air Derby had changed since her previous letter. She now thought it too ambitious a plan, 'and if there is the tiniest mishap, the papers will make such a scare of it'. She agrees with Mrs McQueen that entry should be limited: 'What I am very much afraid of is that some of our younger girls may be induced by large monetary considerations to fly unsound machines and so few of these splendid girls have enough experience behind them to choose for themselves.' She had already written to Cliff Henderson outlining her reservations. Certification by the Department of Commerce 'would rule out dangerous, experimental mortals or specially built racing freaks', she felt. Lady Mary said that she would be back in Wichita the next day for their annual dance and a few days' break; she would then head for Temple, Texas, and after that, California. There she hoped finally to meet Mrs McQueen.

By the end of May, Lady Mary was in Fort Worth, Texas. Between 20,000 and 30,000 spectators had gathered to welcome Reginald L. Robbins and James Kelly back to earth at Winburn Field municipal airfield after they had spent 172 hours 32 minutes 1 second in the air for a new world's endurance record. When they landed, Lady Mary was among the first to congratulate the crew, presenting them with a basket of flowers on behalf of herself and the Texas Aero Corporation. She had arrived at Fort Worth the previous Saturday morning and left for Temple later in the day, returning immediately when she heard that Kelly and Robbins were expected to land on the Sunday. She had taken just an hour to cover the 140 miles between Temple and Forth Worth in her small Avian. 'While Lady Mary is a member of the British peerage, she is also an ardent American. She would have it known that this country is to be her future home, she declared, after catching a glimpse of the glorious possibilities of this Nation,' reported the *Fort Worth Record* reverentially.

The hype surrounding the first woman's air race continued. Among the likely entries were Elinor Smith, Lady Heath, Thea Rasche and Blanche Noyes, while Chubbie Miller was trying to find a suitable machine. The winner would receive the 'Symbol of Flight' trophy from the Cleveland Pneumatic Tool Company and there would be a prize fund of $8,000. All airplanes and pilots entered had to check in at Clover Field early on 17 August for inspection, with final instructions a day later.

Lady Mary may have wangled herself some job with the organisation of the race and perhaps even the National Air Races, though Elinor Smith was doubtful, since she was working for Henderson herself and had been assured by him that she was the only female pilot signed to perform daily. Whatever her role, she somehow acquired official stationery and in a letter written on National Air Races notepaper in June to Mrs McQueen, thanks her for a book after apologising for not replying to a number of letters: 'You are familiar of course with the sorrow which has come to me, and I am sure your thoughtfulness in sending this book to me reflects your appreciation of the fact that my work here requires all the strength and help both physical and spiritual which it is possible to receive.' This presumably was a reference to her problems with her estranged husband.

After her earlier doubts, she was now a committed supporter of the Women's Air Derby: 'The race project this year really holds promise of being the air classic of the century in the truest sense of the word. Many things are happening which will make it stand out as the greatest drama of the aviation industry's progress and your help in bringing the nation to realise that women have their part in aviation is indeed significant.' She seemed to have decided that a mixed race would be a good idea, to judge from a letter sent to her by organiser Cliff Henderson: 'The committee discussed the matter of mixed races thoroughly during their meeting last evening and finally decided that it would not be advisable to have mixed races this year. However several new ladies' events were scheduled as a result, and I trust these events will be in line with your ideas on the subject.'

At the time, Lady Mary was working on the Redpath Chautauqua lecture circuit in the upper New York state area and had recently flown to Niagara, although there is no mention of her in the Institution's archives, nor in an archive of material relating to 4,546 performers (including Amelia Earhart) on the circuit. According to newspaper reports, her 'Chautauqua work' would take her to a different town every evening for eleven weeks. She was using a Great Lakes Trainer with a Cirrus III engine to get around, and carrying 200 pounds of luggage. She did her own mechanical work and used filling station gasoline to keep herself airborne. A book on the Chautauqua Circuit refers to her briefly: 'Mary Heath, who piloted her own aircraft from circuit engagement to circuit engagement, presented a lecture entitled the "Conquest of the Air".' The author does not give the date of the lecture.

Articles presenting her views continued to appear in numerous American newspapers and magazines. 'Women belong in aviation when they have the necessary strength, that is, when they have the mental and physical fitness for flying,' she told the author of one article, stressing that because of the speed of their machines, pilots must be at their best physically. She believed the best pilots were 'nervous': 'It is totally wrong to suppose that a pilot "without nerves" is the best. A pilot who does not recognise danger and take consequent care is bound to have accidents. The best pilot appears to be one who is distinctly "nervous" but whose nerves compel her always to jump in the right direction.'

Pilots also needed a good ear: 'Next to the eye, a keen ear is important to the woman pilot, for it enables her to tell the slightest change of note in the engine. By the sound, a pilot can tell whether her machine is climbing, gliding or side-slipping, no matter how little.' She reckoned that about three out of every four women were fit for flying lessons, though generations of domestic life had left women with 'less effective co-ordination'. Dressed in a smart grey sports frock and small grey beret to complement the colour of her 'steady and sure' eyes, Lady Mary clearly made a strong impression on this particular reporter: 'Lady Heath speaks in an unusually soft, well modulated tone. Her appeal is distinctly feminine, pleasingly in contrast with the newspaper impression she may have created with many because of her amazing prowess in the sports arena.' She is the ideal prototype of the modern woman 'who plays outdoor games, who rides, flies, swims; who does a man's mental or physical labour, perhaps, but who, outwardly at least, sacrifices nothing in the way of loveliness or personal charm'.

But Lady Mary, charmer of journalists and brilliant manipulator of the media though she was, had met her equal in the publisher George Putnam, who was ruthlessly sweeping aside all threats to Amelia Earhart's position as the female face of American aviation. When Lady Mary had arrived in New York, Earhart had gathered as many women pilots as possible to honour the woman who had been so kind to her just a few months earlier in London. At a special dinner party, Putnam questioned her closely about her plans, and, guilelessly, Lady Mary told him about her Chautauqua booking. Like other women pilots of the time, Lady Heath was to regret sharing her confidences. When she set off on her much-anticipated tour, accompanied by Bill Lancaster, who was still convalescing after his crash, she found that most of her engagements had been cancelled owing to 'lack of interest', with Amelia Earhart replacing her. Yet the American public was clamouring to honour Lady Mary for her flight from Cape Town to London and Bill Lancaster and Chubbie Miller for their historic odyssey from London to Australia.

Lancaster had experience of George Putnam's determination to see Earhart firmly established as the top woman pilot of the day. As her celebrity had increased, Earhart had started travelling with a secretary and press agent and so needed a larger plane than the Avian she had bought from Lady Mary. But because she was not yet experienced enough to pilot such a machine, Lancaster was hired as back-up. Publicly he was described as a 'mechanic' but he told Lady Mary that he flew the plane on most of these flights and had been sworn to secrecy.

In a conversation with Elinor Smith, Lady Mary revealed that she felt Putnam had engineered the cancellation of dates on her tour, but that because of her husband's disapproval of litigation, not to mention her ongoing marital problems, she could not sue. Whether this was true or not, her friendship with Earhart quickly cooled. Over the summer, Lady Mary made the best of it, continuing her lecture tour when she could and attempting to keep her name before the public as an outstanding pilot and campaigner for the rights of women pilots. In a July telegram to her secretary that was made public, she revealed that the FAI (*Fédération Aéronautique Internationale*) had agreed to recognise separate aviation records in endurance, speed and altitude categories for women. Presumably, she had been canvassing for this.

Towards the end of that month, she was due to arrive at the Hartwick Seminary as part of her Redpath Chautauqua tour, but overshot her mark, landing instead at the County Poorhouse in Cooperstown, New York. Those awaiting her at the seminary field jumped in their motorcars to follow her after they heard the plane go overhead. When they got to the poorhouse, they found Lady Mary happily chatting to the aged inhabitants, explaining some elementary aspects of aviation and promising to leave her plane with them until she resumed her tour the following day.

By then, the entire nation was talking of the Women's Air Derby. Confirmed as the opening event in the National Air Races, it would include two classes: one for heavier faster planes and one for smaller 'sport' types (110 hp or less). The race was to be supervised and its prizes financed by the National Exchange Clubs, a men's service club committed to aviation. Although Lady Mary had filed an entry for the race, in the end she opted out because her own plane was too light and too slow and she failed to find anyone prepared to sponsor her in something faster: 'Her "superior" attitude didn't always sit well with many people which was really too bad,' said Elinor Smith, also left without a plane. George Putnam's all-pervading influence could not be discounted, though he didn't manage to prevent the country's top two female pilots, Louise Thaden and Phoebe Omlie, from entering a race he desperately wanted Amelia Earhart to win.

A steady stream of stories on the Women's Air Derby continued to appear in the newspapers. With a month to go until the start, the organisers made it clear that men would not be permitted to fly as passengers in any plane entering the race; only women who had never flown solo would be allowed as passengers. The move was to discourage small-time Hollywood starlets and other publicity-seekers from teaming

A visit to the Lockheed factory in Burbank, California shortly before her near-fatal accident in Cleveland.

up with a male 'mechanic'. Pilots signing on had to prove their skill by producing an FAI licence and evidence of least a hundred hours of flying, half of that cross-country.

As late as 3 August, Lady Mary was still listed among the entries, along with Marvel Crossan, Ruth Elder, Louise Thaden, Bobbie Trout and Amelia Earhart. The build-up to the race and the National Air Show continued, with an Ohio Chamber of Commerce Goodwill Tour of 30 planes setting off to visit all the state's airports in early August. On 13 August, just before she headed for Cleveland, Lady Mary damaged the strut of her DH Moth while landing at Billings Fields near the Canadian border at Ogdensburg after flying in from Thousand Island Park nearby. She had escaped injury, but because of the strut cracking, the fabric was torn and she was forced to stay put until the plane was repaired.

On 18 August 1929, nineteen planes lined out for the start of the Women's Air Derby in Clover Field, Santa Monica. The ex-Ziegfeld Follies star and actor Will Rogers was compere. Befitting a man best known for his ability to talk while swinging a lasso, he kept the tone humorous, and the newspapers quickly followed his lead, dubbing the race 'the powder puff derby' and the women competitors as 'ladybirds', 'angels', 'sweethearts of the air' or even the 'flying flappers'. As Amelia Earhart commented acidly: 'We are still trying to get ourselves called just "pilots".' In fairness, Rogers himself was a staunch supporter of women in aviation: 'If flying is dangerous, pass a law and stop it. But don't divide our nation between a class that should fly and one that shouldn't. Aviation is not a fad, it's a necessity….'

The race provided mixed publicity for the women embarking on the 4,320-kilometre journey. Few members of the public believed that the women aviators were capable of such a long flight and their fears appeared justified when Marvel Crossan was killed; she had blacked out from carbon monoxide poisoning because of a fault in her plane; Louise Thaden had suffered from the same problem earlier. Others lost their way, ran out of fuel or were forced down with engine trouble. Blanche Noyes landed in a desolate and mosquito-infested area of Texas when she discovered that the baggage compartment of her plane was on fire. She brought the plane down without damaging it, put out the fire and took off again. Also in Texas, Pancho Barnes survived unscathed after overshooting a runway and ploughing into a parked car. There were calls for the race to be abandoned, especially after Crossan's death, but these were ignored and, after eight adventurous days, Louise Thaden was the first to cross the finish line in Cleveland, followed by Gladys O'Donnell and Amelia Earhart. Phoebe Omlie, a skilled pilot who ran a flying school with her husband in Memphis, won the light plane class. Of the nineteen women that started, sixteen finished.

The women's race was just one of a number of publicity-grabbing gimmicks introduced to the National Air Races programme that year. For the shorter races, there was a 'racehorse' start. Previously, planes had taken off one by one, but in Cleveland, they lined up fifteen metres apart in front of the grandstands, took off together and flew to a special scattering pylon. In all, there were 35 closed-course races scheduled, including five for women only,[1] as well as cross-country races from points all over the United States. In downtown Cleveland, the 1929 National Air Races and Aeronautical Exposition was launched in spectacular fashion, with a man in a tiger skin portraying Adam leading a cavalcade of marching units, bands and a hundred floats depicting the history of transportation, through the streets. In the sky, squadrons of wheeling aircraft battled for air space with sedate blimps. Over 80,000 citizens watched enthralled.

The centre of racing activity was nineteen kilometres away at the newly renovated Cleveland Airport. Cliff Henderson had asked Elinor Smith to do a daily radio spot during the races; she agreed because, like Lady Mary, she had failed to find a suitable plane for the air derby. With the women now safely home, the programme of closed-circuit races began.

Lady Mary had planned to compete in the first race for light aeroplanes and immediately got herself into trouble. When she discovered that she was the only experienced pilot entered, she pulled out, tactlessly telling a reporter that if she competed 'it wouldn't be fair to the other girls – they're all amateurs you see'. She had a point: like Thaden, Omlie and Smith, she was a professional pilot and had an unfair advantage over young women who flew simply because they could afford to. But she – or the journalist concerned – could have worded it better and the atmosphere was tense when she met a number of the other women pilots after she arrived at the airfield with Elinor Smith. Checking the start sheet, Lady Mary noticed that Phoebe Omlie, an excellent and much respected pilot, had signed on for the race. Now of course she would fly, proclaimed Lady Mary, flinging her arms around Omlie as soon as she saw her.

Immediately after the race started, Lady Mary, flying a Great Lakes trainer, went into the lead, shaving the first pylon with no more than an inch to spare. Her style attracted an admiring report in *Aviation* magazine:

> A conspicuous feature of the race was the flying of Lady Heath, who was seldom overshooting the pylon by more than twenty yards during any part of a turn. She was completing each turn, from passing the pylon at the finish of one leg to swinging around and passing it again straightened out for the next leg, in approximately four seconds, which only half a dozen or so of the male pilots were able to beat consistently. Some of the least experienced of her compatriots were using as much as twelve seconds for each turn, in itself enough to cost them 6 or 8 mph of average speed on a five-mile triangular course. Lady Heath, who, of course, had had very extended racing experience in handicap events in England, was banking about 60 degrees and diving steadily around the turn for a total loss of altitude of some 75 feet on each one. Mrs Omlie banked her Monocoupe only about 35 degrees and climbed into each turn and dove out of it, a method common to many of the pilots. Mrs Miller's turns were noticeably good, although not up to the standard of her British rival's.

Lady Mary seemed to have won the race easily, but when the figures were added up, it turned out that Phoebe Omlie in the Monocoupe had put in an average time of 111.63 mph, compared to Lady Mary's 95.7 mph. One of the judges insisted however that Omlie had failed to round a pylon early in the race and declared Lady Mary the winner. Lady Mary was adamant that she had seen Omlie go back to re-circle the missed pylon and this was substantiated by Chubbie Miller. Her sportsmanship may have lost her the race, but it went a long way to dissolving the resentment caused by the pre-race newspaper article.

Later, Elinor Smith asked Lady Mary about the incident. She had just started working for the Great Lakes Company and losing a race the very first day at Cleveland would hardly have impressed her new employers. Puffing one of her scented Turkish cigarettes, Lady Mary pointed out to her young colleague that since she planned on spending more time in the United States, she could not afford to make enemies among her sister pilots. She knew from the expressions of their faces when the pylon business came up that they were ready to hate her forever unless she did something to clear the air. She confessed that she had no idea whether Omlie had circled the pylon or not: 'Who looks back during a race for goodness sakes?' Smith marvelled at her ability to turn a tactless mistake to her advantage: 'One thing was for sure: when opportunity knocked on the door, Lady Mary was right there with her hand on the knob.'

Before that first race, Amelia Earhart had called a meeting of women pilots in her hotel suite, where she outlined a plan formulated by herself, Louise Thaden, Gladys O'Donnell and Phoebe Omlie, following on an idea put forward by Neva Paris. To commemorate the first ever women's derby, they would set up an organisation of women pilots, since it would be a shame to let the energy and enthusiasm generated by the derby dissipate. Everyone was on her side until she brought up the subject of equality with men in the free-for-all races with big racing purses. Lady Mary, along with Elinor Smith and Phoebe Omlie, objected to this on safety grounds, arguing that few women had experience of flying the larger, more powerful machines used in racing. These were popularly known as 'widow-makers' because their huge engines and small wings made them difficult to control and many fatal crashes had resulted. To expose themselves to this level of competition and its potential for disaster would do the image of women pilots no good.

The three got some support from other women and the discussion remained friendly. Out of that meeting came the Ninety-Nines Club, the first organisation of women pilots. Lady Mary would have little to do with it. By the time it was formally established, her aviation career was effectively finished.

CHAPTER 16

Crash-Landing

ON 29 AUGUST, the fifth day of the air races, Lady Mary dominated the headlines, but certainly not as she would have wished. At the worst possible moment, her luck had finally run out. 'Lady Mary Heath, Ireland's premier woman flyer and one of the world's greatest woman pilots, was near death at the Emergency Clinic Hospital, 928E 152nd Street from injuries suffered when her plane crashed through the roof of the Mills Company's factory at 965 Wayside road this afternoon,' said a local newspaper. The factory was located beside the flying field of the Great Lakes Aircraft Corporation.

Unconscious when taken from the plane, Lady Mary was rushed to the Emergency Clinic Hospital in Cleveland. She was not expected to live. At the hospital, Dr A.R. Miller said that an x-ray examination disclosed two fractures of the skull, a broken nose, a fractured jaw and other injuries. With Lady Mary when the plane crashed was Erwin Kirk, a 28-year-old mechanic. He escaped serious injuries by leaping from the plane to the roof of the building just after impact. He then jumped through the hole in the roof to help rescue the stricken Lady Heath. He lost a finger and broke his ankle, but was capable of walking from the scene.

The plane, a Cirrus-engined Great Lakes Trainer, was manufactured by the Great Lakes Aircraft Corporation of Cleveland and had been flown into the city earlier in the week by Bert Hassel, when he finished seventh in the Miami Beach to Cleveland derby race. That morning, Lady Mary had excused herself at breakfast to visit the Great Lakes Aircraft factory and, after arriving at the airfield, had made two flights before bringing Kirk with her on a third, perhaps because the engine was giving trouble and she needed his advice. After he climbed into the back seat, she took off from the short runway beside the factory.

She may have been practising a dead-stick landing, since at about 100 feet she attempted one of her trademark vertical 'side-slips' before the plane went into a nose dive. Although Lady Mary struggled frantically with the controls, the plane failed to straighten before crashing into the factory, its wings completely sheared off when it

A large crowd at the National Air Races in Cleveland.

burst through the heavy timbers. Several workmen had a lucky escape when she came crashing through the ceiling. Just moments earlier, they had been seated where the plane fell, taking a break from work. They immediately rushed to help, but had difficulty extricating Lady Mary from the wreckage since, unlike Kirk, she was securely strapped into the machine.

An eyewitness to the crash was Captain Daniel Glasser of Chicago, an auto parts salesman: 'I saw the plane make a sudden dive. It looked as though it would crash into a tall stack. It swerved away from the stack and then dropped through the roof of the building.' On the roof when the plane crashed was Joe Patrick. He said the plane appeared to be making a turn around the chimney when it plummeted to earth, hitting the roof less than eight metres from where he stood. C.F. van Sicklen, vice-president of the Great Lakes Corporation, promised an immediate investigation. 'We do not know what happened. It may be that Lady Heath pulled the stick the wrong way. She was practising dead-stick landings and was about to take part in the dead-stick landing contest,' he said. In such competitions, pilots cut the power of their machines and land as close as possible to a special mark. Despite her many public utterances on safety and care, Lady Heath was well known for her daredevil flying; it was this along with her ability to turn at speed that made her such a good racer, but it also increased the risk of an accident.

In later reports, it was suggested that while banking her plane to circle the chimney of the Mills factory, Lady Mary had come too close and hit one of the support wires attaching the chimney to the building. Most likely, she had failed to notice the chimneystack wires and crashed while attempting to avoid them. Elinor Smith was sceptical: 'She must have known about the smokestack – all had been avoiding it for the past week. Whether her attention wandered or the stack was blotted out by a wing, no-one knew….'

For the first couple of days, chances of saving Lady Mary's life appeared slim. A three-hour operation was required to remove a portion of the jawbone that had been forced upwards against her brain. There was a risk of spinal meningitis and a fear that she would lose her eyesight. But just a day after the crash, on 30 August, she regained consciousness. 'She withstood the operation well and is taking a liquid diet with apparent relish,' said the surgeon, Dr Elliott C. Cutler, in one bulletin. 'Sleeps most of the time, but responds when aroused and answers questions with yes or no,' he added. Her temperature was now at 100 degrees fahrenheit, her pulse 108 and her respiration 36. A number of other women pilots had already visited her in hospital.

Bill Lancaster immediately informed her husband of the accident by cablegram: 'Regret to inform you that Lady Heath seriously injured in airplane accident here this morning,' it said. When contacted later at his London home, Sir James said he had no news other than what he had read in the newspapers. Asked what he planned to do, Sir James replied: 'There is nothing I can do!'

Elinor Smith heard about her friend's accident the morning after a night on the town. When she came down for breakfast in her hotel, Deke Lynam, aviation editor of the *New York Times*, and another friend, the journalist C.B. Allen, gave her the bad news. The three immediately set off for the hospital by taxi, where they met Lancaster. While they sat in the hospital waiting room, Lancaster showed Smith the cable he had just received from Sir James saying that he had no plans to come to America at this time, even though his wife was close to death. The crash cast a pall over that afternoon's racing, but by next day, spectators were again thrilling to the feats of aces like Jimmy Doolittle and Al Williams. By then, Lady Mary was improving. Her temperature had dropped and she was resting comfortably and was capable of talking rationally. Her first words when she regained consciousness concerned the women who were to have competed against her in the dead-stick landing competition. This had been cancelled because of the accident.

A day later, medical reports were not so optimistic. 'Hope for Lady Heath less; is now only semi-conscious' was the headline on the *New York Times* report. She slipped in and out of consciousness for the next day or so, but was soon out of danger, though still very ill. Doctors doubted that she would ever fly again. There were reports of serious relapses in early September but these were later denied. As early as a week after her accident, she had been well enough to dictate a letter to Elinor Smith, thanking her for a bouquet of her favourite red roses and apologising for her late reply.

In mid-September, Lady Mary featured in the newspapers on an altogether different matter. Immigration authorities at the Greenwich hospital in Connecticut had arrested her former maid, twenty-year-old Kathleen O'Connor, who had come to the United States with Lady Mary but had deserted her the previous July. When she found work as a ward maid at Greenwich hospital, she neglected to tell the immigration authorities about her move. Nor had she said anything to Lady Mary, who had asked immigration to find her. O'Connor, described as blonde and pretty, was sent to Boston to await deportation to England and charged with overstaying her leave of six months.

Later in the month, a frantically worried Aunt Cis received a letter from Eliott C. Cutler at the Lakeside Hospital reporting on Lady Mary's condition: 'I am glad to drop you a line about Lady Mary Heath. She has made an excellent recovery. Everything is now healed and she gets out of bed today or tomorrow. Her damage is purely in the frontal lobe where she lost a considerable amount of brain. She sustained a compound, comminuted fracture of her skull and completely sheared off the face and both superior maxillae from the base of the skull.' He bluntly warned of possible side-effects: 'The only disability which might remain would be some loss of her intellectual capacity such as disposition, will power or qualities of one's psyche.'

Her aunt, Aphra 'Effie' Pepper, living in Canada at the time, had already written to Cis, seemingly in reply to a message, probably a telegram, from Ballybunion. Living just a day's journey away, she had been keeping in touch with the hospital and had herself received a telegram from Dr Cutler informing her that Lady Mary was greatly improved and that a complete recovery was expected 'unless something unusual happens'.

Although her aunt was confident she was getting the best of medical attention, and was determined to keep in touch, she wasn't so happy about the people surrounding her celebrated niece: 'I have no idea what all the rest of the world is doing about her as she is surrounded no doubt with her own sort of friends and I'm beyond their pale, but "blood is thicker than water" and she may be glad I am near when she is herself again. She will have to keep on terra firma now I fancy if she is spared and that will ease all our minds....'

In early October, Lady Mary was photographed at the Lakeside Hospital in a fur coat, along with a pilot's cap and glasses, something she normally never wore when photographers were about. The outlandish garb only exaggerated her self-consciousness and distress at her scarred appearance. She had been told that it would be six months before she could take any active exercise. A muscle in one eye was permanently damaged and not even plastic surgery could correct the disfigurement. A few weeks later, her chances of ever again earning a good living in the United States took a further battering when Wall Street crashed with devastating repercussions for the world economy over the next few years.

Since her marriage to Sir James Heath had now irretrievably broken down, money was again, as so often in her life, a primary concern for Lady Mary. At the end of October, she was recognised by reporters in Reno, Nevada, a long way from Baltimore. She had taken out a three-month lease on an apartment, but she refused to respond to her name when approached and would not confirm that she was there to petition for divorce under Nevada state laws, which required a residential qualification of just three months.

With terrible timing, the case of *Christobel Russell* v. *Sir James and Lady Heath* was heard in London's High Court, King's Division, before Mr Justice Talbot in late November. When she had been contacted about the forthcoming case, Lady Mary had allegedly replied, 'Don't sue me. Sue my husband. He is liable'. She was not represented in court.

The court heard that in October 1927 Mrs Eliott-Lynn married Sir James Heath and that soon after, they left for South Africa. Before they went, Lady Heath bought an evening dress from Christobel Russell, Court dressmakers, and when Sir James returned from South Africa in April 1928, he paid for that dress. Later in the year, Lady Heath ordered other items and paid £50 of the bill, with Sir James paying the balance of £20. In October 1928, Lady Heath had gone to Russell's shop on Curzon Street and bought two silver evening dresses, a black beaded evening gown, a taffeta gown, a brocade jumper, two scarves and a leather coat, for a total cost of £210. She had asked that the bill be sent to her husband but he refused to honour it. A month later, she left for the United States.

'It is now known that, at the time, the matrimonial relations between Lady Heath and her husband were considerably strained, but Mrs Russell was unaware of it until a day or two before Lady Heath left the country on November 4,' counsel told the court.

Mrs Christobel Russell, in evidence, said that she had met Lady Heath before her marriage for flying lessons: 'I think I went five times. I disliked it intensely.' She had dined with Sir James and Lady Heath once or twice but never noticed that relations between the two were anything other than friendly. Later, Lady Heath had told her that there was trouble between her and Sir James and that she was leaving for the United States.

Sir James's case, outlined by Mr Rayner Goddard, was that on marrying his wife he had set aside £20,000 for her, enough to provide an annual income of £925. Since her marriage, she had received over £2,000 extra; Sir James had paid the usual household bills and bought his wife a light aeroplane. When asked if she was earning a living from her flying, he replied that there was no question about that, since she was lecturing and giving lessons. Although her husband did not like this, 'she is not the sort of lady whom Sir James could easily control'.

Solicitor Eric Ernest Stammers, a trustee for Lady Heath's settlement, said that she had insisted that a formal settlement be signed before the marriage. Indeed, she had failed to turn up at the church on the original date fixed for the wedding because the settlement had yet to be finalised. He told of a meeting between Sir James and Lady Heath, with solicitors present, when Sir James had told his wife that she must make do with her settlement and no more. In October 1928, Lady Mary told Stammers that if Sir James agreed to a certain course of action (presumably if he cleared her debts), she would cancel her trip to the United States. If he did not agree, she would spend as much money as possible before clearing off. 'I'll sting the old swine,' he quoted her as saying.

Stammers told her that he would report the conversation to Sir James and would advise him to put a notice in the newspapers at once forbidding her to pledge his credit. Lady Heath replied that she did not care. The notice was delayed until 17 November, to prevent Lady Heath being held up by the American immigration authorities at Ellis Island, because, annoyed though he was, Sir James did not wish to stand in the way of his wife earning her living in America. Under cross-examination, Stammers said the trouble between the couple was not just financial. Explaining a payment sent to Lady Heath in the United States by the trustees in December, Mr Stammers said she had cabled for money.

In his evidence, Sir James said that his annual income after tax was about £7,000 at the time of his marriage and that it had since declined. He agreed that his marriage to Mrs Eliott-Lynn was his 'third venture in matrimony'. After he had returned to England from South Africa in April 1928, he paid bills for his wife totalling £1,000, including the cost of an aeroplane: 'These people were clamouring to be paid and I didn't want my wife's name messed about in connection with unpaid bills.'

Questioned about his wife's departure for America, Sir James said she had asked him to go with her; he had replied that he would think it over. About two days later, before he had made any decision, he saw her trunks in the hall. When asked whether or not his wife made money from aviation, his views on her activities were made clear. He believed she made some money from lecturing, he said, but did not think she earned anything by teaching pupils – at least he hoped not, since he would regard that as 'rather undignified'. Her flying he regarded not as a career but as a hobby.

Asked if it was true that his wife had paid his bridge debts for him and had been so hard up that she had to borrow from friends and servants to pay her lecture expenses, he denied both claims. On one occasion, however, she was going to Birmingham and sent round to a friend of his living in Berkeley Square to borrow 30 shillings. 'She did that on purpose to put me in the wrong,' he declared, before the case was adjourned for the day. The story made all the daily newspapers, with Lady Mary's alleged 'I'll sting the old swine' comment widely quoted. When telephoned in Reno about the sensational revelations heard in court, Lady Mary was reported to have fainted with shock.

The following day, judgment was found in favour of Sir James. Mr Justice Talbot said that the case turned solely on questions of fact. On whether or not Sir James had authorised his wife to buy the goods claimed for on his credit, he was of the opinion that he did not. Although he had paid Christobel Russell before, this was no reason to suppose that he would do so again. He gave judgment against Lady Heath for £239 8s, plus costs.

Already desperately trying to come to terms with the after-effects of her accident, Lady Mary was deeply affected by the case and uncharacteristically muted in her response. 'I have nothing to say,' she told journalists seeking her side of the story. Most unsettling was the 'vile expression' attributed to her. This, her nurse Florence Madden loyally affirmed, was totally at variance with her character. She asked that no attempts be made to interview Lady Mary until she had recovered her health.[1]

She was still in Reno at the start of December, when she dictated a short note to her Aunt Cis, addressed to 'Bally Bullion, County Cary' by the confused typist. In this, she thanked her aunt for her letter of a few weeks earlier and promised to write 'a nice long letter' as soon as she got time. As usual, she signed herself 'Baby'.

Whether or not she attended the first meeting of the Ninety-Nines at Curtiss Field is doubtful. Following the gathering after the Women's Air Derby, invitations to a

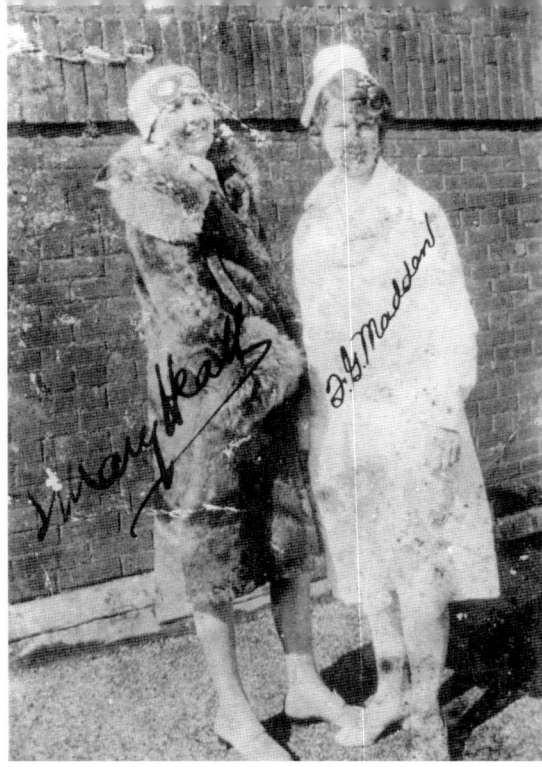

Lady Mary with her nurse, Florence Madden. *(Cussen Collection)*

meeting on 2 November at Curtiss Field were sent to 117 women pilots by Neva Paris. About 26 turned up, balancing tea and biscuits on a spare-parts wagon in a hangar and struggling to make themselves heard over the din of a Wright Whirlybird being taken apart in the background. First item on the agenda was the name of the new organisation, and after 'Gad Flies', 'Climbing Vines' and 'Bird Women' were dismissed, Amelia Earhart suggested calling the club after the number of its charter members. Affirmative replies rolled in from 76, then 86, 97 and, finally, 99 women pilots, with Lady Mary's name among them. So the organisation became the Ninety-Nines, with Neva Paris as temporary chairman and Louise Thaden as secretary until formal elections were held in 1931, when Earhart was elected president.

Lady Mary had written to Elinor Smith after her return to New York: 'They are sending me up to Boston for a bit of face changing. Who knows? I may come out of this looking like one of your film stars! I'll have to stay there a while – six weeks or more.' After Christmas, Smith took the train to Boston to visit her old mentor. Lady Mary was in a small private hospital and Smith was shocked by her appearance. One of her eyes was not focusing and it was obvious that her cheekbone had been shattered. She insisted that she was in 'absolutely superb' condition and that she could not wait to get flying again. The loyal Bill Lancaster was flying up every week to visit and other friends were concerned about her situation. A court case against the Great Lakes Corporation had started and she hoped to get some money from that.

When Lady Mary dozed off, her nurse told Smith that she was a lot weaker than she pretended and, to make matters worse, she was sleeping badly. They were giving her strong drugs to knock her out, but even if she got stronger, the plastic surgery was unlikely to do much for her appearance. Once again, she was penniless and the medical staff was worried about the effect of her private worries on her morale.

The following January, Lady Mary filed for divorce in Reno's district court, charging extreme cruelty. In her complaint, she had cited the difference in age, her husband being 75 and she less than 30 when they had married. Her husband, though extremely wealthy, was penurious and found fault with her expenditures. After authorising her to make purchases, he would repudiate them. In September 1928, he was ready to come with her to the United States, but backed out on the grounds that it was too expensive. Her aeroplane was in a hangar under her orders, but he still tried to sell it. As they had left the church following their wedding, her husband had told her that he had rewritten his will the day before, leaving her nothing. She also claimed that Sir James threatened to deny paternity if a child was born, contending that it was too expensive to bring up children.

Two months later, in March, it was announced that Lady Mary would receive her divorce a few days later. Sir James had accepted service of the divorce notice through the American Consul in London, with the answer filed though a Reno attorney. In early May, the legality of the divorce was questioned in London since the English courts did not generally recognise foreign divorces granted to citizens living in England, particularly when granted on grounds considered insufficient in Britain. Since the wife takes the husband's domicile, in this case England, lawyers argued that Lady Mary's divorce was unofficial and that neither she nor Sir James was entitled to marry again, in England at least.

Lady Mary's life took several bizarre twists as she attempted to come to terms with her dreadful accident and its consequences. In March 1930, she received $3,000 from the Workmen's Compensation Bureau in Jersey City in compensation for her accident. Since she was working for the Cirrus Motor Company based in New Jersey at the time of the accident, she had been entitled to petition the Bureau. The Cirrus company also agreed to pay $350 in legal fees and $500 towards her medical expenses.

Later that year, in late July, she was back in Cleveland and alleged to be mentally incompetent in an application by her nurse and companion, Florence Madden, to be appointed her guardian. The application revealed that Lady Mary had entered the Delhurst Sanitorium at Mentor, near Cleveland, a few days earlier for treatment. Staff said she was suffering from a nervous condition, which appeared to be a result of her accident; Elinor Smith had spoken of the desperation and depression her friend felt every time she looked in a mirror. She was no longer able to look after herself and her only means consisted of a trust fund from which she received an annual income of $3,500. Lady Mary may not have felt that was a lot but a companion on minimal wages might have thought otherwise.

Since her accident, she had developed a disturbing pattern of disappearing for days and sometimes weeks at a time. One day, Elinor Smith was surprised to hear her familiar tones at the end of the telephone line and asked her how she was keeping: 'Her cheery greeting of "Ma-h-velous m'deah, simply ma-h-velous" indicated to me that she was about to pick up just where we'd left off weeks ago and had no intention of disclosing where she'd been or what she'd been doing.' She did tell Smith that she was planning to marry again. 'Don't tell Willie [Bill Lancaster]. He doesn't approve – my age and all. Silly boy … one is never too old to be happy is one?'

In March 1931, she was back in the New York area and took her first flight since her accident at Curtiss Field. With John Trunk at the controls, she was in the air for half an hour and started to think of taking a refresher course. Her commercial pilot's licence had lapsed, but rather than re-take the rigorous exams, she opted to apply for a simple private licence. She duly passed her written and flight exams, but was denied the customary temporary licence from the Department of Commerce until her official licence came through because of a silly stunt. While waiting for Inspector George D. Ream to return from his office, she had taken a plane up at the request of a few photographers, just clearing the school hangar where the Department of Commerce offices were located, and zooming over the heads of cameraman. For this 'dangerous and foolish' act, she was brought before Sanford L. Willits, the district supervisor, and was told to return the following day. Although she would then be granted her licence, she would be 'grounded' for fifteen days.

About a week later, also at Curtiss Field, Reginald 'Jack' Williams, secretary to Lady Mary, made his first solo flight after little more than an hour of dual instruction. Williams, in a Curtiss Fledgling, flew for eleven minutes and made three perfect landings, said instructor John Trunk. He had taken only two lessons, one a week before and one earlier that same day.

George Anthony Reginald Williams, a small, handsome man born to a wealthy family on the Caribbean island of St Lucia, and usually called either 'Reggie' or 'Jack', was already secretly engaged to Lady Mary and would become her third husband. They had met at a horse show somewhere in the United States, she would tell young admirers at Kildonan a few years later. Williams was a keen horseman, and while competing in a show-jumping competition, his horse was startled by the movements of a woman in a red dress. After losing the top prize, he made his way in a fury towards the woman who had spoiled his chances. It was Lady Mary.

A few weeks later, Lady Mary was back in trouble when she failed to appear in magistrate's court in Windsor, Ontario, to face trial on a charge of drunkenness, which sadly was to become the first of many in the years to come. She had spoken at two meetings the previous night, one at the YMCA and the second a private dinner. Later, two policemen came across a traffic-jam at a busy junction, caused by a car blocking the road. In the car, they found Lady Mary intoxicated and quarrelling loudly with her secretary, Reginald Williams. Both were arrested.

Booked by the police as Mary Heath, she had spent six hours the previous night on a narrow wooden bench in the local jail before being released on bond of $16.50. Williams was released without charge.

When Lady Mary neglected to show up in court the following morning, Magistrate D.M. Brodie took brief testimony. 'She was in a very drunken condition,' testified Constable Alfred Carter, one of the arresting officers. The fine and costs were entered against her. When found by police at her hotel, Lady Mary pleaded ignorance: because she had paid the $16.50, she had thought the incident closed.

Dressed in bright green pyjamas, Lady Mary received reporters in her hotel later that day: 'I had been to a little party before the scene occurred, but all I had to drink was two glasses of beer and a glass of whiskey'. For 'chivalrous reasons', she refused to divulge her host's name. 'Honour bright, I wasn't drunk. Why, I wasn't even cheery. It is just a mean dirty old trick.' When she and Williams left the party, it was raining: 'Reginald was driving and I leaned over to turn on the windshield wiper. As I did so, my arm caught and that's what caused the trouble.'

Lady Mary rolled up her sleeve to display two bruises on her left forearm, caused when her arm got caught; Williams confirmed her story. A couple of days later, she retained a counsel to investigate the circumstances of her arrest. She hoped to reopen the case and possibly appeal it.

She continued to write for magazines and later that year was pleading for more airports to be opened in an article on 'Woman and Her Place in Aviation' published in the *Washington Post*. She described a frightening experience when she and a mechanic called Davis had got caught in a storm while airborne. After leaving Cincinnati, they were nearing the Indiana-Illinois border when the sky ahead turned black. Headwinds were slowing the plane dangerously, while forked lightning 'warned us to stop, look and listen!' They landed safely in a field and Davis jumped out of the cockpit, while Lady Mary turned the tiny craft in the direction of some nearby haystacks. Just then, they were hit by a huge gust of wind that lifted the plane out of Davis's grasp: 'We were lifted aloft like nothing more than a bit of fluttering paper. Twenty feet we rose, straight into the air.' When the plane hit ground again, the tail snapped off and the machine flipped over, with Lady Mary huddled in the cockpit, holding on for grim life. Since the aeroplane was badly damaged, said Lady Mary, she and her mechanic were forced to hitch a ride in a truck to the nearby town of Terre Haute.

Had there been an airport nearby, she argued, she would have been spared this forced landing. Every city and town should have an airport: 'In this great country of nearly three-million square miles, there are scarcely a thousand airfields in fair-to-good condition'. She felt there should be an airport 'every five miles along the airways'.

After her Reno divorce, Lady Mary became Mrs G.A.R. Williams in November 1931, but not without difficulty. Sir James Heath was vigorously contesting her divorce through the London courts and refused to accept the Reno decision. In Lexington, where the couple were staying, two local parsons refused to conduct the ceremony because they disapproved of remarriage for divorced people. Eventually, a Baptist pastor agreed to marry the pair. 'This is the first time I've married a younger man,' said the new bride. She gave her age as 34 and that of Mr Williams as 33; in fact, she was a year older and he a year younger.[2] The state governor of Kentucky was among the guests at the reception. The couple set off on honeymoon, and when they arrived in Mexico City by car in mid-December, visited the wife of President Ortiz Rubio, who promised them the use of a military plane during their stay. Lady Mary continued to be treated like a celebrity and became the second woman to be granted a Mexican flying licence.

Whether or not she loved her new husband was open to question. Elinor Smith certainly thought not: 'I'm not sure at all she ever knew what real love was all about. I think her feelings for this man were based on his promises to take care of her. He had already been supportive when her drinking got out of hand.' Certainly she was never to drop her title, remaining 'Lady Mary' to the end of her short life, despite many protestations that it meant nothing to her. While on honeymoon, the pair made the news when they sportingly promised to help China in its battle with Japan. After invading Manchuria in November 1929, Japan had captured Shanghai in January 1931. Since there was a substantial foreign population in the city, troops were sent by the United States of America, Great Britain, Italy and France to protect their citizens and Lady Mary (or the reporter quoting her) clearly felt her piloting skills might be of some use, though it is unlikely the Chinese ever formally received her offer, which smacked of a desperate need for attention.

She was still president of the Women's International Association of Aeronautics and in January 1932 wrote to Elizabeth McQueen from Mexico with the news that a Mexican branch had been established 'with some of the finest, richest people in it'. The local aero club had become involved, along with two local aeronautic companies: 'We have formed quite a strong body of "compañeros" of the men who can push their wives on to help, and we have roped in a number of very able American women who live in the city to help.' She was not entirely impressed by the local women: 'Quite frankly, the Mexican women are extremely slack in anything in which Push and Go are needed.'

Nonetheless, Señora Ortiz Rubio, the President's wife, had agreed to become a patron of the new association. 'General Escarette's wife is becoming president and we have other big names roped in,' she added. These included Señora Robinson, the late President Calle's daughter; Señora Acosta, the American wife of a Mexican general, who volunteered to chair the entertainment committee, and Major Farrell the man in charge of civil aviation locally. She also sent a letter to the association's secretary, Edith Weir, asking for an association badge to replace one she had lost, preferably in the form of a bracelet since the previous version had fallen off so often.

With her reputation still intact in the United States, an article she had written on 'Why I believe Women Pilots Can't Fly the Atlantic' appeared in *Liberty* magazine on 21 May 1932. Even during her own Cape to London flight, she had disliked flying over water and believed it should be done only in a seaplane. In a note sent with the article, she wrote: '…do make an appeal if you can for women not to fly the Atlantic, even if you can't use my scribble. It is madness for them to attempt it and at least the first dozen will be drowned.' The article was remarkably patronising. 'Four woman plan and really hope to fly the big pond this summer unchaperoned. It is plain suicide for any woman today,' she began. She proposed a test: 'Lay out a course between New York and Los Angeles, some 2,500 miles. Some fine day (when bad weather is due), load a good ship with all the gas she will carry. Put a good man pilot in the rear cockpit, with orders not to take the stick except to save the ship from cracking up.'

The pilot should take off and, after a 100 miles or so to get settled, should have her cockpit blacked out. With no visual aids from her surroundings, the pilot would have to work out her course and compute her fuel consumption, using only compasses, air-speed and turn-and-back indicators, altimeter, tachometer, gauges, thermometers, artificial horizon and radio beacon, if any. No woman and few men could land a plane under such conditions within 100 miles of Los Angeles, Lady

Mary contended. Add in 'impossible ocean weather', and the difficulties of flying the Atlantic became apparent. Of the seven women who had attempted an Atlantic crossing, only one had made it 'and she did no piloting'.

Lady Mary was sadly unaware of that particular woman's plans and, with catastrophic timing, her article was printed on the very day Amelia Earhart set off on her historic flight across the Atlantic. Less than fifteen hours later she would land in a County Derry field and, almost instantly, become a twentieth century icon. Because of her almost pathological fear of flying over water, Lady Mary had got it badly wrong.

CHAPTER 17

Back in Ireland

In July 1932 in London, Sir James Heath was granted a decree nisi from his wife, Lady Mary, on the grounds of her adultery with Reginald Williams. No defence was offered.

By then in his 80s, he took a fourth wife in 1935. She was Dorothy Mary Hodgson, a scientist from Hampshire, and when they married there was a congratulatory telegram 'from the first Mary to the second'.

After her dreadful accident, Lady Mary had decided to leave the United States, where, with aviation in a slump because of the Great Depression, she could no longer earn a living. Somewhat surprisingly, she opted to return not to Britain, where she had made her name, but to the calmer backwaters of Ireland. By then her native country had a well-founded reputation as a launching pad for some of the great aviation adventures of the early twentieth century and the contribution to flying made by the country's citizens, many of them personal friends.

Lady Mary had returned to Ireland in the summer of 1932 and, in mid-August, was photographed at Portmarnock strand, near Dublin, when Jim Mollison set off for the United States in a DH 80A Puss Moth, 'The Heart's Content'. Though dressed smartly, she looked heavier than in the past and a hat was pulled down over her eyes. Standing beside her was Mollison's new wife, the even more celebrated aviator, Amy Johnson, with her sister Molly.

A month later, Lady Mary went through a second marriage ceremony with Reginald Williams at the registry office in Tralee, with their address given as care of Miss Peirce, Ballybunion. On the wedding certificate, he is described as a 32-year-old bachelor, a pilot by profession, and son of the Honourable George Williams, retired. She, Sophia Mary Heath (otherwise Peirce-Evans), a 34-year-old divorcee, gives no profession. She had pared a year off her age; in 1932, she was just a month off 36. Aunt Cis was one of the witnesses to the wedding, along with Kate Flynn, her maid. The registrar, William H. Giles, performed the brief ceremony. Afterwards, the pair settled in Dublin, and, according to one report, bought a butcher's shop in Finglas, although there is no firm evidence for this. She was to spend a lot of time flitting

Lady Mary (left) along with Amy Johnson (centre) and her sister Molly (right) watch Amy's husband Jim Mollison take off for the USA from Velvet Strand, Portmarnock watched by an *Irish Times* journalist. *(D.M. MacCarron Collection)*

between England and Ireland for the next few years, unable to abandon her gypsy-like existence.

A valid reason for her frequent trips across the Irish Sea was the problem Lady Mary was having renewing her British pilot's licence. In February 1933, she had visited the Air Ministry in London, wanting to know whether she could re-qualify for a 'B' or commercial licence by simply taking a medical examination and carrying out flying tests. She seemed reluctant to undergo the technical examinations. Lady Mary told officials at the Ministry that she had not held a commercial licence for the previous two years, although she had qualified for both Mexican and US licences. She had also undergone a medical examination in Dublin the previous autumn. In her application, from a London address, she stated that she had flown about seventy hours over the past two years, approximately fifty of them since April 1931. In the previous six months, she had flown about fifteen hours, and held an Irish private pilot's licence.

The authorities were not impressed. Her last technical examinations dated back to 1926 and therefore fresh examinations were necessary, although she would be

Marriage certificate of Lady Mary and G.A.R. Williams

excused some of the flying tests: 'We are aware that she has carried out a fair deal of flying in America since the licence lapsed'.

There were further problems when it came to her medical examination and, at a test dated 15 March 1933, she was found to be 'temporarily unfit', although she could apply to be re-examined in three months' time. The reasons were unexplained; according to a distraught letter she immediately wrote to Colonel Shelmerdine, the Director of Civil Aviation, she was given a clear bill of health by all the doctors, including a brain specialist, who said that the effects of her accident were entirely gone. But when it came to the granting of the licence, the president of the examining committee turned her down. She begged Colonel Shelmerdine for an immediate interview: 'Can my country do nothing more for me, who has worked so hard and given so much to the cause of aviation?'

Following her request, she was granted an appointment a few days later, showing that she still had some friends in high places. What resulted is not entirely clear, but by June, Lady Mary was back in Ireland and was flying under an Irish commercial licence. She wrote again to Colonel Shelmerdine requesting another medical examination: 'At the moment, I am assistant manager to Iona National Airways Ltd and am their only B licensed pilot. I have a great deal of instruction, joyriding, and charter work to do and am kept pretty busy'.

She admits that, at her previous medical examination, she had been warned that her blood pressure was high but that this was now back to normal for a woman of her age. 'I have the offer of two jobs in England now, and I very much hope that you will please

Lady Mary and her husband Jack Williams with the greyhound presented to them by Ballybunion breeder Jim Clarke. *(Cussen Collection)*

help the first woman in the world who got a B in England to retain it', she pleads.

Lady Mary's appeal was not in vain and she was given a July date for her test. Whatever was going on in her life at the time, she then scribbled a note to Colonel Shelmerdine asking to defer this. By August, it was clear that she wanted the British authorities to validate her Irish licence without the need to take further tests, a request that was refused until she passed a medical examination.

While all this was going on, she was kept busy in Ireland. In April 1933, she received an invitation from her old friend Oliver St John Gogarty to visit him at his home in Renvyle, Connemara, which had reopened as a hotel in 1930. With the news of the impending closure of the Galway to Clifden railway, Gogarty had revived his long-held plan to establish an air link from Dublin to Connemara. Lady Mary arrived with her husband Jack Williams in one of Iona Airway's DH Gypsy Moths to carry out a survey of possible sites for an airstrip. They stayed overnight in the hotel and gardaí were sent from Letterfrack to provide overnight security for the aircraft. Over the next few months, minor levelling work was carried out on a strip of land near the sea and Lord de Ramsey, who lived in nearby Ballyconneely, announced his plan to start a weekly air service from Dublin to Renvyle. Although a few private aircraft did land on the strip, the grandiose plan for a regular service came to nothing and the site is now part of the hotel golf course.[1]

Helen Allott, a distant cousin on the Locke side of the family (her father was a third cousin of Lady Mary's), was a child when her famous relative returned to Ireland: 'I was fascinated by her and always felt she was so glamorous. She put my hand on her head one day and said, "There is nothing between it and my brain but a bit of tin". I also met her husband and he was very nice and good to her. She seemed to me to be tall and beautifully dressed and very vivacious compared to the usual attenders at tea parties.'

Lady Mary had returned to Ireland at a time when civil aviation was in its infancy. Before Iona National Air Taxis was founded in 1930, only three private aircraft carried Irish registration marks, no commercial airline existed and the few aircraft operated by the Irish Army Air Force were rarely seen by the local population. Abroad, by comparison, Imperial Airways was setting up routes all over the British Empire, Air France and KLM were flying to the Far East, while Lufthansa and Swiss Air were establishing European networks. In the USA, air mail pilots were bringing aviation to every large town on the continent.

In Ireland, the only aerodrome was at Baldonnel, an old British base to the west of Dublin, evacuated in February 1922 and left almost derelict for the fledgling Irish army that took over. Inadequate though it was, and plagued by grazing sheep, Baldonnel continued to play a pivotal role in Irish aviation for the next decade, since all aircraft coming into the country had to land there to clear customs. Attempts to interest the government in this new form of transport were in vain, with even Colonel Charles Russell's groundbreaking mail flights from Galway to London and later Galway to Berlin largely ignored.

In November 1930, Ireland belatedly introduced its own registration scheme for pilots, with the country's first two Class A licences issued to Dr George Pepper of Dublin and James Milo St John 'Bill' Kearney, an instructor with the Irish Aero Club; in July 1931, the third went to Paddy Saul, navigator on Sir Charles Kingsford Smith's transatlantic flight from Portmarnock a year earlier. Learning to fly was not prohibitively expensive for Aero Club members. Annual membership cost £5, with instruction 30 shillings (£1.50) an hour and a solo trip five shillings (25p). With an average of fifteen flying hours required, a club member could acquire a licence for little more than £20.

An enthusiastic member of the club was Hugh Cahill, owner of the Iona garage at Cross Gun's Bridge in the northside Dublin suburb of Drumcondra. Convinced of the need for a commercial air service in Ireland, he visited the Desoutter aircraft factory at Croydon near London in 1930 with fellow club member J.C. Malone. There he bought a Desoutter Mark II, which was registered as EI-AAD. With 'Iona National Air Taxis and Flying School' painted on its fuselage, it became the country's first commercial aircraft. Cahill, a true pioneer with a good nose for business, had also bought a de Havilland Gypsy Moth and, in this machine, dozens of Irish Aero Club members learned to fly.

Iona began its operations at Baldonnel in August 1930, offering a number of services – joyrides at five shillings a go, air taxi services at a shilling a mile, aerial photography of towns and factories, and banner towing. On one memorable occasion, a ball was dropped from the sky to start a GAA football match at Croke Park in Dublin. But there were always problems at Baldonnel, which was used by the Air Corps until 4.30 each day. Finding a time-slot was a frustrating business for private planes, although Cahill managed to maintain a cordial relationship with the military.

In 1931, after an intensive search all over the Dublin area, Cahill leased a site at Kildonan House near Finglas village on the north of Dublin city. Kildonan belonged to the Fitzpatrick family and they gave the fledgling airline their blessing, allowing Hugh Cahill to build a hangar that could fit twenty aircraft, plus parts. Beside the hangar was a comfortable clubhouse for staff and visitors. John J. Dunne, a frequent visitor as a boy, later described the place: 'The "aerodrome" was simply a large grassy field, flat enough to be used for the take-off and landing of the tiny aircraft of the day, mostly primitive Puss Moths and Gypsy Moths, some with small cabins but usually with open cockpits.' The hangar was no more than a large shed; close by, there was a petrol pump and a white canvas bolster attached to a pole, serving as a windsock.

By June 1932, the site was approved for use by civil and commercial aircraft and became Ireland's first commercial aerodrome; no longer would all planes coming into Ireland have to land at Baldonnel. Kildonan would have a crucial part to play in the development of aviation, not just in Ireland but further afield; among the early employees were Captain Oliver Eric 'Paddy' Armstrong, later to become the first Aer Lingus pilot, and the ground engineer John Robert Currie, designer of the Currie Wat aircraft; another Aer Lingus pioneering pilot, Ivan Hammond, was to learn to fly at the small Finglas aerodrome and got his job thanks to a glowing recommendation from Lady Mary. Notable regulars at the airfield included the local Roman Catholic curate, Father Joseph Furlong, dubbed inevitably 'The Flying Priest' and a feature at air shows all around the country with his ever-present dog, a red setter called 'Bruno', probably Ireland's first flying dog. In an earlier life, Father Furlong had served as a chaplain in World War 1 and suffered from shell shock for the remainder of his life.

The Roman Catholic Eucharistic Congress of June 1932 truly put the small aerodrome on the map. Aeroplanes based at Kildonan transported the various dignitaries and gave joyrides over the city during the congress, which included hugely supported religious services in the Phoenix Park and at O'Connell Bridge, the like of which would not be seen again until the visit of Pope John Paul II in 1979. Kildonan

An air show at Kildonan. *(Irish Independent)*

also provided much of the aerial photography that still exists from this extraordinary outpouring of religious fervour. At Kildonan, Cahill, ever the entrepreneur, also attempted to initiate a mail service to Berlin but, like Colonel Charles Russell a few years earlier, when he flew mail from Galway to London, was well ahead of his time and could not persuade officialdom to subsidise a service which would soon be regarded as routine.

In the spring of 1933, Hugh Cahill approached Lady Mary to join Iona National Airways as an instructor in the women's school of aviation, according to her version of the story at least. Lady Mary was already disenchanted with her treatment at Baldonnel, where she had garaged the DH-Moth she had brought over from England and where, despite her international reputation, she had been charged for routine maintenance of her plane. Like many others, she had an uneasy relationship with the male-dominated and stuffy Irish Aero Club; a proposal at one meeting to award her a small plaque in honour of her achievements and to acknowledge her considerable contribution to Irish aviation was not acted upon and she was never once invited to a club function or meeting, even as an honoured guest. Kildonan, with its welcoming

Pilots of the future take instruction from Lady Mary, by then in her forties. *(Weston Photo)*

and relaxed atmosphere, was altogether more to her taste and already three young women had 'signed on' for flying lessons, while ten men were also learning to fly.

There was plenty of interest in the National Junior Aviation Club she founded soon after, with hundreds of flying-mad local teenagers attending lectures and practical demonstrations in the art of flying given by famous names, including Paddy Saul and Charles Russell, former head of the Air Corps and a pivotal influence in Irish aviation at the time. Modelled on similar organisations in the USA, it was the first such club for youngsters in Europe and proved an enduring success, thanks to Lady Mary's immense organisational skills. Among the original vice-presidents were Sir Alan Cobham, Amy Johnson and Jim Mollison, even though Johnson was always cool with Lady Mary, whom she felt had denigrated her friend Lady Bailey's African flight in her book *Women and Flying*.

'Every Friday in summer, we cycled out to Kildonan, or took the single-decker bus that then alone served Finglas village and trudged the remaining mile along the Ashbourne road to the aerodrome. There, the airmen and engineers working for Iona lectured us on various aspects of flying, using the firm's aircraft and equipment for

National Junior Aviation Club members cluster around Lady Mary, during one of her talks. *(Weston Photo)*

demonstration purposes, while occasionally, distinguished aviators would come,' said John J. Dunne. In winter, the visits to Kildonan were replaced by lectures in the old Moira Hotel in Dublin's Trinity Street. The present-day Irish Aviation Authority, the governing body for aviation in Ireland, grew out of the National Irish Junior Aviation Club, as indeed did the Model Aeronautics Council of Ireland and the Limerick Flying Club.

For the youngsters enraptured by flying, Lady Mary was their own homebred heroine. They were well versed in all her achievements and could not hear enough of the stories she told them of her days flying around Europe, Africa and the USA. Always full of ideas, she also helped set up the Dublin Aero Club, the Irish Gliding Association and the Dublin Tramway Club, an organisation designed to give tramway employees a chance to fly, during her time at Kildonan.

Chris Bruton was a prominent member and later secretary of the National Irish Junior Aviation Club. In this role, he would meet Lady Mary perhaps once a week

Lady Mary and her husband Jack Williams in front of the DH moth 'The Silver Lining'. *(Weston Photo)*

and remembered her as a large but graceful woman with a prominent English accent, like most people from her background. In her ability to organise and marshal those around her, she was exceptional, said Bruton:

> She was an extremely charming woman and knew her stuff, especially on navigation and meteorology, though it was hard to keep her on the subject. As the club built up steam, we relied more and more on her. She got all kinds of famous speakers to talk to the junior club – she would drag someone in by the hair of the head. There were also prizes, such as cinema tickets, if you answered questions correctly.

But although young, he was aware of the other more erratic side to her personality:

> Her personal life was not at all organised. She was very mercurial and unreliable. I think a lot of her problems were due not so much to the drink as the unstable life she led – a bit like theatrical people. They're in bed during the day and working when

other people want entertainment, so they don't mix with normal people. Even when she was here, you didn't known if you had her. It was a life with no normal keel to it.

Bruton remembered Jack Williams as a short man who suddenly appeared in Dublin and seemed to have become a pilot because of his wife. With a friendly word for everyone, he became well known and liked, though his dark colouring attracted the occasional racist comment. Two DH Moths were registered to Lady Mary's name during this period – EI-AAW, called 'The Silver Lining', the plane she had brought with her from England and initially kept at Baldonnel, and EI-ABE registered on 1 March 1935.

In May 1933, Lady Mary was one of a number of vice-presidents elected to the inaugural committee of the National Aero Club (Irish Free State), set up for pupils of the Iona Flying School. Lady Kathleen Nelson was elected chairman and president. A few weeks later, on Whit Monday, 5 June 1933, she took part in an air race put on as part of an 'Air Pageant' organised by Iona at Kildonan and including Air Corps personnel for the first time. Highlight of the day was a breath-taking parachute jump at 2,700 feet by Air Corps engineer Joseph Gilmore, who coolly side-slipped a clump of trees just before landing; less than two months earlier at Baldonnel, Gilmore had performed the first parachute jump ever in Ireland while testing out a new parachute. Thrilling the 15,000 strong crowd was an exhibition of formation flying by the Air Corps, an aerobatic display by three Air Corps pilots and 'crazy flying' by the Irish Aero Club's chief instructor, a popular ex-RAF pilot from England called William Elliott.

Four other pilots lined up with Lady Mary for the 'Irish Cup' race, which was won by C.F French, assistant instructor of the Irish Aero Club, who finished just ahead of his boss, William Elliott. Lady Mary was fifth and last, underlining the loss of her considerable skills as a racing pilot. Afterwards, the planes were surrounded by hundreds of spectators seeking joyrides at five shillings a time. Lady Mary also took part in a novelty obstacle race. In this, participants stood 25 yards away from their planes, put on flying garb, and then ran to their machines carrying a glass of water before starting them up and setting off. Elliott emerged as winner of the canteen of cutlery presented by Hugh Cahill.

While she settled into Dublin life, taking a basement flat at Fitzwilliam Street and later at Pembroke Road, Lady Mary attempted to revive her social life in the city she had so enjoyed as a schoolgirl and student. In 1934, she and her husband were admitted as members of the Arts Club, where her old neighbour from Newcastle West, the artist Dermod O'Brien, still played a pivotal role. Since her student days, she had maintained her links with the club, and a cartoon from the 1931 Christmas dinner programme featured Lady Mary, dressed in her trademark fur-trimmed coat, flying in the clouds above the club's more earth-bound members.

In 1933, Ireland had truly earned her wings, with a long summer of air shows, pageants and displays. Spectators thronged to eagerly awaited air shows all over the country and gazed in awe skywards as the daredevils of the sky risked their lives with spectator stunts in their still-flimsy machines. When they lined up afterwards in their thousands to take a short 'spin', they were ensuring handsome profits for the show organisers.

Highlight of the year came at the end of June when British aviation legend Sir Alan Cobham visited Ireland with his Air Circus. Because Baldonnel, as a military base, was off limits, Hugh Cahill invited Sir Alan and his troupe to stay at Kildonan. The world-renowned aviator, who had been knighted in 1926 following his epic flights to South Africa and Australia, brought Dublin to a standstill when his ten aeroplanes flew over the city on the way to Finglas, accompanied on the ground by a convoy of caravans and trailers, all painted in distinctive cream and red livery. One report described several women in the crowd fainting with excitement. Sir Alan later attracted a capacity crowd to a talk in Clerys department store on O'Connell Street, underlining the huge public interest in aviation at the time. The tour was organised in conjunction with the Irish Aero Club, whose two DH Moths flew with the Air Circus, offering pleasure flights and trial lessons. Over 14,000 spectators packed Kildonan for the first show of the tour, thrilled by the daring young men and women looping the loop, walking on the flimsy canvas wings of their tiny aircraft, spinning and rolling their craft, and dropping from the air in parachutes.

After Dublin, the show planned to visit Waterford, Clonmel, Cork, Limerick, Galway, Bundoran, Derry, Belfast and Dundalk in a two-week tour, but a tragic accident in Limerick brought the cavalcade to an abrupt halt. Geoffrey Tyson, star of the Air Circus, was flying a DH Fox Moth with four passengers when he saw debris from his machine falling earthwards after he had made a dramatic swoop with his plane. Realising that somehow his undercarriage had been sheared off, he landed carefully in soft grass with the minimum of panic. Only then, he claimed afterwards, did he discover that another pilot in a DH Moth had flown underneath him and sliced off his landing wheels and undercarriage.

This proved to be the Irish Aero Club's chief instructor, William Elliott, and his passenger, William Ower, a motor mechanic from Lady Mary's home town of Newcastle West. Flying in the opposite direction and blinded by the sun, Elliott had flown into the bigger plane's undercarriage when it had made its dive. His plane spiralled to the ground and both pilot and passenger were killed. It turned out that there was a history of bad blood between the two pilots, going back to their time in the RAF, and many observers felt the accident could have been avoided. Later that evening, members of the Cobham show needed to call on the police to protect them from an angry crowd, particularly angered by the death of one of their own.

The remains of William Elliott were returned to England for burial and when the cortege reached Kildare on its way to the ferry port of Dun Laoghaire, it was escorted by a number of mourners from the Irish Aero Club and friends from Kildonan, including Lady Mary and her husband Jack Williams. An 'In Memoriam' poem, written by Oliver St John Gogarty, describing himself as 'a pupil', paid tribute to a 'simple character, cheerful, trustworthy, clean and bold'. But sentiment played little part in the air display business and, in Limerick, the Cobham show concluded the following evening after Sir Alan had made a public speech extending his sympathy to the families of the dead men. Members of the Irish Aero Club took no further part in the display although they did rejoin the air circus in Galway. Later, at a public inquiry, Tyson was lucky to find himself exonerated of all blame for the incident.

In September, Cobham's air show was back, starting with a visit to Carlow and, among other towns, visiting Newcastle West. Locals remember Lady Mary as part of the show – a tall, somewhat butch woman descending from her plane, was how one young observer described her. During a hectic summer, an air show in Dublin's Phoenix Park, attracting a crowd of 30,000, had produced three tragic deaths. Air Corps pilot Jim Twohig died just days before the show during a rehearsal, while on the day itself, another Air Corps pilot, Oscar Heron, and his observer, Richard Tobin, crashed and died. Not one single pilot from Kildonan was asked to take part in the show, which caused Captain Paddy Armstrong, for one, to resign his membership of the Irish Aero Club in frustration.

The begrudging attitude of the aviation 'establishment' and the lack of support from the State, which refused to subsidise air clubs like the British government had done, were the reasons behind Hugh Cahill's decision to close Iona down in November 1933. The Irish government believed that flying clubs could become a security risk and felt flying should be confined to the defence forces. Not even the establishment-friendly Irish Aero Club could persuade it otherwise, although key member of the Air Corps, particularly Charles Russell, were arguing strenuously for the formation of a national aviation company. They would eventually get their way, but in the meantime private enterprises struggled on.

In February 1934, Lady Mary was declared 'unfit' to fly by the British Air Ministry because of her 'below standard' sight and history of 'morbid mental trouble' since her American accident. She was told emphatically never again to apply for a commercial licence and wrote another pleading letter to Colonel Shelmerdine: 'As I have been failed twice, and never having passed the examination better than the last time I took it last year, I am reluctantly obliged to consider that there must be some personal animosity in the matter.'

Colonel Shelmerdine's reply must have come as a crushing blow: '…the result of my enquiries indicate without doubt that as you are well below the I.C.A.N standards of eyesight, you are permanently unfit for the grant of either an "A" or a "B" licence'. In a revealing private note, he described the letter from 'Mrs Williams (the lady has no right to call herself "Lady Heath"), as 'hardly the letter of a normal person'. She made one more appeal to him from her bed at West London Hospital, Hammersmith, where she was spending a fortnight because of what she claimed was a bad dose of bronchitis, but it was clear that her flying career was over.

Her alcoholism and other personal problems had made her something of an embarrassment and might help explain an exchange of letters concerning the foundation of the Irish Gliding Association in September 1934. Gliding was the latest flying craze with a number of clubs in the Leinster area; the Irish Junior Club was just one that was planning to build its own glider. At Baldonnel, ex-RAF pilot Johnny Maher, later chief engineer with Aer Lingus, had been one of the pioneers of this new sport and been instrumental in setting up the first Irish Gliding Club. Lady Mary was presumably involved and in four letters held by the Irish Military Archives in Dublin, wrote to Frank Aiken, the Minister for Defence, inviting him to attend the inaugural meeting of the new association and, later, reporting back to him on how it went.

In the first three letters, she signs herself as 'president', but in the fourth, she thanks Mr Aiken for agreeing to become president of the new association and makes it clear that she had not attended the meeting herself: 'I do so wish I had had a notice of the meeting as I would have absolutely loved to be present,' she writes, adding that even the Irish Junior Club had neglected to keep her informed. One theory is that the Irish air force, which still had considerable influence over local aviation matters, wished to keep this new organisation under its control and wanted nothing to do with the maverick Lady Mary. An alternative view is that Lady Mary was by now incapable of taking on any position of authority. While she may have been eager to become involved with the burgeoning sport of gliding, those involved wanted to keep her well out of it.

CHAPTER 18

Her Final Days

WITH IONA GONE, Everson Flying Services, a short-lived company formed by the prominent aviator and socialite Lady Catherine Nelson and her lover, a jockey called George Everett, had taken over Kildonan in December 1933. Aircraft used by the company remained registered in the names of the various private owners based at the airfield and John Currie was appointed manager in charge of flying services, with Fred Griffith as chief pilot. The principal occupation of Everson was flying instruction and, in early 1935, it had more than a 100 would-be aviators on its books. In February 1935, Everson was reorganised, first as Free State Air Ferries and, shortly after, as Dublin Air Ferries, a company formed by Lady Mary with her husband in an attempt to save the airfield. Around the same time, the Dublin Aero Club for pupils of the flying school at Kildonan was founded, with Lady Mary and Jack Williams co-opted as members; some 140 quickly joined.

On 2 March 1935, the new company was inaugurated with an air display at Kildonan. Applauding the Lord Mayor of Dublin, Alderman Alfie Byrne, when he launched the new company, were representatives of the Irish Aero Club, the Cork Aero Club, Newtownards Flying School, the new National University College (Dublin) Aero Club, the United Ireland Aero Club, the National Irish Junior Aviation Club, the Dublin Gliding Club and officers from Baldonnel.[1] Public interest in aviation was clearly still high.

Machines on view included the Monospan, the big Stinson owned by Lady Nelson, a Klemm Swallow owned by Cork Aer Club and a number of DH Moths. The company owned four aircraft – three DH Gypsy Moths and the ex-Iona DH Fox Moth, fondly remembered by regulars at the airfield as 'Alpha Papa' (EI-AAP). Three pilots were employed, mostly on charter work, and newspaper photographs of the day show Lady Mary wearing her trademark leopardskin overcoat over a smart, navy uniform.

Among the special courses planned were one for ground engineers and another for navigators, to be given by Paddy Saul. Engineers were George Bell, an Englishman, Mick Brady from Dublin and Prativa Ghosh from India. A highlight of the week,

ABOVE: Lady Mary and her husband Jack Williams (to her left), with the Lithuanian pilot Felix Vaitkus in Ballinrobe chatting to a local journalist in 1935. *(D.M. MacCarron Collection)*

RIGHT: Prominent pilot members of Dublin Air Ferries were Lieutenant Andy Woods, Irish Army Air Corps; Captain Jack Williams, Lady Mary's husband; George Kennedy and John Currie.

remembered by Oonagh Hammond, came on Sundays when members flew over Dublin city in formation. Weekends were also the time for 'joy-riding' at five shillings a time, mostly over Glasnevin graveyard a few miles south of the airfield. The small group that assembled there felt like part of a select band of pioneers and never minded the long waits for a chance to fly, caused either by poor weather or bad landings by pupils, which meant minor repairs to the planes. Jack Williams was the chief instructor, keeping a stern though benevolent eye on his charges.

The company got plenty of good publicity in the first months of its existence and there was speculation that it planned a regular service to the UK. In late April, Jack Williams flew to Manchester with exclusive photographs of the fire at the Hospital Sweepstakes premises for the British press. In May, the new company held an aviation camp at Kildonan that went on for a fortnight, with lectures, practical demonstrations and social events, both in the club house and a number of tents pitched nearby.

The camp coincided with National Aviation Day, which took place in the

Phoenix Park after a similar event, planned by the Irish Aero Club the previous August, had been cancelled because of a newspaper strike. This was the largest air display ever seen in the country, with the Air Corps, the Irish Aero Club and Sir Alan Cobham's Air Circus all in action. Some 60,000 spectators packed the flat, open spaces of the 'Fifteen Acres', paying admittance fees of ten shillings for a car or one shilling per person. The Irish Aero Club made £2,966 from the day and like in 1933, not a single plane from Kildonan was invited.

Afterwards, Cobham spent three weeks touring the country, although a day in Limerick was cancelled because of gale force winds. It was to be his last visit. Later that year, a horrific mid-air crash, similar to the one in Limerick two years earlier, persuaded him to give up the business. He sold out to Scott's Circus, which was to visit Dublin the following year, attracting a much smaller crowd.

Lady Mary continued to court publicity whenever she could. On 22 September 1935, the Lithuanian pilot, Felix Vaitkus, crash-landed near Ballinrobe, County Mayo when attempting to fly from New York to Lithuania in a Lockheed Vega. With Williams as pilot, Lady Mary hurried to the scene in 'The Silver Lining' to see what Dublin Air Ferries could do to help. Unfortunately, their plane was damaged while landing in a nearby field and had to be sent back to Dublin by lorry for repairs.

Williams continued to do most of the charter work from the airfield and just two months later, in November, had a lucky escape. While on a flight to Croydon in 'The Silver Lining', with passenger Nora Wilson, he was forced to make an emergency landing at Stone in Staffordshire when the plane's engine caught fire. No sooner had the pair raced clear than the plane burst into flames and was destroyed.

Dublin Air Ferries continued to sponsor and control the National Irish Junior Aviation Club, with dances and camping trips, as well as lectures on engines, rigging, navigation, theory of flight, maintenance of aircraft, ambulance drill, hygiene and sanitation, fire drill and gliding. From this, the more enthusiastic graduated to flying lessons at 30 shillings an hour with many going on to become pilots.

By now, Lady Mary's drinking was out of control. She would drink anything, so long as it was strong and alcoholic. 'She was always drunk,' remembered the late Sister Katherine Bayley-Butler, who, inspired by the first visit of Sir Alan Cobham's Flying Circus, spent most weekends at Kildonan between 1933 and 1936. 'Young people would come out from Dublin to meet the famous Lady Heath and she would be slumped in a corner with her bottle. We would be so ashamed.'

Every now and then, her husband would book her into the local Farnham House clinic, described on contemporary maps as a 'mental hospital', to dry out. 'She was what we called a dipsomaniac in those days — a hopeless alcoholic,' said Sister

Katherine. She had lost her looks. 'We always thought of her as a lot older than she was. She had been very attractive in her young days, but by the time she came to us, her face was all dragged and haggard. But she could still be charming.'

Others saw her differently. As a teenager, Pearse Cahill had been with his father, Hugh, on Iona's very first flight into Kildonan. 'She was a sad case by the time we knew her. Her face was distorted, as she had a lot of plastic surgery after the accident, though she was still a fine big woman.' Although Lady Mary had stopped flying by this time, she occasionally got the notion to take a machine up. The young aviators came to dread these occasions: 'You would try and put her off or avoid her, but sometimes nothing would work. I remember having to go up with her once and when it came to landing the plane, she started shouting and swearing. I was terrified it was two months before I even had my licence. I learned a few new words that day I'm telling you!'

Sister Katherine remembered the occasion: 'The instructor's stick had been removed they did that when you were going solo and no-one had put it back. So Pearse, who was only a boy at the time, had to take over.' Jack Williams did his best for his wife: 'He was terribly good to her. She really would get herself into an awful state and he would clean up after her with no fuss,' said Sister Katherine, who was presented very quietly with a set of rosary beads by Williams when she entered the convent in January 1936. 'He was a nice man, though not always a good man. He looked after Lady Mary, but always had a bit extra going on the side, and while we were very innocent at the time, we would have known enough to guess what he was up to.'

By now, the swash-buckling days were over, as aviation evolved into the multinational business it is today. In November 1935, the governments of Ireland, Canada, Great Britain and Newfoundland had met in Ottawa to discuss establishing a transatlantic air service. As the first stop in Europe, Ireland had a key role to play in such a plan and Charles Lindbergh was among those visiting Ireland in search of a suitable site for both sea and land aircraft. Soon after, Kilcrony, a small village in County Clare, began its transformation into Shannon International Airport.

Postscript

Just before Christmas 1935 came Lady Mary's first arrest for drunkenness since the episode in Canada four years earlier. When charged at Paddington Police Station with being drunk in a public place, she had given her name not as Mrs Williams but as Lady Mary Heath. A day later, when she failed to appear in Marylebone Police Court, enquiries made at the address she had given revealed that she was no longer living there and so a warrant was issued for her arrest.

Two days later, she was picked up again and charged with another offence of being found drunk in a public place. This time she gave her name as Sophie Mary Williams, of no fixed abode. In court, the magistrate dismissed the case, imposing costs. A Harley Street doctor, Elizabeth Sloan Chesser, spoke on her behalf and said that Mrs Williams wished to return to her native Ireland. She agreed to pay the costs and said she would look after Mrs Williams until her return to Ireland. She appears to have made it back to Dublin because it was only in 1936 that the Irish Tramway Club was established, allowing tram and transport workers to try aviation and following a pattern already well established among large companies in Britain of setting up flying clubs. Soon the club, which offered flying instruction at 30 shillings an hour and had the use of Father Furlong's Aeronca plane,[1] had 80 members. It was to last only a year. By August 1936, Lady Mary was back in England with an address in Surrey. In a barely decipherable typed letter to Ivan Hammond, congratulating him on the birth of a son, she says that she had found a job as secretary and possibly something called 'bridge hostess' to the Aviation Club in London. Members of the Dublin club will always be welcome there, she added.

On 27 May 1936, the first flight of the newly established national airline, Aer Lingus, took place when a wood and canvas DH 84 Dragon biplane called 'Iolar', the Gaelic for Eagle, flew from Baldonnel to Bristol with Kildonan graduate Captain O.E. Armstrong at the controls. So began a regular service that was soon extended to Croydon and attracted 1,800 passengers in its first year.

In September 1936, probably because of Lady Mary's increasing health problems, Dublin Air Ferries shut down for a 'change of direction and reorganisation'. It wasn't quite the end and, in March 1937, the company, now with three aircraft, re-emerged with an entirely new board led by J.M. Clarke as managing director. Neither Lady

Mary nor Jack Williams had any involvement with the company, which was plagued with bad luck from the start: one plane was sold and the other two grounded following minor accidents soon after it reopened.

So it was not altogether surprising that Dublin Air Ferries ceased operations in August 1938, when the last of its three planes, the venerable 'Alpha Papa' (EI-AAP), was put up for sale. By now, Irish aviation was moving on, and it was left to Darby Kennedy to continue the fight for private aviation when he set up Weston Aerodrome and Flying School at Leixlip, County Kildare, in 1938, with members of Dublin Aero Club transferring to this venue.

Work by now had begun on a new airport at Collinstown, an old British Army base in north County Dublin which had been turned over to the Irish Army. In January 1940, Dublin Airport officially opened. While Baldonnel would survive, there was little hope for nearby Kildonan and it duly closed down. Jack Williams left Ireland when Kildonan folded, although he was to return briefly in the late 1940s or early 1950s to buy horses. 'During the war, he went back to Trinidad and set up a huge flying school there, preparing lads to be cannon fodder, as I said to him,' said Pearse Cahill, remembering 'a very pleasant character'. Williams had indeed returned to the Caribbean, where as Flight Lieutenant George Williams, he became second-in-command of the Empire Training School at Piarco aerodrome in Trinidad. After the war, he returned to England, remarried, and lived in Surrey until his death in 1987.[2]

Now estranged from her husband, Lady Mary headed for England. With no one to stop her, she was drunk all the time. On one occasion, police were alerted when she disappeared from a house at Hucclecote, Gloucestershire. She had left the house saying that she was going to change her library book at a shop nearby. A boy saw her get a bus going to Gloucester, but when the bus reached its destination, she was not aboard.

In December 1937, she was found drunk in London's Gerrard Street and remanded in custody at Bow Street. A policeman said he had found Mrs Williams sitting at the foot of a flight of stairs. He helped her into the street but she was incapable of taking care of herself. He brought her to Vine Street station where a doctor reported that she had a black eye, bruised knee and sprained wrist. In her possession she had one penny, a handbag and half a bottle of rum. Mrs Williams said that she had gone to a café in Kingston to meet a close friend after receiving a letter from him.

'After that, I remember absolutely nothing until I found myself unconscious in an outhouse in Kingston. I picked up the bottle not knowing what it was. My eye was shut up and I was in great pain. My knee was badly cut. I thought of getting back to

Lady Mary featured in a series of cigarette cards in 1936.

where I was staying. I could not get any help. I went into town by getting a lift on a lorry,' she told the court.

When in town, she went into a hotel and had two glasses of beer. After sleeping for a bit, she said that she had been seen by a doctor, who bandaged her eye and knee and told her to rest. Since she was still in pain, she later sought another doctor. Soon after, the police picked her up. The magistrate pointed out with some exasperation that she had lost one entire day in her fragmented account and requested a further report on her mental state.

As Lady Mary made more frequent appearances in front of the judges, their patience finally wore out and she ended up in jail. In a newspaper article written shortly before her death, she remembered two days spent in Holloway Prison:

> I was recently sentenced to 28 days in Holloway for drunkenness. I was there for two days, then someone got me out. I wish they had left me there. It was the first time in my life that I had been really happy. I loved being among the other women there. They were so kind.

She spoke of her drink problem: 'People wonder why I took to drink after I had been fearless and rose from a poor Irish girl to become a titled lady. It was the failure of my struggles for happiness. My frequent romances have ruined my life.' She knew she had to start again: 'Now I have given up drink forever. I went to church last Sunday and now I am studying my medicine and surgery books again. I shall start life all over again and be what I wanted to be when I was a girl – a doctor.'

It was not to be. On 7 May 1939, a shabbily dressed woman boarded a tram car at Highgate Hill, some way from her then residence in Princes Square, Paddington, and went up the stairs to the top deck. When the conductor Alfred Stokes came to collect her fare, she failed to respond to him and seemed 'very vacant'. Later he found her dozing in her seat and when he woke her up, she burst out laughing. He asked her where she was going and she said that she had a date in the East End. In that case, he told her, she should get off at Old Street. He then went back to the platform and gave the signal to start moving. The tram set off again with no noticeable jerking or bumping.

He then heard a noise. 'I was still on the platform when I heard a commotion on the stairs and a thud I shall never forget,' he told the inquest a few days later. The shabbily dressed woman had fallen down the steps: 'Her head was lying on the controller, her body was on the stairs and her feet on the staircase.' The woman, still not identified, was rushed to St Leonard's Hospital, Shoreditch, that evening. She died within a day. Her identity was not established until she was recognised by a police officer as a woman he had seen many times before the court.

At the inquest, the coroner, Hervey Wyall, was shown Mrs Williams shoes after Stokes had commented that the heels were high. He found them 'somewhat high but not abnormally so'. A cousin, Francis Carnegie Peirce of Eaton Terrace, London, said he had not seen Mrs Williams for eighteen months but had heard of her and that, as far as he was concerned, her health was 'all right'. The court head that she had not been 'quite right' since the accident of 1929, although she was able to walk quite normally afterwards.

Dr Cedric Keith Simpson gave his medical opinion: 'I found nothing which would indicate that the dead woman was under the influence of alcohol. I found an old depressed fracture on the left side of the head consistent with an old injury. Underneath it was an old blood clot pressing on the brain. This clot could have caused epilepsy, black-out and unconsciousness for a short time or led to her fall.' After evidence from the car driver that the tram had started normally and without a jerk and had travelled only about thirty yards when the accident occurred, the jury returned a verdict of accidental death, exonerating the driver and conductor from blame.

Present at the inquest was an old friend and legal advisor of the dead woman, Colonel S.H. White. 'We all knew that she suffered from the effects of an air-crash through the concrete roof of a factory while flying in the United States in 1929,' he told the *Daily Mail*. He added that, in accordance with what relatives and friends felt would be her wish, the body would be cremated at Golder's Green Crematorium on

15 May. Afterwards, her ashes would be taken back to Ireland and scattered over her home town of Newcastle West from an aeroplane.

She was remembered kindly in many obituaries. 'She never knew fear, was daring to the point of recklessness,' said the *Weekly News*:

> Her feats got her name into the headlines both in this country and in America. Of late years, she had received a different kind of publicity – an unpleasant kind. From time to time, she appeared at London police courts on charges of drunkenness. Several times she was placed on probation and sent to nursing homes where she could be properly looked after. I met her many times during this unhappy period in her life. She told me bitterly that she was unable to help herself. 'I never used to be like it,' she said. 'There was a time when I scarcely touched drink at all, and if I did, I knew when to stop. Now if I take intoxicants at all, I seem to lose my powers of restraint.' I try to think of her as she once was – a commanding figure among the world's women. These later years – when she became but a shadow of her real self – I want to forget. It is not fair to remember them. I know that she was powerless to prevent the incidents, which have brought her into unfavourable limelight. The London Magistrates knew it too. They nearly always treated her with leniency, and probation officers strove hard to recapture the strong personality, which had once been hers. They were attempting the impossible.

Flight magazine also opted to remember her at her best: as a woman who took on men on their own terms and often beat them.

There is a codicil to Lady Mary's story, possibly apocryphal, but still a good yarn. The ashes of Mrs Williams were duly brought back to Ireland, according to the wishes of her family, most notably her beloved Aunt Cis, still alive at the time, and to whom she had left all her worldly goods – a total of £204 7s 10d.³ Lady Mary had apparently requested that her ashes be scattered over the houses adjoining the southwest side of the square at 12 noon precisely. At the time, the houses here consisted of the former Peirce home, by then a bank, and the house of Captain Richbel Curling, agent of the Earl of Devon's Limerick lands and a man she had disliked intensely as a child. At an angle was a Church of Ireland chapel, enclosed by a stone wall facing the square. Every day at noon, Curling would emerge from his house, stroll over to the church wall and lean against it to survey the passing scene.

At midday precisely, a small plane passed overhead and all

An Post's first day issue of their series of 'Pioneers of Irish Aviation', 1998.

A signed portrait of Lady Mary, kept by Chris Bruton.

that remained of the town's most famous daughter drifted slowly earthwards. The captain, in his usual position, could not escape inhaling the scattered ashes, which caused a prolonged coughing fit. He soon learned why the plane had caused such a commotion and, in later years, when the wind picked up and raised the dust around the square, the captain, in his usual position, would salute passers by saying, 'There's that Peirce lady at it again. Will I ever be clear of her?'

APPENDIX I

SOPHIE'S ATHLETIC CAREER

1921

Date	Event	Discipline	Result
July 7	Moate Sports, Co Westmeath	High jump (exhib)	1.24 (4ft 1ins)
July 9	Birr Sports, Co Offaly	High jump (exhib)	1.35 (4ft 5ins)
July 31	Tramway Sports, Lansdowne Rd, Dublin	High jump	1st, 1.22 (4ft)
Aug 2	Clara Sports, Co Offaly	220 yds	2nd, 31 secs (est.)
Aug 6	Clonliffe Sports, Lansdowne Rd, Dublin	High jump	1st, 1.37 (4ft 6ins)
Aug 21	Ballygar Sports, Co Galway	High jump (exhib)	1.45 (4ft 9ins)
Sept 21	Rathmines Sports Carnival, Leinster CC Grounds	100 yds open h'cap	1 Betty Magee 12.0 2 Sophie, inches
		High jump	1st, 1.37 (4ft 6ins)

1922

Date	Event	Discipline	Result
May 13	King's College Sports, Mitcham, London	220 yds	1st, 30.6
		High jump	1st, 1.4 (4ft 7ins)
		Long jump	3rd, 4.04 (13ft 3ins)
Jun 13	Kensington	100 yds 1st,	12.2
Jul 20	Lee, London	High jump	3rd, 1.4 (4ft 8)
Aug 2	Torquay High jump 1st,	1.47 (4ft 10ins)	
		Shot (4.5kg)	2nd, 7.51 (24ft 8ins)
Aug 11	Paddington, London	High jump	2nd, 1.39 (4ft 7ins)
		100 yd hurdles	3rd, 16.9 (est.)
Shot		(1-hand in 2 hand comp)	7.90 (25ft 11ins)
		Javelin (800g)	2nd 34.40 (112ft 10ins); 17.12 (56ft 2ins) 1-hand
Aug 20	Women's World Games Paris		
		Shot (3.6kg) 2-hand	9th, 14.32 (47ft)
Sept 23	Waddon, Croydon	Shot (3.6kg)	2nd, 7.73 (25ft 4.5ins)

APPENDIX I

Sept 30	British Legion Rally, Crystal Palace	High jump	2nd (no record of height)
1923			
Apr 5	3rd Monte Carlo Games	High jump	3rd, 1.40 (4ft 7ins)
		Long jump	3.95 (13ft)
		Javelin (2-hand)	3rd, 25.33 (83ft 1in)
May 21	Torquay	Javelin 800g	1st 19.91 (65ft 4ins)
Jul 14	Woolwich, London	High jump	1.47 (4ft 10ins)
Jul 26	Lee, London	Shot	3rd, 8.70 (28ft 6.5ins)
Aug 6	Brentwood	High jump (?)	2nd no ht (yet rec of 1.48/4ft 10.5ins endorsed by FSFI)
		Javelin	26.30
Aug 18	1st WAA C'ships, Bromley	Shot (8lb, 2-hand)	3rd, 15.78 (51ft 10ins)
		Javelin (800g; 2-hand)	1st 35.76 (117ft 4ins)
		120 yd hurdles	ht 3, w/o; final 2nd (only 2)
Aug 19	GB v France, Paris	100 yd hurdles	2nd, 15.9e
		Javelin (800g, 2-hand)	2nd, 36.65 (120ft 3ins)
1924			
May 28	Stamford Bridge	High jump	1st, 1.42 (4ft 8ins),
		Shot (8 lb, 2-hand)	2nd, 14.70 (47ft 7ins)
Jun 28	WAA C'ships, Woolwich	High jump	1st, 1.44 (4ft 9ins)
		Discus	3rd, 19.59 (64ft 3.75ins)
		Javelin	1st, 52.78 (173ft 2ins) 1-hand: 32.83 (108ft 9 ins)
Aug 20	Stamford Bridge	Long jump	3.13 (13ft 6.5ins)
		Shot (8lb, 2-hand; h'cap)	1st, 16.47 (53ft 11.5ins) 1st 1-hand 4.13 (13ft 6.5ins)
		Javelin (800g, 2-hand)	1st 38.93 (127ft 8.5ins)
1925			
May 16	Battersea Park	100 yd hurdles	2nd, 16.9 e
		Shot	2nd, 15.49 (50ft 10ins)
		Javelin	43.32 (142ft 1.5ins)

Jun 6	Daily Mirror Trophy, Stamford Bridge	Shot (8lb, 2-hand)	4th, 15.69 (51ft 4ins)
		Javelin (800g, 2-hand)	2nd, 44.65 (146ft 5.5ins)
Jul 11	WAAA C'ships, Stamford Bridge	Javelin (800g, 2-hand)	2nd, 40.42 (132ft 7.5 ins)
		High jump	3rd, 1.38 (4ft 6ins)
		Discus	7th 20.72 (66ft 3ins)
Jul 25	Battersea Park	Discus (1kg)	2nd, 22.55 (74ft)
Aug 1	Stamford Bridge	Javelin (800g, 2-hand)	43.25 (141ft 9.5ins)
Aug 22	Torquay	Long jump	2nd, 4.29 (14ft 1ins)
		Javelin (800g, 2-hand)	1st, 42.44 (139ft 3ins)
Sept 20	Göteborg, Sweden	High jump	3rd, 1.40 (4ft 7ins)
		Javelin	1st, 27.12 (88ft 11ins)
Sept 22	Falkenburg, Sweden	Shot (8lb, 3.6kg)	3rd, 7.82 (25ft 8ins)
		Discus	3rd, 19.52 (64ft)
		Javelin	2nd, 24.22 (79ft 5ins)

1926

Jun 5	Stamford Bridge	Javelin	2nd, 38.05 (128ft 1ins)
Jul 28	Stamford Bridge	Javelin	1st, 41.72 (136ft 10ins)
Aug 28	World Games, Göteborg, Sweden	Javelin	4th, 44.63 (7th, 24.21 1-hand) (146ft 5ins/79ft 5ins)
Aug 31	Post-World Games, Stockholm	Javelin	2nd, 44.67 (25.58 1-hand) (146ft 6.5ins/83ft 11ins)
		High jump	5th, 1.35 (4ft 5ins)

1927

May 13	London (venue unknown)	Pentathlon	(80m H, HJ, SP, LJ, 200m 1,724 points

NOTE: Heights and distances given in metric measurements, which is standard for international athletics. Since British athletics was still using imperial measurements in the 1920s, these are also given.

APPENDIX 2

LADY MARY'S FLYING CAREER

1925

19 Aug	First flying lessons.
18 Oct	Flew solo.
4 Nov	Qualified for A or private flying licence (Cert No 7975).

1926

3 Apr	First woman to make parachute jump from a plane.
9 Jun	Qualified for B or commercial licence.
24 Jul	Yorkshire Pageant, in Sherburn. Crashed in relay; 1st Yorkshire Evening News Cup, for private owners.
9-15 Aug	Concours d'avions économique, Orly, Paris. Won three of seven tests; 7th overall.
22 Aug	Bournemouth Meet; 1st Light Aeroplane Club Members' Handicap; 2nd Private Clubs Handicap, 3rd Private Owners Handicap.
9 Sept	Lympne Air Meeting. 10th (off scr) in Open Handicap.
2 Oct	Yorkshire Meeting 2nd Open Handicap.
27 Oct	Gave demo of DH Moth at Air Display in Croydon.

1927

18 May	With Lady Bailey, sets altitude record for light aircraft, of 16,000ft in an Avian from Southampton.
4 Jun	Bournemouth Air Show, 1st ladies' race.
16 Jul	Birmingham Air Pageant; 2nd behind Lady Bailey; the two women beat 13 men ; 5th in Air League Cup (120 miles).
19 Jul	Flight around Britain making 79 landings, 1,250 miles, av speed 80mph.
24 Jul	Yorkshire Air Pagent, Sherburn.
1 Aug	Royal Aero Club's Meeting at Hucknell (King's Cup meet); pulled out of King's Cup. 1st Grosvenor Cup in a DH Moth prototype (60hp Cirrus 1 engine), beating Colonel the Master of Semphill. Also 1st Ladies Purse,
Mid- Aug	Middle European tour in Avro Avian; participated in Zurich Flying Club meet.
24 Sept	Hooton Park, Liverpool. 1st Ladies Cup; 1st High Power Handicap.
1-2 Oct	York Club's Pageant. 1st Ladies' Consolation Race; 2nd President's Light Airplane Handicap; 3rd Open Handicap.
8 Oct	Equalled Lady Bailey's altitude record (set 5 July) of 17,284ft in an Alpha Avian at Woodford, Cheshire.

1928

5 Jan	Left Capetown for tour of South African aerodromes.
22 Jan	Left Johannesburg for Cairo and then London in Avro Avian G-EBUG.

17 May	Arrived back in Croydon.
10 Jul	Seaplane altitude record of 13,400ft in a Shorts with Sicele O'Brien.
20-22 Jul	1st at Waalhaven Aviation Festival Netherlands in a DH Moth.
4 Oct	Altitude record of 24,700ft in DH Moth at Croydon; height not ratified.
1 Dec	Failed altitude record attempt from Curtiss Field, New York.

1929

Early Jan	Air Races, Miami.
6-13 Feb	Aviation Show, Grand Central Palace, New York.
Feb	First woman to qualify for mechanic's licence in USA.
29 Aug	Crashes into factory roof with mechanic Irwin Kirk while practising for air race at National Air Races, Cleveland.

1931

20 Mar	Private licence restored.

1933

May	Joins Iona National Air Taxis in Dublin as instructor; founds National Junior Aviation Club.

1934

Sept	Accepts position of president with newly-formed Irish Gliding Club.

1935

2 Mar	Dublin Air Ferries launched at Kildonan.

1938

Aug	Dublin Air Ferries folds

APPENDIX 3

FROM CAPE TOWN TO LONDON 5 JAN – 17 MAY 1928

5 Jan	Cape Town
	Port Elizabeth
9 January	East London
Durban	
	Tsolo
	Umtata
11 January	Durban
13 January	Pietermaritzburg
22 January	Johannesburg
24 February	Pretoria
25 February	Fort Usher (crash)
26 February	Bulawayo
28 February	Livingstone
1 March	Broken Hill
4 March	Ndola
4 March	Abercorn (Mbala)
	Tabora
	Mwanza
14 March	Nairobi
22 March	Kisumu
29 March	Mongella
30 March	Malakal
30 March	Kosti
31 March	Khartoum
2 April	Atbara
2 April	Wadi Halfa
4 April	Cairo
15 April	Sollum
23 April	Benghazi
24 April	Sirte (Surt)
25 April	Tripoli
5 May	Sfax
5 May	Tunis
6 May	Catania
6 May	Naples
7 May	Rome
14 May	Marseilles
15 May	Dijon
16 May	Paris
	Lympne
17 May	Croydon

[243]

Sources and Bibliography

CHAPTER 1
Trawling through the *Limerick Chronicle* and the *Limerick Leader* provided much of the material on the Peirce murder trial, while the legal papers from the Power rape case of a few years earlier, part of the Sophie Peirce Archive held by John Cussen, graphically outlined the tragic life of Jackie Peirce in fastidious copperplate handwriting.

CHAPTER 2
Clues to Sophie's early life appear in Eric Cowe's superb *Early Women's Athletics: Statistics and History, Vol. 1*; Helping to build the picture was the article from *School-Days* quoted by Mary Cadogan in *Women with Wings*, a revealing conversation with Pat Richardson, a past pupil of St Margaret's, and chats with distant cousins, Helen Allott and R.O.V. Lloyd.

CHAPTER 3
Original documents held by the National Library, including issues of *The Torch*, a student magazine published 1916-17, plus a call to UCD's archives department, provided most of the information on the Royal College of Science for Ireland.

CHAPTER 4
Background on World War 1 came from Braybon and Summerfield's *Out of the Cage* and Marlow's *Virago Book of Women and the Great War*. Susie and Meirion Herries's book *The War Artists* filled in the story of Sir John Lavery. Eliott-Lynn's war records are held at the Public Records Office in Kew, while his long and interesting letter from Africa was kept all her life by Cis Peirce and is part of the Sophie Peirce Archive.

CHAPTER 5
Allen Guttman's *Women's Sport, a History* was the starting point for research into the early days of women's sport, with Gertrud Pfister providing additional material on the remarkable Alice Milliatt. Books by F.A.M. Webster, Mel Watman and Peter Lovesey provided much of the British angle, but apart from Eric Cowe's excellent books and Sophie's own writings, John Brand's *Irish Women's Athletics 1891-1946*, a truly comprehensive piece of work, proved the best source of material on Sophie's athletic achievements. Greg Moon's illuminating thesis on women's athletics in Britain provided useful background material, while sports historian, Dave Terry, filled in the gaps concerning Middlesex Athletic Club. Local newspapers such as *Sport*, the *Irish Times* and the *Irish Independent*, as well as the provincial press, were all consulted.

CHAPTER 6
Much of the background material for this chapter is held by the Sophie Peirce Archive – her own books, as well as press clippings that her Aunt Cis had saved. Mary Scanlan's thesis, *The Life and Achievements of Sophie Peirce*, provided a valuable starting point, while Robert Cussen's widely disseminated article 'Sophie Peirce' painted a colourful picture of her early life.

SOURCES AND BIBLIOGRAPHY

CHAPTER 7
Moon, Cowe, and Webster, plus articles printed in *The Times*, helped unravel the tangled web of deliberations before women athletes were accepted at the Olympic Games.

CHAPTER 8
Newspapers and magazines of the time comprehensively covered Sophie's flying adventures, in particular, the *Daily Mail* and *The Times*, while specialist magazines, *Aeroplane* and *Flight*, provided much of the more technical detail. In Elinor Smith's autobiography, *Aviatrix*, Sophie leaps from the pages, Turkish cigarettes and strangled vowels intact. Biographies of Amy Johnson by Constance Babington-Smith and, more recently, Midge Gillies, provided evocative descriptions of the early days at Stag Lane.

CHAPTER 9
The 'other Lady Mary', Lady Mary Bailey, has had her life absorbingly chronicled in Jane Falloon's *Throttle Full Open*. This chapter was based on many secondary sources: *Aeroplane*, *Flight*, *L'air*, the *Yorkshire Evening News*, the *Liverpool Post & Mercury*, the *Daily Mail*, the *Irish Independent*, Harald Penrose's *British Aviation: The Adventuring Years 1920-1929*, the *Illustrated Encyclopaedia of Aviation*, Wendy Boase's *The Sky's the Limit*, articles held in the McQueen Archive at the University of Southern California and other material from the Royal Aeronautical Society, plus contact by telephone and letter with Nuala Costello in Ballybunion and Penelope Dent, an aviation historian. The continuing athletics story draws on Moon and Webster.

CHAPTER 10-11
A hint in Eric Cowe's book sent me to the *Rand Daily Mail*, held by the British Library at Colindale, where Sophie was front-page news almost daily in the early months of 1928. Combining this material, plus later accounts in the British press, with her own account of the trip in *Women and Flying* hopefully gives a more objective view of the flight. Beryl Markham's classic *West With the Wind* supplied good background on flying conditions in Africa.

CHAPTER 12
The McQueen Archive, plus newspapers, and *Flight* and *Aeroplane* magazines, are the sources of much of this chapter.

CHAPTER 13
Lovell's biography of Amelia Earhart proved definitive and illuminating. An article Sophie wrote on her KLM experiences for *Air*, the journal of the Air League of the British Empire, held at the Royal Aeronautical Society, was a valuable find. Giving the other side of the story was the information, including images and translations of Dutch newspaper articles, generously supplied by Ed Nolte, of the Aviodrome Documentation Centre, Lelystad, the Netherlands. Ulick O'Connor's *Oliver St John Gogarty*, Hayden Lawford's *In Galway Skies* and the pages of the *Irish Independent* added to her own account of the trip to the west of Ireland, published by *Flight*. Much of the material relating to her American experiences is held by the International Women's Air and Space Archive, while the *New York Times* made following her movements a lot easier.

CHAPTER 14-15
Sir James's letter appeared in many newspapers; I found it in the *Glasgow Herald*. Barker's *Verdict on a Lost Flyer* gives the story of Bill Lancaster; Amelia Earhart's *The Fun Of It* is a breezily written book on her own adventures. Elinor Smith replied patiently and with insight to many questions by

e-mail and letter and, again, the *New York Times* proved its worth as a newspaper of record, while the McQueen and International Women's Air and Space Archive put the story in context.

CHAPTER 16
The accounts of Sophie's accident come from material held by the International Women's Air and Space Archive; from Elinor Smith, the *New York Times* and the Sophie Peirce Archive.

CHAPTER 17
Lady Mary's stint at Kildonan was described by the late Katherine Butler in her article 'Kildonan 1933-1936: A Memory'; by John Haughton in *Silver Lining* and by John J. Dunne in an article called 'Where Dublin Won Its Wings'. Background on Irish aviation came from several histories, most notably Michael Traynor's *Through the Clouds Over Limerick and Beyond*, Donal MacCarron's *A View From Above,* Liam Byrne's *History of Aviation in Ireland* and Haughton's invaluable book. Vicki Kanhai in at Piarco Airport in Trinidad kindly researched Jack William's movements during World War 2, while interviews with Chris Bruton, Kathleen Butler and Pearse Cahill rounded out the picture of a remarkable if occasionally difficult woman.

BIBLIOGRAPHY

Primary source:
Cusssen Collection (Sophie Peirce Archive), Newcastle West, County Limerick, Ireland.

By LADY MARY HEATH

BOOKS
Eliott-Lynn, Sophie, *Athletics for Women and Girls* (Robert Scott, London, 1925)
Eliott-Lynn, Sophie, *East African Nights* (Robert Scott, London, 1925)
Heath, Lady Mary and Wolfe, Stella, *Women and Flying* (John Long, London, 1929)

ARTICLES
'My Seaplane Record Flight', *Flight*, London, 19 July 1928
'A West of Ireland Tour', *Flight*, London, 18 October 1928
'Flying with the KLM', *Air*, London, Vol. 1, No 11, October 1928
'Record Hunting', *Air*, London, Vol. 1, No 12, November 1928
'Short Distance Racing and Handicapping', *Aviation*, New York, Vol. 26, No 3, 19 January 1929,
'Why I Always Fly Solo', *Pictorial Review*, New York, March, 1929
'Why I Believe Women Pilots Can't Fly the Atlantic', *Liberty*, 21 May 1932

OTHER SOURCES

GENERAL
Becket, J.C., *The Anglo Irish Tradition* (Faber & Faber, London, 1976)
Bence-Jones, Mark, *Twilight of the Ascendancy* (Constable, London, 1987)
Bowen, Kurt, *Protestants in a Catholic State* (Gill and Macmillan, Dublin, 1983)
Braybon, Gail and Summerfield, Penny, *Out of the Cage: Women's Experiences in Two World Wars* (Pandora, London, 1987)
Farmer, Tony, *Ordinary Lives: Three Generations of Irish Middle Class Experience, 1907, 1932, 1962* (Gill and Macmillan, Dublin, 1991)
Harries, Susie and Meirion, *The War Artists* (Michael Joseph, London, 1983)
Holt, Richard, *Sport and the British* (Oxford University Press, Oxford, 1989)
Leder, Jane, *Grace and Glory: A Century of Women in the Olympics* (Triumph, Chicago, 1996)
Loughrey, Patrick (ed.), *The People of Ireland* (Appletree/BBC, Belfast, 1988)
Lyons, FSL, *Culture and Anarchy in Ireland 1890-1939* (Clarenden Press, Oxford, 1979)
Marlow, Joyce (ed.), *The Virago Book of Women and the Great War* (Virago, London, 1998)
McConville, Michael, *Ascendancy to Oblivion: The Story of the Anglo-Irish* (Quartet, London, 1986)
Parkes, Susan M. (ed.), *A Danger to Men? A History of Women in Trinity College Dublin 1904-2004* (Lilliput Press, Dublin, 2004)
Steel, Nigel and Hart, Peter, *Tumult in the Clouds: The British Experience of the War in the Air, 1914-1918* (Hodder and Stoughton, London, 1997)
Weinalb, Ben and Hibbert, Christopher (ed.), *The London Encyclopaedia* (Papermac, London 1983)
Woodcock, Caroline, *An Officer's Wife in Ireland* (Dublin, 1921 and 1994)

Athletics
Brand, John W., *Irish Women's Athletics 1891-1946* (Hull, 2000)
Cowe, Eric L., *International Women's Athletics 1890-1940* (Bingley, 1985)
—, *Early Women's Athletics: Statistics and History, Vol 1* (Bingley, 1999)

Daniels, Stephanie and Tedder, Anita, *A Proper Spectacle: Women Olympians 1900-1936* (ZeNaNa, Bedfordshire, 2000)
Eyquem, Marie Thérèse, *La Femme et le Sport* (Paris, 1944)
Guttman, Allen, *Women's Sport, a History* (Columbia University Press, New York, 1991)
Henry, Noel, *From Sophie to Sonia - A History of Women's Athletics* (Dublin, 1997)
Lovesey, Peter, *The Official Centenary History of the AAA* (Guinness Superlatives, London, 1979)
Moon, Greg, *A New Dawn Rising: An Empirical Social Study Concerning the Emergence and Development of English Women's Athletics until 1980* (unpublished thesis, Roehampton, 1997)
Pozzoli, Peter, *Irish Women Athletics* (Enfield, 1977)
Wallechinsky, David, *The Complete Book of the Olympics* (Aurum, London, 2000)
Watman, Mel, *History of British Athletics* (Robert Hale, London, 1968)
Webster, F.A.M., *Athletics of Today for Women* (Warne, London, 1930)

AVIATION

Aitken, Maria, *A Girdle Round the Earth - Women Travellers and Adventurers* (Robinson Publishing, London, 1984)
Angelucci, Enzo and Matricardi, Paolo, *World Aircraft 1918-1935* (Samson Low, Maidenhead, 1977)
Babington Smith, Constance, *Amy Johnson* (Collins, London, 1967)
Barker, Ralph, *Verdict on a Lost Flyer* (Harrap, London, 1969)
Barry, Michael, *Great Aviation Stories, Vols. 1 and 2* (Saturn Books, Fermoy, 1993 and 1997)
Bedford, John, Duke of, *The Flying Duchess* (Macdonald, London, 1968)
Boase, Wendy, *The Sky's The Limit, Women Pioneers in Aviation: The Women's Decade* (Osprey London, 1979)
Byrne, Liam, *History of Aviation in Ireland* (Blackwater, Dublin, 1980)
Cadogan, Mary, *Women With Wings: Female Flyers in Fact and Fiction* (Macmillan, London, 1992)
Cobham, Sir Alan, *A Time to Fly* (Shepheard-Walwyn (Publications) Ltd, London, 1978)
Corn, Joseph J., *The Winged Gospel: America's Romance with Aviation 1900-1950* (Oxford University Press, New York, 1983)
Coster, Graham, *Corsairville* (Penguin Books, London 2001)
de Barnardi, Fiorenza (ed.), *Pink Line: A Gallery of European Women Pilots* (Aeritalia, 1984)
de Havilland, Geoffrey, *Sky Fever* (Airlife Publishing, Shrewsbury, 1999)
Earhart, Amelia, *The Fun of It* (Harcourt Brace Jovanovich, New York, 1932)
Falloon, Jane, *Throttle Full Open* (Lilliput Press, Dublin, 1999)
Gallagher, Desmond, *Shooting Suns and Things: Transatlantic Fliers at Portmarnock* (Kingford Press, Portmarnock, Co. Dublin, 1986)
Gillies, Midge, *Amy Johnson, Queen of the Air* (Weidenfeld & Nicholson, London, 2003)
Haughton, John, *The Silver Lining* (Finglas Environmental Project, Dublin, 2003)
Haynsworth, Leslie and Toomey, David, *Amelia Earhart's Daughters* (William Morrow & Company, New York, 1998)
Jessen, Gene Nora, *The Powder Puff Derby of 1929* (Sourcebooks, Illinois, 2002)
Lomax, Judy, *Women of the Air* (John Murray, London, 1986)
Longyard, William H., *Who's Who in Aviation History* (Airlife, Shrewsbury, 1994)
Lovell, Mary S., *The Sound of Wings: The Biography of Amelia Earhart* (Hutchinson, London, 1989)
MacCarron, Donal, *A View from Above: 200 Years of Aviation in Ireland* (O'Brien, Dublin, 2000)
Markham, Beryl, *West with the Wind* (Virago, London, 1984)
Mittelholzer, Walter; Gouzy, René and Heim, Arnold, *RAST en Hydravion de Zurich au Cap de Bonne-Espérance* (Editions de la Baconnière, Neuchâtel, 1927)
Moolman, Valerie, *Women Aloft* (Time Life Books, Virginia, 1981)

O'Connor, Ulick, *Oliver St John Gogarty* (New English Library, London, 1967)
O'Neill, Paul, *Barnstormers and Speed Kings* (Time-Life Books, Virginia, 1981)
O'Rourke, Madeleine, *Air Spectaculars: Air Displays in Ireland* (Glendale, Sandycove, Co Dublin, 1989)
Penrose, Harald, *British Aviation: The Adventuring Years 1920-1929* (Putnam, London, 1973)
Russell, Mary, *The Blessings of a Good Thick Skirt* (TJ Press, Cornwall, 1986)
Scanlan, Mary, *The Life and Work of Sophie Peirce* (Unpublished thesis, University of Limerick, 1995)
Liam M. Skinner and Tom Cranitch (ed.), *Ireland and World Aviation: The Complete Story* (Universities Press, Dublin, no date)
Smith, Elinor, *Aviatrix* (Harcourt, Brace, Jovanovich, New York and London, 1981)
Taylor, Michael and Mondey, David, *The Guinness Book of Aircraft Records, Facts and Feats* (Guinness, Enfield, 1992)
Traynor, Michael, *Through the Clouds Over Limerick and Beyond: A History of Aviation in Limerick* (Dublin, 1997)

IRELAND/LIMERICK

Barrington, T.J., *Discovering Kerry: Its History, Heritage and Topography* (Collins Press, Cork, 1999)
Boylan, Patricia, *All Cultivated People: A History of the United Arts Club Dublin* (Colin Smythe, Buckinghamshire, 1988)
Kemmy, Jim (ed.), *The Limerick Compendium* (Gill and Macmillan, Dublin, 1997)
Lenihan, *History of Limerick* (1866; reprinted Mercier, Cork, 1967)
Lewis, Samuel, *A History and Topography of Limerick City and County* (1837; reprinted Mercier, Cork, 1980)
MacCarthy-Morrogh, Michael, *The Munster Plantation: English Migration to Southern Ireland 1583-1641* (Clarendon Press, Oxford, 1986)
O'Connor, Patrick J., *Exploring Limerick's Past* (Oireacht na Mumhan Books, Coolanoran, Newcastle West, 1987)
Royal College of Science in Ireland Student Handbook, 1921-1922

FAMILY HISTORY

Burke, Bernard, *A Visitation of the Seats and Arms of the Noblemen and Gentlemen of Great Britain and Ireland* (London, 1855)
Hickson, Mary (ed.), *Selections from Old Kerry Records* (London, 1872 and 1874)
Lodge, J., *The Peerage of Ireland; or a Geneological History of the Present Nobility of that Kingdom* (Dublin, 1754)
O'Hart, J., *Irish and Anglo-Irish Gentry When Cromwell Came to Ireland* (Dublin, 1884, 1892)
— *Irish Landed Gentry, Appendices, Addenda, Corrigenda and Index*
Pender, Seamus (ed.), *A Census of Ireland c.1659* (Irish Manuscripts Commission, 1939)
Ryan, James G. (ed.), *Irish Church Records. Their History, Availability and Use in Family and Local History Research* (Dublin, 1992)
G.E.C., *The Complete Peerage of England, Scotland, Ireland, GB and UK* (St Catherine's Press, London, 1916)
Thom's Official Directory (Dublin)
Who Was Who, Vols. 1-7 (Adam and Charles Black, London, 1981)

KENYA

Carberry, Juanita, with Tyrer, Nicola, *Child of Happy Valley* (Heineman, London, 1999)
Fox, James, *White Mischief* (Jonathan Cape, London 1982; Mandarin, London, 1998)
Markham, Beryl, *West With The Night* (Virago, London, 1983)

Miller, Norman, N, *Kenya The Quest for Prosperity* (Gower Publishing Company, Aldershot, 1984)
Trzebinski, Errol, *The Lives of Beryl Markham* (Mandarin, London 1994);
—*The Kenya Pioneers* (Mandarin, London, 1991)

ARTICLES

'Sophie Peirce', Robert J. Cussen (*The Annual Observer,* Newcastle West Historical Society, June 1983 & *The Limerick Compendium,* Gill and Macmillan, Dublin, 1997)
'Kildonan 1933-1936: A Memory', Sister Katherine Butler (*Dublin Historical Record* Vol. XXXVII Nos. 3 & 4, Jun-Sept 1984)
'Kildonan Aerodrome', John Haughton (*Finglas - A Celebration*, ed. Aidan Kelly, Dublin, 1998)
'The Flying Lady Heath', P.D. O'Donnell, (*Kerryman/Corkman*, 16 Sept 1983)
'The Flying Irish Woman', Mary Scanlan (*Stars, Shells and Bluebells: Women Scientists and Pioneers,* WITS, Dublin, 1997)
'Capetown-England Flight: Lady Heath's Return', *Flight,* Vol. 20, No. 21, London, 24 May 1928
'Wings for Women' by Courtenay D. Marvin, International Women's Air and Space Museum archive, dated September 1929.
Untitled and undated article by Carol Bird, International Women's Air and Space Museum archive.
'Olympia nur für Männer?' by Gertrud Pfister; Auseinandersetzungen über die Beteiligung von Frauen an den Olympischen Spielen. In: Krüger, M. (Hrsg.): Olympische Spiele: Bilanz und Perspektiven im 21. Jahrhundert. Münster: Lit 2001, 48-69
'Do "Air-Minded" Women Make Unsatisfactory Wives ?" Undated and uncredited article, McQueen Archive, USC.

NEWSPAPERS

Algemeen Handelsblad, Rotterdam
Daily Express, London
Daily Mail, London
Daily Telegraph, London
East African Standard, Nairobi
Evening Herald, Dublin
Freeman's Journal, Dublin
Glasgow Herald, Glasgow
Het Vliegveld, Rotterdam
Irish Citizen, Dublin
Irish Independent, Dublin
Irish Times, Dublin
Irish Weekly Mail and Sports, Dublin
Kerryman/Corkman, Tralee
Limerick Chronicle, Limerick
Limerick Leader, Limerick
Limerick Reporter and Tipperary Vindicator, Limerick
Munster News
New York Times, New York
Rand Daily Mail, Johannesburg
Sport, Dublin
Sunday Independent, Dublin
The Times, London
Yorkshire Evening News, Leeds
Yorkshire Post, Leeds

SOURCES AND BIBLIOGRAPHY

MAGAZINES
Aerial Register and Gazette
Aeroplane, London
Air, London
L'air, Paris
Aviation, New York
Cara, Dublin
Flight, London
The Torch, student magazine Royal College of Science for Ireland, 1916-17
World Sport

JOURNALS
Dublin Historical Record, Dublin
Newcastle West Observer, Newcastle West

LIBRARIES/ARCHIVES

British Library Newspaper Library, Colindale
Chautauqua Institute
City of Westminster Public Libraries
Dublin Central Library
Dun Laoghaire and Rathdown Public Libraries
Family Records Centre, London
Gilbert Library, Dublin
Imperial War Museum, London
International Women's Air and Space Museum, Cleveland, USA (Joan Hrubec)
National Archives, Dublin
National Library of Ireland
Public Records Office, London
Royal Aeronautical Society, London
Royal Geographical Society, London
University College Dublin Archives
University of Aberdeen
University of Southern California Special Collections (John Ahouse)

INTERVIEWS/CORRESPONDENCE

Helen L. Alott
John Brant
Chris Bruton
Sister Katherine Butler
Pearse Cahill
Eric Cowe
John Cussen
Penelope Dent
Jane Falloon
Noel Henry
Vicki Kanhai
R.O.V. Lloyd

Jayne Loader
Ed Nolte
Gertrud Pfister
Patricia Richardson
Elinor Smith
Dave Terry

AND FINALLY...

For editing, encouragement and sound advice during five long years, very special thanks to Jessie Naughton, John Naughton, Mary Butler, Risteard O Gallchobhair, Gerry Ronan, John Cussen, Sean Liston, the people of Newcastle West and Knockaderry, Meabh Warbuton, David Naughton, Ed Nolte, John Haughton and, above all, Jonathan Williams.

At Ashfield Press, thanks to John Davey, Judith Elmes, Linda Longmore and Susan Waine for their enthusiasm and support.

Endnotes

CHAPTER 1 A Family Tragedy
1   His brother, John established himself in Liverpool following his graduation. The story goes that when he died, he left a large sum to Liverpool Hospital, on condition that they set aside a bed in the hospital free of charge to anyone who came from Newcastle West. Another brother emigrated to Australia after he graduated and was never heard of again. There was also Robert, who was to live at Castleview House and who died on 1 January 1920 in Copenhagen, and Francis, to whom Robert left Castleview.
2   The D'Arcy family had lived in Knockaderry since the early eighteenth century. James Conyers D'Arcy probably built the present house, still just about standing, a few decades later. His daughter, Catherine, married Reverend Thomas Waller Evans, the rector of Dunmanway, County Cork; their son Thomas assumed the name D'Arcy Evans on inheriting Knockaderry. His brother, James, was Sophie's maternal great-grandfather.
3   Poor Law Unions were set up under the Poor Law Relief Act of 1839. Rates, or land-based taxes, were collected within these areas for the maintenance of the local poor in 'workhouses'.
4   'On many occasions, when they were in Newcastle West, her manner and attitude towards her husband were of a most aggravating nature.' *Limerick Chronicle*, 9 December 1897

CHAPTER 2 Growing up in Newcastle West
1   By the mid-nineteenth century, an agent of the Earl of Devon called Curling occupied the castle at Newcastle West, succeeding Alfred Furlong and earlier, Sophie's great-grandfather, Reverend Thomas Locke, who had a detailed plan of the town drawn up in 1776. On this is clearly marked a well known chalybeate spring, protected by a covered building. This has since become the source of the world-renowned Ballygowan mineral water industry based in the town.
2   Between 1911 and 1926, there was a 34 per cent decline in the Protestant population living in Ireland, a fall in numbers from 249,535 to 164,215, although those in rural areas were less inclined to leave.
3   A number of well-known personalities contributed memories of their school days to this magazine, published in December 1928 and quoted by Mary Cadogan in her book *Women with Wings* (London 1992).
4   A portrait of Dr Badham can be seen in Alexandra College, Dublin.

CHAPTER 3 College Days in Dublin
1   The city's population was 371,936.
2   The building, designed by the London architect, St Aston Webb, and the Dublin architect, Thomas Manly Deane, was taken over by the Provisional Government in 1922 and now houses the Department of the Taoiseach.
3   In 1926, the RCSc.I was incorporated into University College Dublin, then located at Earlsfort Terrace.
4   William Davies Lynn – the Eliott was his father's name and added later – was born on 12 June 1875. His father, William Eliott Lynn, was a Baptist minister and his mother the former Sarah

Davies. Their address was given as 26 Woodville Terrace, Everton, a suburb of Liverpool.
5 Just a week later, on 19 December, her father's long-suffering neighbour, William Power, also died, aged 74.

CHAPTER 4 The War Years
1 The Lavery portrait ended up with Cis Peirce in Ballybunion and remains in a private collection.
2 Clearly the accident happened in Dublin, but that is all we know.

CHAPTER 5 Mrs Eliott-Lynn, Athlete
1 Although international athletics then (as now) used the metric system, in Britain and the USA, imperial measurements were still used in domestic competition and so we use them here when appropriate.
2 Other notable women athletes in Aberdeen at the time were Christian Battisby, a maths teacher and long jumper, and Matilda Fisher Menzies, a qualified doctor, who held Scottish and British records at 220 yards, 440 yards and high jump.
3 Won by Daisy Wright and Mary Lines respectively.
4 'By courtesy of a firm of film people I have been allowed to examine a reel of my javelin throw and I find that I run to within 2 or 2 yards of the throwing-line, carrying the javelin low across me, parallel to the ground. On reaching the throwing-point, when my left leg is raised for the next stride, I appear to throw my weight back on to my right foot, which is in the usual running position, and hop, coming down with the foot at right angles to the direction of the run, at the same time bending the body well back and bringing the javelin into the throwing position.'

CHAPTER 7 Olympic Arguments
1 In this, Sophie is wrong; amenorrhoea can lead to osteoporosis, or brittle bone syndrome, in later years.
2 The resolutions of the Medical Sub-Committee of the Olympic Congress on the 'Participation of Women' were published on 1 June 1925.
They were:
   1. The special functions in life of woman make it necessary that she should not do anything to injure her special organisation.
   2. Her sports must be carefully chosen and only those suitable for women can be proposed for training and competition.
   3. The conditions for women in competition and practice must be reduced considerably from those arranged for men.
   4. Medical tests are absolutely necessary both before, and periodically during training.
   5. Those sports not fit for women must be cut out. Boxing, wrestling and rugby. The majority of the Commission are against football.
   6. Clothing regulations are very necessary and must be made by each nation to prevent regrettable exhibitions.

3 Peter O'Connor's remarkable achievements are chronicled in Mark Quinn's *The King of Spring* (The Liffey Press, Dublin 2004).

CHAPTER 8 Sophie Takes Flight
1 Commissioned in the Royal Artillery in 1896, Sefton Brancker (1870-1930) learned to fly in 1913 and the next year, became deputy director of military aeronautics in Britain and steadily moved

up the ranks. In 1922, he became director of Civil Aviation; his vision was to unite all of Britain's colonies with a network of airways. He died in the tragic crash of the R101 airship in 1930. From William H. Longyard, *Who's Who in Aviation History* (Airlife, Shrewsbury, 1994).
2   In London, Newcastle, the Midlands, Lancashire and Yorkshire.
3   Before the war, Mrs Hewlett, wife of the novelist Maurice, ran her own school and aircraft factory at Brooklands, while Quimby, a Boston journalist, became the first woman to fly the English Channel on 16 April 1912 in a Blériot monoplane.

CHAPTER 9 Wings Over Europe
1   On 8 January 1928, the FSFI international committee accepted the principle of women in the Olympics athletics programme, but asked that ten events be included. At the fifth congress of the FSFI, held from 1 to 3 August in Amsterdam, Sigfrid Edstrom of the IAAF stated his belief that a compete athletics programme should be included at the next Games in Los Angeles. The 9th Congress of the IAAF, held a few days after the games, did not agree. Although it was voted by sixteen to six to retain a women's programme, the request for a fuller programme was rejected by fourteen votes to eight. At the 1932 Games, the high and long jumps would be added to the programme but the 800m would be dropped. Britain again was one of the dissenting voices, along with Ireland, Canada, Finland Hungary and Italy. It meant that until 1948, when the 200m was added, the 100m was the longest race for women on the Olympic programme. The struggle by the FSFI for proper recognition of women's athletics continued until 1936, when Alice Milliatt agreed to dissolve the organisation and allow the IAAF control women's athletics.
2   That particular Moth, named 'Miss Kenya', was the first to be registered in Kenya and was active there for nearly 40 years; it is now kept at the Old Warden airfield, near Bedford in England.
3   In a list printed that November, Lady Mary was reported as owning three planes: an Avro Avian G-EBQL, registered on 20 September of that year, the SE 5a Viper G-EBPA, registered on 30 July 1926, and a Gypsy Moth G-EBMV, registered on 11 July 1927, which she sold a few months later.

CHAPTER 11 The Flight from the Cape
1   A nursing home was named after her.
2   Ironically, the only pilot to make a forced landing in the Sudd was a man. Ernst Udet had run out of petrol and was forced to land on a ridge of hardened mud. After several anxious days, a search party, found him none the worse for his experience, though his mechanic was near death from mosquito bites.
3   Jane Falloon in *Throttle Full Open*, the biography of Lady Bailey, confirms that she had difficulty reading a compass.

CHAPTER 13 After Earhart
1   The first Imperial Airways flight to Karachi, via Cairo, had taken place in December 1927; a regular service would follow in March 1929.
2   Lady Mary is a bit mixed up here. Renvyle House, burned down during the Civil War in 1923, had not yet been rebuilt. Gogarty was living in a smaller house located on Freillaun Island in the middle of Tully Lough, a few miles inland from Renvyle, near the village of Tully Cross. He had acquired the eleven-acre island at the same time as he had bought Renvyle.

CHAPTER 14 The New World
1   The American pilot Richard Evelyn Byrd (1888-1957) made a disputed first flight over the North Pole in 1926, since discredited, and later flew over the South Pole to much media acclaim.

2   Just north of present-day Kennedy Airport.
3   The result was that Smith was named 'Best Woman Pilot in the USA' in 1930, because she was forced to set many different kinds of aviation records in order to circumvent Putnam's influence.
4   She took a lover, who died in mysterious circumstances; Lancaster was tried but found not guilty of murder.

CHAPTER 15 The Women's Air Derby

1   No. 1 was a 50-mile race 'free for all' for planes less than 510 cubic inches, consisting of ten five-mile laps with a top prize of $1,000; No. 28 was a 12 x 5 mile lap race for planes with engines of between 510 and 800 cubic inches with a prize fund of $1,250; No. 29 was a dead stick landing contest, taking place on 29 and 31 August and 2 September, while races No. 30 and 31 were Australian Pursuit races, scheduled for 30 August and 1 September.

CHAPTER 16 Crash landing

1   Later in the year, the case was notorious enough, even in the USA, to be cited in an action to recover the cost of a typewriter by a husband from his separated wife. The husband was still liable if he had not settled a sufficient allowance on his wife, even if they were separated, was the opinion.
2   Williams was born on 15 October 1900.

CHAPTER 17 Back in Ireland

1   Originally planned and laid out by my father, Ben Naughton.

CHAPTER 18 Her Final Days

1   The gathering included Lord and Lady Glenavy, the Belgian consul-general M. Groot, Lady Nelson, Major General MacNeill and Mrs MacNeill, Commandant. J. Carroll, officer commanding Air Corps, Major Liston (officer commanding Baldonnel), District Justice and Mrs Reddin, Rotary president Keith Eason, Major A.J. Dease, C.H. Gates, the Misses Dillon, F.W. Griffiths, Patrick Hyland, Miss Hallinan, Miss Oonagh Scannell, B. Hyland, W. Good, Mr Bryant, Grattan Osmonde TD, Mr French, Captain and Mrs Quirke, A. Dease, Chris Bruton, Ivan Hammond, James Bell and Sergeant Maher.

POSTSCRIPT

1   The Aeronca C3 EI-ABN, a Japanese monoplane, was part-owned by Lady Mary. A low powered aircraft, with only 38bhp, it had an enclosed cabin, which allowed pilot and passenger to sit side-by-side. Because of its low carriage it was tricky to land.
2   With his second wife Muriel Marjorie, he lived at 14 Cherimoya Gardens, West Molesey, Surrey until his death from pneumonia at the age of 87 on 13 December 1987.
3   Cis was to die aged 77 on 27 May 1942.

Index

Numbers in bold refer to photographs.
Numbers in italics refer to quotes by and about Lady Mary.

AAA 58
Abercorn, South Africa (*later* Mbala) 119–20, 131
Abrahams, Harold 84
accidents, flying 102, 107, 134–5, 148–9, 187, 190, 197, 225–6, 230
    Lady Mary 200–4, 208–9
Acosta, Señora 212
Adelaide Road, Dublin 50
adventure, love of *112*. see also flying career
Aerial Activities Company 189
Aerial Oaks (race) 103
Aer Lingus 232
Aeroplane magazine 100, 165
Africa, Lady Mary in
    farming in 62–73
    solo flight from South Africa to London 112–24, 125–42, 143–56
        distance **124**, 125, 142, **148**
        flying with Bentleys *130, 138*
        preparations and difficulties *112*, 119–20, 136–9, 140–1, 143, 145
        returns home 11–12, *153–6*
        sights and animals 128, 129, *130, 133–4, 138*
        weather conditions *129, 130–2, 134, 145, 152*
Agricultural Debating Society 37
Agriculture and Technical Instruction of Ireland, Department of 37, 48
Ahouse, John 8
Aiken, Frank 227
Air Circus 225–6, 230
Aircraft Disposal Company 142, 174, 182
air festivals 87, 97, 99, 135, 159, 190–9, **220**, 225, 230
Air France 218
Air League of the British Empire 110–11, 155
    Ladies' Committee formed 156
Air Ministry, London 83, 92, 100, 163, 215, 227
'Airwoman's At Home' celebration 94
alcoholism, Lady Mary's 210, 227, *230–1, 233–5*
Algrove, Belfast 105
Allen, C.B. 202

Allott, Helen 30, *217–18*
'Alpha Papa' aeroplane 228, 233
altitude record
    Elinor Smith challenges Lady Mary 180
    Lady Mary's flying 101, *159–60*, 173–5, 181
Amateur Athletic Association (AAA) 58
Amateur Athletic Union 180
America. *see* United States of America
American Army Air Corps 177
American Cirrus Engines 182, 185–6
American Counsul, London 208
Amsiate, fort of 145
Amsterdam Olympics 161, 167
Aristocrat aeroplane 188
Arkle, Mr 139–40
Armstrong, Captain Oliver Eric 'Paddy' 164, 219, 226, 232
Arnold Constable and Company 179
arrested, Lady Mary 210, 232, 233–4
ashes, Lady Mary's 236–7
Astor, Lady 84, 91
Atbara, Sudan 141
athletic career, Lady Mary's 54–61, 65–8, 71
    high-jump 55–7, 65–**6**, 67, 74, 87, 238–40
    javelin throwing 59, 60–1, 65–6, 67, 74, 81–2, 87, 238–40
Athletics for Women and Girls 53, 74, 78–81, 84
Atlantic flights 157, 167–8
A.V. Roe Company 103, 110, 142
Avian Cirrus MK II,
    Lady Mary's 11, 89, 101, 103, 105–7, 110, 113, *173–4*
        problems 129, 137, 144–5, 146, 149, 150
            leak in petrol tank 115, 116, 121, 123, 134, 136
    sold 158
Aviation magazine 186, 188, 190, *198*
Avro Avian Cirrus MK II aeroplane. *see* Avian Cirrus Mk II

[257]

Badham, Dr Edith F 33, 34
Bailey, Lady Mary 62, 88, 101, 110, 111, 114, 156
    African trip 112, **113**, *140*
    altitude record 103, 110
    receives International Union of Aviators award 115
    rival **95**, 102–3, 106, 115
Bailey, Sir Abe 88, 95, 114
Balbo, General 151
Baldonnel, County Dublin 105, 167, 169, 172, 218, 219, 220, 233
Ballybunion, County Kerry *31*, 39, **40**
    Lady Mary finds herself in difficulty at sea in 49–50
    Lady Mary flies plane to 104–5, 169–70
Ballygar, County Galway 56–7
ban, women pilots 91–4, 95
Baragwanath aerodrome, South Africa 118
Barnes, Pancho 197
Batavia (*later* Jakarta) 161, 163, 165, 166
Bayley-Butler, Sister Katherine 230–1
beauty and glamour *71–3*, *117*, *154*
Bedford, Duchess of 156
Belfast 169
Belgium 97
Bell, George 228
Bellanca aeroplane 177
Belleville, New Jersey 185
Bellin, Lieutenant G.W. 118–19, 121, 123
Benghazi, Libya 146–7
Bennett, Lottie 121
Bennett, Myrtle 121
Bentley, Dorys (nee Oldfield) 129–30, 132, 134, 136–7, 154
Bentley, Lieutenant Richard (*later* Captain) 114, 118–19, 120, 140, 145, 149
    accompanies Lady Mary from Cape Town to London 114, 118, 122, 129–30, 131–2, 136–40, 150–1
    honoured with Britannia Trophy 155
Bewley's, Dublin 35
Billings Field, Ogdensburg 196
Binks, Joe 75
Birchenough, Florence 57–8, 73, **98**
Birmingham 103
Birr, County Offaly 55
Blackpool air pageant 159
Blanc, Camille 54
Blanchard, Madeline Sophie 88
Bob, C.V. 177

Bolland, Madame 91
Bonini, Signor 133, 134, 143
Boston 181
Bouchier-Hayes, Dr John 19
Bournemouth 97, 101–2
Bouwer, G.S. 114
Bowyer, E.C. 150
Brady, Mick 228
Brancker, Sir Sefton 83, 92, 93, 145, 155, 162
    flying with Lady Mary 93
Brand, John 7
Bremen (aeroplane) 167–8
Brentwood, England 65
Breslau, Germany 106
Britain 97, 98, 167, 211
British Aircraft Constructors, Society of 155
British Olympic Council 78
British Private Aircraft Owners' Club 88
Brodie, Magistrate D.M. 210
Broken Hill, Zambia (*later* Kabwe) 129
Brown, Mr 174
Brunner, Sir John 84
Bruton, Chris
    and Lady Mary 222–4
buffalo 133–4
Bulawayo, Zimbabwe 123, 125, 128
Bulawayo Chronicle 128
Burry Port, Wales 157
Busoga, Uganda 133–4
Byrd, Commander 177
Byrne, Alfie (Lord Mayor of Dublin) 228

Café Cairo, Dublin 35
Cahill, Hugh 218, 219, 220, 224, 225, 226
Cahill, Pearse *231*, 233
Cahirmoyle House 28
Cairo, Egypt, Africa 11–12, 141, 142
    Lady Mary flying into Cairo *141*
California 158, 192
camera seized, Lady Mary's 146
Canada 167
Canadian Avro Company 182
Canadian Vickers Company 190
Cancianotti, Commandant 151
Cape Bon, Tunisia 150
Cape Town, South Africa 11, 113
Carberry, John 100, 112, 134–5
Carberry, Maïa 134–*6*
Carlton Hotel, Johannesburg, Africa 122

INDEX

Carter, Constable Alfred 210
Carthage, Tunisia 150
Castleview House 28
Catania aerodrome, Sicily 151
Catholics 28, 29
Central Park South, (112), New York 189
Chamberlain, Mrs Clarence 179, 187
Charleston, United States of America 184
Chesser, Elizabeth Sloan 232
Chesterfield House, County Limerick 19
children, Lady Mary and *69–70*
China 211
Christ Church, Mayfair, London 109
Christobel Russell v. Sir James Heath and Lady Heath (court case) 204–6
Chrysler Cape to London Motorcar Speed Dash 114, 119, *131*
    Lady Mary travels with expedition 119–20, 121, *131*
        preparations 122–3
Churchtown Cemetery, County Limerick 26
cigarette cards **234**
Cincinnati, United States of America 210
Cirrus engine 182, 185–6
Cirrus Motor Company 208
citizenship, Lady Mary applies for American 186
Civil Aviation Advisory Board 83
Clarke, Jim 217, 232
Cleveland 190, 196, 197, 208
Cleveland Pneumatic Tool Company 192
Clifden, County Galway 171
Clonliffe Harriers Sports, Lansdowne Road, Dublin 56
Clover Field, Santa Monica 192, 196
Cobham, Lady 156
Cobham, Sir Alan 84, 113, 159, 221, 225, 226, 230
Collinstown, County Dublin 233
Commerce, Department of 187, 192, 209
commercial flights 161
    Lady Mary flies with KLM 164–6
Concours d'avions économique 97
conforming, Lady Mary and 64
Connaught Tribune 170
Connemara, County Galway 171–2
Coolidge, Mrs 177
Coolidge, President 177
Cooperstown Poorhouse, New York 195
corsets *79–80*
Cosgrave, President W.T. 167
Coubertin, Baron Pierre de 54

court case, Lady Mary's 204–6, 210, 234–5
Cowes, Eric 7
Cowie, Dudley 135
Cox, P.J. 189
crash-landings, Lady Mary and 126–7, 200–4
Criminal Lunatic Asylum, Dublin 13, 26–7
Crosfield, Sir Arthur 84
Crossan, Marvel 196, 197
cross-country running *80*
Crouch, Goodman 186
Croydon 153, 158, 164, 174
Croydon Sports Club 60
culture, Irish 35
Curling, Richbel 31, **104**, 236–7
Currie, John Robert 219, 228, **229**
Curtiss Falcon aeroplanes 177
Curtiss Field, aerodrome, Long Island 180, 187, 206–7
Curtiss Fledgling aeroplanes 209
Cussen, John 7
Cussen, Robert 49
custom officials, Lady Mary and 176
Cutler, Dr Elliott C. 202, 203
Czechoslovakia 95, 97

Daily Chronicle 73
Daily Mail 101, 235
Daily Mirror 71–2
Daily Mirror Trophy 81
Daily News 150, 180
D'Arcy, Rosie **104**
D'Arcy-Evans, Catherine 14
D'Arcy-Evans, John 35
D'Arcy Evans, Thomas (Old Tom Evans) 15, 16
Darnah, Libya 146
Daytona, Florida 184
Deal, Kent 153
de Havilland, Geoffrey 85, 88, 173, 190
de Havilland, Louie 103, 110, 173
de Havilland Moth. *see* DH Moth
de Havilland School of Flying 85
Delhurst Sanitorium, Mentor, Ohio 208
depression 30, *69*
Derg, Lough 169
Desoutter Mark II 218
Devon, Earl of 14
    sells estate 28
DH Moth 83, 87, 88, **99**, 118–19, 214, 219
    Captain Bentley's 114, 116, 129, 150

[259]

Gypsy Moths 158, 219, 228
   Lady Mary's 161–2, **163, 164,** *173–4, 176,* 228
      problems 172, 184, 196
      races **96–7,** 161–2, 184–5
      'The Silver Lining' **223,** 224, 230
Dickson, J.M. 23
Dijon, France 152
dispatch driver in World War I, Lady Mary 43, 44–6, **47**
divorce, Lady Mary files for 208, 214
Dollymount strand 169
Dooling, Catherine Teresa (*later* Peirce-Evans, Mrs Catherine) 13
   background 13–14
   children 18–19, 20
   court case and imprisonment 20–1
   murdered 22–6
   relationship with 'Jackie' 18–20, 21–2
Doolittle, Jimmy 202
Doon Bay, County Clare 170
Doon Cottage, Ballybunion, County Kerry 41, 49
Dornier Merkur seaplane 114
Douglas, Mr 118
driver in World War I, Lady Mary 43, 44–6, **47**
Dublin 35, 169, 172, 214
Dublin Aero Club 222, 228, 233
Dublin Air Ferries 228–30, 232
Dublin Airport 233
Dublin Arts Club 224–5
Dublin Registry Office 20
Dublin Tramway Club 222
Dublin Tramway Sports, Lansdowne Road, Dublin 56
Dundee aerodrome, South Africa 116
Dunne, John J 221–2
Dunne, John J. 219
Durban, South Africa 115
Durban Light Aeroplane Club 115

Earhart, Amelia 176, 180, 183, 187, 196, 197, 199, 207
   flight across Atlantic 157, 213
   friendship with Lady Mary 157–8, 194–5
East African Nights 63–4, 76
East Africa Standard 135
East London, South Africa 114–15
Eastwood, Mr 156
Eclectic Club 180
Edmonde, Osmond Grattan 168

Egypt, Africa 143
Egypt, High Commissioner of 143–4
Eielson, Carl 160
Elder, Ruth 196
Eliott-Lynn, Captain William Davies (*later* Major) 7, 39, 183
   in Africa 47, 50, 51, 62–3, 65, 68–71
      contracts malaria 47, *70–1*
   drowning and inquest 100–1
   letters to Aunt Cis 50–1, 52–3
   letter to War Office 46–7, 48
   marriage and finances 50–3
Elliott, William 224–5
Ellison, Dorothy 107
Emergency Clinic Hospital, Cleveland 200
Emerson, Mr 141
engine, Cirrus 182, 185–6
English Channel 153
English Women's Athletics Championships 60, 65–6, 74, 96
English Women's Track and Field Championships 161
Entebbe, Uganda 137
Eucharistic Congress 219
Evans, Mrs Samuel 118
Evans D'Arcy. *see* D'Arcy Evans
Evans Peirce. *see* Peirce-Evans
Evening Herald 22, **23**
Everett, George 228
Everson Flying Services 228
examination, Lady Mary's flying
   physical 92, 156, 163, 215–17
   technical *187,* 215–16

FAI 159, 195
Falkenberg, Sweden 87
family origins, Lady Mary inquires about *186*
farming in Africa, Lady Mary 62–73, *70–1*
Farran, Dr 109
Farrell, Major 212
Fawcett, Louise 98
Fayetteville, North Carolina 184
Fédération Aéronautique International (FAI) 159, 195
Fédération Sportive Feminine International (FSFI) 54, 57, 65, 67, 76, 78
   conference 59, 60, 74, 96, 98–9, 167
      anger at experimental Olympic programme 98–9

INDEX

Lady Mary as vice-president 121, 180
finances, Lady Mary's 34, 50–3, 73, 85, 88, 178–9, 185–6, 208–9
Finglas, Dublin 214
Finland 167
Fitzmaurice, Commandant (*later* Colonel) 105, 167–8, 169
    flew across Atlantic 167–8
Fitzwilliam Street, Dublin 224
Fletcher, Mr Pat 127
Flight magazine 102–3, 110, 157, 159–60, 169, 236
Flint, Wales 105
Florida, United States of America 183
flying career, Lady Mary's 83–94, 107, 209, 210–11. *see also* licence, flying
    accident 200–4, 208–9
    first female commercial pilot 92–4
    flies to Ireland 105, 168–72
    flying in Europe 95–211
    instructor 220–4
    involved in controversy 106, 175
    new altitude record 101, 109–10, 159–60
    pleasure of 6, 83, 86, 89, 90, 117–18, 177–8
    solo flight (*see under* Africa)
    79 stop trip around England **102**, 103–4
    wins open race against men 106
flying lessons 85–6
Flynn, Kate 214
Fokker aeroplane 157, 164, *164–5*
Folkstone, Kent 46
'Fortitude' (poem) 69
Fort Usher, Zimbabwe 126
Fort Worth Record 192
France 45–6, 95, 97, 211
French, C.F. 224
French Air Association
    Concours d'avions économique 97
'Friendship' (aeroplane) 157
Frodsham, Cheshire 110
From Sophie To Sonia 7
FSFI. *see* Fédération Sportive Feminine International
Fuld, Edgar 163
Furlong, Father Joseph 219

Galway 170–2
Garden City Hotel, Long Island 182
Gardner, G. McLean 188
Garelli, Colonel 147

G-EBUG. *see* Avian MK II
General Aeroplane Corporation 188
ghibli (storm) 145, 146, 148
Ghosh, Prativa 228
Giles, William H. 214
Gillman, Mr 116
Gilmore, Joseph 224
Glasser, Captain Daniel 201
Glenville, Jane Langford 186
gliding 227
Goddard, Mr Rayner 205
Godwin, Pauline 8
Gogarty, Oliver St John 168, **171**, 226
    friendship with Lady Mary 171–2, 217
Golder's Green Crematorium 235
Good Hope, Cape of 150
Goold, Mrs 59
Gordon, Lou 157
Gothenburg, Sweden 87, 97
Govern, Michael 37
Gowers, Sir William (Governor of Uganda) 137
Grafton Street, Dublin **36**
Grand Central Station 187
Grand Hotel, Tripoli, Egypt 149
grants, Lady Mary applies for 48–9
Gray, Thomas 64
Great Depression 214
Great Lakes Aircraft Corporation 185, 190, 199, 200, 207
Great Lakes Trainer aeroplane 190, 193, 198, 200–1
Green, Colonel 144
Greenly Island 167–8
Greenwich hospital, Connecticut 203
Grey, C.G. 100, 165
Griffiths, Fred 228
Grigg, Sir Edward 136
Groslimond, Louise 75
Grosvenor Cup, Lady Mary wins 106
Groves, General P.R.C. 111
Guest, Amy 157, 158

Hadley Field, New Jersey 177
Hamble aerodrome 101
Hammond, Ivan 219, 232
Hammond, Oonagh 229
Hampshire Air Club 176
Hannon, Annie 24
Hannon, Kate 24

Hannon, Thomas (junior) 23–4, 25, 27
Hannon, Thomas (senior) 24, 27
Hansen, Maurice de 189
Harley-Davidson motorbike 42, 43
Harmon, Clifford 153
Harrisburg, South Africa 116
Harrison, June 192
Harrold, Mrs 20
Hartford, Connecticut 181
Hartley and Company, 100, 101
Hartwich Seminary 195
Hassel, Bert 200
Hatt, Hilda 65, 74
Havilland, Geoffrey de 85, 88, 173, 190
Havilland, Louie de 103, 110, 173
health, Lady Mary's 72, 126–8, 147, 149, 152. see also alcoholism
'The Heart's Content' (aeroplane) 214
Heath, Lady Mary 2
    achievements (see athletic career; flying career)
    in Africa (see Africa)
    appearance **2**, 31–2, **237**
    background and childhood 13, 21, 22, 27, 28–34, 30–1, **32**
    career (see athletic career; flying career)
    character 32, 38, 49–50, 51, 70
    education 32–4, 35–8, 39, 48–9, 53
    marriages (see marriage)
Heath, Sir James **108**–9, 154, 171, 172, 183
    marriage to Lady Mary 109
        difficulties 176, *178*–9, 202, 204–6, 208, 214
Heathfield House 28
Heath Flying Scholarship 172–3
Heliopolis aerodrome 141, 143
Hemmings, Major Harold 102
Henderson, Cliff 191, 192, 193, 197
Henderson, Colonel 120
Henry, Noel 7
Hensman, Miss 33
Hereford, Lady Mary's parachute jump at **93**
Heron, Oscar 226
Het Vliegveld (The Airfield) 161–2, 163
Hewlett, Hilda 88, 107
Hewson, Henrietta Georgina 15
high-jump, Lady Mary and 55–7, 65–**6,** 67, 74, 87, 238–40
Hill, Dr Leonard 79
Hitomi, Kinue 161
Hoare, Sir Samuel (Minister for Civil Aviation) 91, 92
Hodgson, Dorothy Mary 214
Hollingdrake, Henry 105, 106–7
Hooton Park 107
Hope, Captain W.L. 106
houses, big 28
Howard, Edward P. 187
Hrubec, Joan 8
Hucknall, Nottinghamshire 106
Hudson, Dame Beatrix 84
Huella, Manco 88
Hunefeld, Gunter von 167, **168**
Hungary 167
hunting, Lady Mary and 62–3
Hyde, Douglas 29

immigration authorities 203
Imperial Airways 161, 218
India, commercial flight to 161
inquest 100–1, 235–6
International Aeronautical Association 191
International Aeronautics Exposition 191, 197
International Commission for Air Navigation resolution 146 banning women commercial pilots 91–4
International Conference on Civil Aviation 176, 177
International Olympic Committee 78, 99
International Union of Aviators 115
'Iolar' aeroplane 232
Iona Flying School 224
Iona National Air Taxis 218–19
Iona National Airways Ltd 216, 220
Ireland 35, 98, 167
    first commercial aircraft 218
    Lady Mary flies to Ireland 105, 168–72
    Lady Mary returns to Ireland 214–31
Irish Aero Club 168, 169, 173, 218, 220, 226, 228, 230
Irish Air Corps 167
Irish Air Force 171
Irish Aviation Authority 222
Irish Cup (race) 224
Irish Gliding Association 222, 227
Irish Independent 172
Irish Land Act 29
Irish Military Archives, Dublin 227
Irish Tramway Club 232
Irish Weekly Mail and Sports 56

Italians, Lady Mary impressed by 145, 147, 151–2
Italy 167, 211

Jacksonville Journal 184
Jacksonville, Florida 184
Jakarta, commercial flight to 161
Japan 97, 211
javelin throwing, Lady Mary and 59, 60–1, 65–6, 67, 74, 81–2, 87, 238–40
Jeffcott, Dean H.H. 37
Jelfe, Mrs 131
Jeppe, Sir Julius 121, 123
Jinja aerodrome, Uganda 137
Johannesburg, South Africa 114, 116, 123
Johannesburg Light Aeroplane Club 118, 152
Johannesburg Star 114
'John' 67
Johnson, Amy 85, 214, **215,** 221
Johnson, Molly 214, **215**
Jones, N.H. 88
Junkers monoplane 167–8

Kabwe, Zambia (*formerly* Broken Hill) 129
Kafue, river 129
Kampolombo, Lake 130
Keane, Catherine 17
Kearney, James Milo St John 84, 218
Kelly, James 192
Kelly, Violet C. 41
Kennedy, Darby 233
Kennedy, George **229**
Kensington Ladies 60
Kensington Town Hall 71
Kentish, Brigadier General R.J. 78–9, 84
Kettel, David 83
Khartoum, Sudan 139, 140
Kilcrony, County Clare 231
Kildonan aerodrome, County Dublin 219, **220**–2, 228, 233
King's College, Mitcham, London 59
King's Cup (race) 106, 161, **162, 163**
King's Division, High Court, London 204–6
King's Royal Rifles 132
Kirk, Erwin 200
Kirkcudbright, Scotland 105
Kisumu, Kenya 137
Kitty Hawk, North Carolina 179
KLM 161, 163–4, 165–6, 218

Knockaderry, County Limerick **15,** 17
Knockaderry House, County Limerick 13, **16,** 21
  sold 27, 30
Knowles, Ted 55, 57–8, 71
Kohl, Herman 167, **168**
Koolhoven, Frederick **165, 166**
Kusti, Sudan 139

Ladies' Athenaeum Club 76
Ladies '89 Pioneer Club 122
Ladies Purse (race) 106
Lady Mary. *see* Heath, Lady Mary
Lakeside Hospital 204
Lancashire Aero Club 159
Lancashire School of Aviation 168
Lancaster, Bill 8, 181–2, 184–**5,** 187, 190, 194–5, 202, 207
Lancaster, Kiki 182, 184, 185
landlords 28–9
Land Purchase Acts 27
Lang, Captain, N. 173
Langford, Creagh 49
Larden, Lieutenant G.H.N. 99
Larkin's Field, Ballybunion, County Kerry 104
Laroche, Baroness de 88
Latvia 97
Lavery, Sir John 47, 48
Lawson, Captain 93
League of American Penwomen's, New York 186–7
Le Bourget airport, Paris 153
lectures, Lady Mary 173
  in Africa 113, 115, 118, 122
  in America 180, 193, 194, 195
Leinster Road, (127), Rathmines, Dublin 35
Leith, Miss 161, **164**
Lenglen, Suzanne 54
Letterfrack, County Galway 217
letters, Lady Mary's 76, 78, 91, 93, 227
  to Aunt Cis 66–7, 186, 189
  to Colonel Shelmerdine 216–17
  to Elinor Smith 203, 207
  to Mrs McQueen 191–2, 193, 212
  to Royal Aeronautical Society 110, 160
Letts, Sir William 105
Leviathan (ship) 176
Lewis, Samuel 13
Lewis-Crosby, Reverend E.H. 41
Lexington, Kentucky 211

[263]

Liberman, Issac 179
Liberty magazine 212
licence, Lady Mary's flying 85
    declared unfit to fly 227
    needs to renew licences 163, 209, 215–17
    preparation and obstacles of B licence 87–8, 90, 91–4, 215–17
    receives A licence 87
    receives Mexican licence 211
Light Aeroplane Club Members' Scratch 97
Limerick Chronicle 22
Limerick Flying Club 222
Limerick Prison 26
Lindbergh, Charles 101, 115, 231
Lindi, Tanganyika 47
Lines, Mary 55, 57, 60, 75
Liston, John 18
Liston, Patrick T. 23
Livingstone, Zambia 128–9
Lloyd, Edward Locke 28
Lloyd, Lady 143
Lloyd, Lord 143
Lloyd, Robert Oliver Villiers 34
Lloyd, Thomas E. 28, 30
Loader, Jayne 8
Locke, Frances 14
Locke, Thomas 14, 28
Lockheed factory, Burbank, California **196**
London Aero Club, Stag Lane 82, 83, 85, 87, 99
London County Council 84
London's Ladies Army and Navy Club 176
Long, John 88
Long Island airfield 180, 181
Lord, Flight Sergeant 141
Lowman, Ivy 65, 74
Lufthansa 218
Lympne aerodrome, Kent 99, 153
Lynam, Deke 202
Lyons 152

Mackey, Elsa 111
Madden, Florence 206, **207–8**, 209
Magistrate's Court, Windsor, Ontario 210
Maher, Johnny 227
Mahoney, Dr 17
Mail, Captain Douglas 127, 128
Makula, Zambia 126–7
Malakal, Sudan 139
Malone, J.C. 218

Manchester 105
Manning, Wing Commander 150
maps 102, 120, **124**, **144**, **148**
Marchant, Major W.B. 55, 57–8, **98**
Markievicz, Count 35
marriage certificate, Lady Mary's **216**
marriages, Lady Mary's
    to Captain Eliott-Lynn 39–41, 50–3, 62, *68–9*, 71
    to Jack Williams 209–10, 211, 214, 230, 231
    to Sir James Heath 108–9, 178–9, 193
Marseilles 152
Mary, Lady. *see* Heath, Lady Mary
Mason, George William 101
Matoni, Capitane 145
Mayers, Mr 115, 116
Mayfair Hotel, London 154–5
Mbala (*formerly* Abercorn) 119–20, 131
McGovern, Molly 168
McLean, Group Captain 141
McQueen, Mrs Ulysses Grant **191–2**, 212
mechanics 129, 145, 150, 210–11
    Lady Mary knowledge of 89, 142, 152, 154
Mediterranean, Lady Mary on 143
Medway, Rochester, Kent 159
Menken, Arthur von Briesen 189
Merrick, Miss 35
Messina, Straits of 151
Mexico City 190, 211
Miami, Florida 182, 184
Middlesex Ladies Athletic Club 71, 88, 94
Miller, Chubbie 181–2, **185**, 190, 199
Miller, Dr A.R. 200
Miller, Major 114, 115, 118–19
Milliatt, Alice 54, 57, 59–60, 65
Millin, Emil 114, 123
Mills Company factory 200–1
Milne, Miss 37
Misratah, Libya 147
'Miss Great Lakes' aeroplane 190, 193, 198, 200–1
Mitchell, Dr Chalmers 113
Moates Sports, County Westmeath 55
Model Aeronautics Council of Ireland 222
Moira Hotel, Trinity Street, Dublin 222
Moisant, Mathilde 88
Mollison, Jim 214, 215, 221
Mombasa, Kenya 134, 135
money problems, Lady Mary's 34, 50–3, 73, 85, 88, 178–9, 185–6, 208–9
Mongalla, Sudan 138–9

INDEX

Mongey, Sergeant Thomas 24
Monocoupe aeroplane 198–9
Monte Carlo, Monaco 54–5, 65, 71
Moon, Greg 7
motorbikes, Lady Mary's love of 42, 43
motorcar speed dash, Cape Town to London 114, 119, *131*
Mount Etna, Italy 151
Moyland, Rose 189
Murdoch, Pat 112–13
Murray, Stella Wolfe 88, 90–1, 92, 152
Mussabini, Sam 55
'Mussel' aeroplane 159–60
Mussolini, Benito 143–4, 151–2
Mwanza, Tanzania 132, 134

Nairobi, Colonial Secretary of 156
Nairobi, Kenya, Africa 125, 134, 135, 136–7
Nakuru, Kenya, Africa 52, 62
Naples, Italy 151
National Aero Club 224
National Aeronautic Association 92
National Air Races 190, 191, 193, 195, 197, **201**, 202
National Aviation Day 229–30
National Exchange Club 195
National Irish Junior Aviation Club **221, 222**, 230
National Physical Laboratory 175
National Playing Fields Association 76, 84
National Women's Party 180
Naturalisation Bureau, Federal Court, New York 186
Naughton, Willie 171
Ndola, Zambia, Africa 130
Nelson, Lady Kathleen 224, 228
Newcastle, England 103
Newcastle West, County Limerick
  Lady Mary's childhood in 28–34
Newfoundland 157
News of the World 75
New York, United States of America 21, 176, 190
New York Aviation Show 187–8
New York State Department of Health and Physical Education 180
New York Times 202, 203
Niagara, North America 193
Nichols, Ruth 176, 180
Nile, river 138, 139, 141
Nimule, Sudan, Africa 138, 139, 140

Ninety-Nines Club 199, 206–7
Northolt, England 158
Norway 95
Noyes, Blanche 192, 197

obituary 236
O'Brien, Dermod 28, 53, 224
O'Brien, Sicele 95, 99, 102–3, 156, 159, 160, 161, **164**
O'Brien, William Smith 28
O'Connor, Constable 18
O'Connor, Kathleen 203
O'Connor, Peter 81
O'Connor, Teresa. *see* Dooling, Catherine Teresa
Oddie, Mr 100, 101
O'Donnell, Gladys 197, 199
O'Dwyer, Dr 17
Ohio Chamber of Commerce Goodwill Tour 196
Oldfield, Dorys (*later* Dorys Bentley) 114, 118, 122. *see also* Bentley, Dorys
Olympiades Feminines 54–5
Olympic Council 54, 76
Omlie, Phoebe 195, 197, 198–9, 199
operation, Lady Mary's 202
Oranmore, County Galway 170, 171
Orly Airport, Paris **96,** 97
Orpen, William 48
O'Shaughnessy, Fr John 17, 18, 20
The Otter (boat) 133
Ower, William 226
Oxo Sports Ground, Bromley 66

Paddington 59
Palmer, Joe 55, 57–8
Pangani, Tanganyika, Africa 52, 62
papers, Lady Mary's (women and sport) 76–8
parachute jump **93,** 224
Paris, France 46, 67, 74, 153
Paris, Neva 199, 207
Patric, Joe 201
Patrick, Major Cochrane 129
Pearson's Magazine 147
Peirce, Ann Maria 'Cis.' *see* Peirce, Cis
Peirce, Aphra Jane 'Effie' (*later* Pepper) 30, 203–4
Peirce, Captain Frances 109
Peirce, Cis 28, 30, 39, 41, 109, 189, 214, 236
  Lady Mary visits favourite aunt 49, 104, 169–70

[265]

letters 50, 52, **186,** 189, 203, 206
Peirce, Frances Thomasina 30
Peirce, Francis Carnegie 235
Peirce, George **14**–15, 19, 23, 28, 30
Peirce, Henrietta 41
Peirce, John 13–14
Peirce, John 'Jackie' (*later* Peirce-Evans, John) 13, 14–16, 17, **18**
   arrest and imprisonment 20, 21, 25, 26
   court appearances 17, 18, 19, 20, 21–2
      murder case 22–6
   death of 39
   relationship with Catherine Dooling 18–20, 21–2
      murders wife 22–6
Peirce, Lou 28, 30, 66–7
Peirce, Margaret 30
Peirce, Robert 28
Peirce, Sophia Louisa 'Lou.' *see* Peirce, Lou
Peirce-Evans, Sophie. *see* Heath, Lady Mary
Pembroke Road, Dublin 224
Pepper, Dr George 218
Percy, Sir James 105
Perrin, Lieutenant Commander Harold 85, 174, 175
Pershing Stadium, Paris 59
Pfister, Gertrud 7
Philadelphia Congress 180
Phoenix Park, Dublin 105, 229–30
Pietermaritzburg, South Africa 116
Pinedo, Marquis de 152
Plesman, Albert 162, **165, 166**
Plevins, Claude 102
poetry, Lady Mary's *31, 63–4, 68–70*
Poland 97
Port Alfred, South Africa 115
Port Elizabeth, South Africa 114
Power, William 19, 20, 21
Power-Berrey, W. 75
Pretoria, South Africa 115, 123, 142
Private Owners' Handicap (race) 97
prohibition 176
Protestant Hospital, Limerick 19
Protestants 28, 29
Provincial Bank, Kilrush, County Clare 15
publications, Lady Mary's. *see Athletics for Women and Girls; Eastern African Nights; The Torch; Women and Flying*
Public Record Office, Kew, England 7
Putman, George 101, 183, 192, 195

Pyramids, Egypt 141, **142**

Quimby, Harriet 88

Ramsey, Lord de 217
Rand Daily Mail 114, 116, 119, 121, 125, 127
Rasche, Thea 192
Rathangan, County Kildare 169
Ream, Inspector George D. 209
Redpath Chautauqua Circuit 180, 193, 194, 195
Regent Street Polytechnic, London 55, 57
Registry Office, Tralee, County Kerry 214
Reid, Captain 83
Reid, Mr 170
Reno, Nevada 204, 206
Renvyle, Connemara 171, 217
rheumatic fever, Lady Mary has 147, 149, 152
Rhodes, Sir Cecil 114, 125
Rhône valley, France 152
Robbins, Reginald L. 192
Robert's Heights, Africa 116, 121, 123, 125
Robinson, Señora 212
Roe, A.V. 103, 110, 142, 155
Rogers, Dr Frederick Rand 180
Rogers, Will 196–7
Rohan, Martin 22
Rome, Italy 151–2
Rosebery, Lord 112
Rossmore, Baron 'Derry' 95
Rotterdam, Lady Mary in **164, 165,** 166
Rotterdam Aeronautical Club 161
Royal Aeronautical Club 85, 155
Royal Aeronautical Society, London 7, 110, 113, 155, 160, 175
Royal Air Force 137, 138, 143, 145
Royal College of Science for Ireland 35, 36–8, 50
Royal Dutch Airlines (KLM) 161, 163–4, 165–6, 218
Royal Geographical Society, Lady Mary nominated **188,** 189
Royal University Act 33
Rubio, Señora Ortiz 211, 212
running, love of *57, 80*
Russell, Christobel 204–5, 206
Russell, Colonel Charles 168, 218, 220, 221
Rye, New York 158
Rynveld, Colonel Sir Pierre van 113, 116, 123, 125
Rynveld, Lady van 118

safari **63**, 133–4
Sanford, Mrs 130
Santa Monica, California 190
Sassoon, Sir Philip (Under Secretary for Air) 83
Saul, Paddy 218, 221, 228
scholarships, flying 156, 172–3
Scholte, J.B. 161, 164
Scotland 107, 169
Scott, Robert 63
Semphill, Colonel (the Master of) 106
Serengeti Plain 134
Sfax aerodrome, Tunisia 149
Shannon Aero Club, Ireland 84
Shannon Airport 231
Shannon estuary 169
Shelmerdine, Colonel F.C. (Director of Civil Aviation) 87, 216–17, 227
Shepherd, J.S. 169
Sherburn aerodrome, Yorkshire 96–7, 99, 107
Short Brothers 159
Shorts seaplane 113, 159–60
Sicily 150–1
Sicklen, C.F. van 201
'The Silver Lining' (aeroplane) **223**, 224, 230
Simpson, Dr Cedric Keith 235
Simpson, John 57
Sister Rigby's Maternity Home 128
Sky Fever 88
Smith, Elinor 8, 46, 108, 109, 180–**1**, 192, 195, 197–8, 199
    friendship with Lady Mary *182–4, 185, 186, 195, 199, 201, 207–9*
Smith, Tom 181
Smyth, Joy Nitch 109
Snijders, General 162
society, Irish 28, 35
Soldier Settlement Scheme 52
Sollum, port of 144
Sopwith, Tommy 155
South African Air Force 123
Southampton 176
South Park, County Galway 170–171170
Spain, port of 190
Sparkes, F.G.M. 83
Sphinx, Egypt 141, **142**
Sponner, Winifrid 156, 160, 161
sport. *see* athletic career
Sport 50, 56
The Square, (1), Newcastle West, County Limerick **29**, 41

Stack, Captain 150, 174
Stamford Bridge, London 58, 74, 81–2, 96, 161
    international women's athletic meet 74–5
Stammers, Eric Ernest 205
stamp, Irish **236**
Stine, Elizabeth 67
Stinson, Katherine 180
Stinson, Majorie 92
St Margaret's Hall, Dublin 33–4
Stock, Cheridah de Beauvoir 88
Stokes, Alfred 235
Stranraer, Scotland 169
Stultz, Wilmer 157
Sturridge, Captain 132
Sudan Defence Force 138
Sullivan, Mr D.B. QC 26
sunstroke, Lady Mary suffers 126–8
Surt, Libya 147
Sutherland, Duke of 84, 110–11, 155, 156
Swayne, R.P.N. 41
Sweden 95
Swiss Air 218
Switzerland 107
Synge, John Millington 29
Syracuse, Sicily 148

Tabora, Tanganyika 132
Talbot, Mr Justice 204, 206
Tanganyika, Lake 130–1
telegrams, Lady Mary's
    congratulated for solo flight 155
    controversy over non-payment 156
    difficulty sending 128, 136
    telegram to Mussolini 143–4
tenants 29
Teruzzi, Attilio 146
Tewkesbury, Gloucestershire 104
Texas Aeronautical Corporation 192
Thaden, Louise 195, 196, 197, 199, 207
The Fun of It 180
Thompson, Mrs Moffat 129
Thompson, Rose 72
The Times 76, 78, 155
Tobin, Richard 226
The Torch 37–8, 40–1, 43, 44
Torquay, Devon, England 59, 71, 82
Town Hall Club, New York 180
Tripoli, Lebanon 147–9
Trout, Bobbie 196

Trumbull, Governor 181
Trunk, John 209
Tsolo, South Africa 115
Tullabawn strand, Lady Mary's plane sinks at 172, **173**
Tunisia, Africa 143, 149
Tunis Tunisia 149–50
Twohig, Jim 226
Tyson, Geoffrey 225–6

Uganda, Africa 136, 137
Umtata, South Africa 115
Ungalla river, Africa 132
United Arts Club, 44, St Stephen's Green, Dublin 50
United States of America 211
    Lady Mary leaves 214
    Lady Mary visits 176–89
University of Aberdeen, Scotland 53
Utah, United States of America 158
Utica, New York 158

Vaitkus, Felix **229**, 230
Vance, Reverend Joseph 21
Vanderbyl, Euphemia Celena 109
Velvet Strand, Portmarnock, County Dublin 214, **215**
Viper aeroplane 95
Voluntary Aid Detachment Motor Convoy 48

WAAA 58, 81–2, 84, 155, 161
Waalhaven Aviation Festival 161–3
Waco aeroplane 181
Wadi Halfa, Sudan 141
Wakefield, Sir Charles 121, 155, 156
Waldorf Hotel, New York 180
Wall Street crash 204
Wankie, Zimbabwe 128
war, women and 43, 44–6, 48
War Office 43, 46
Washington 176, 177, 184
Washington Post 211
water, Lady Mary's fear of 49–50, 125, 143, 150–1, 168–9, 212–13
Webster, F.A.M. 167
Weekly News 236
Weir, Edith 212

Westland Widgeon monoplane 114, 115, 150
West London Hospital, Hammersmith 227
Weston Aerodrome and Flying School 233
White, Captain A.H. 158
White, Colonel S.H. 235
Wilkins, Sir George 160
Williams, Al 202
Williams, George Anthony Reginald 'Jack' **217**, **223**, 224, 228, **229**, 233
    marriage to Lady Mary 209–10, 211, 214, 230, 231
Williams, Harold 84
Williams, Honourable George 214
Williams, Jack. *see* Williams, George Anthony Reginald
Williams, Mrs 110
Willits, Sanford L. 209
Wilson, Nora 230
Wolfe, Stella 108
Women and Flying 88–9, 90–1, 112, 136, 152, 221
Women's Air Derby 190–9
    controversy 197–9
    races 195–9
Women's Amateur Athletic Association (WAAA) 58, 81–2, 84, 155, 161
Women's Auxiliary Army Corps 44, 45
Women's Engineering Society 107
'Women's International and British Games' 75
Women's International Association of Aeronautics 191–2, 212
Women's Modern Olympic Games 59–60, 78
'Women's World Games' 78, 96, 97–9
Woodford aerodrome, England 99, 103, 110
Woods, Lieutenant Andy **229**
Woolwich Stadium, London 74
Workmen's Compensation Bureau 208
Worsech, Major 57
Wright, Catherine 180
Wright, Orville 179
Wyall, Hervey 235

Yale Junior Prom 187
Yeats, William Butler 29, 171
York, Duke of 84
Yorkshire Air Pagent 96–7

Zimbabwe, South Africa 125
Zougha, port of 149